For Polina Chesnokova, food has always been the throughline, a way to make sense of her family history. Born in Ukraine, she was raised in the United States by a Russian mother and Armenian father who met and married in Georgia. *Chesnok*, which translates to a head of garlic, holds together these cloves, in this case, the disparate culinary traditions joined in the uneasy grip of what was the Soviet Union. Azeri plov scented with saffron and studded with dried apricots and chestnuts, pillowy soft Ukrainian dumplings filled with farmer cheese, robust borsch laden with herbs and dolloped with sour cream, luscious Georgian eggplant, fried and then bejeweled with pomegranate seeds, and the towering, and light as air, honey cake are just a few of the recipes included in this gorgeous cookbook.

As Polina, and the millions of others scattered throughout the Soviet diaspora have discovered, a shared culinary heritage is making blini glistening with butter in a sun-drenched kitchen, watching your little boy devour the same semolina kasha you grew up eating, and knowing that food is both the documenter of history, and the delicious path forward.

Chesnok

Chesnok

COOKING FROM MY CORNER OF THE
DIASPORA: RECIPES FROM EASTERN EUROPE,
THE CAUCASUS, AND CENTRAL ASIA

POLINA CHESNAKOVA

PHOTOGRAPHS BY DANE TASHIMA

Hardie Grant

NORTH AMERICA

To my mama and tyetushki, without whom this book wouldn't be complete

INTRODUCTION

A holiday meal in my family is the culmination of weeks of coordinating, delegating, and yes, bickering. By the time we bow our heads for grace, stomachs are growling, mouths are salivating, and our hanger has brought the tension in the room to an all-time high. I know what everyone at the table is thinking. Can we wrap this prayer up already? We're ready to eat.

Gem-colored *pkhali* pushed up against golden, flaky *khachapuri*. Glistening bowls of bright, fermented tomatoes, briny pickles, and sauerkraut generously doused in sunflower oil. And old Soviet favorites like dill-flecked Olivier salad next to platters of smoked salmon, caviar plated with thick slabs of butter, *kolbasa*, cheese, all served with warm crusty lavash or bread. Chicken two ways: one roasted, *adjika*-spiced, and the second dressed in a fragrant walnut sauce and spooned over hot, cheesy *mamalyga*.

Then the *actual* main dishes debut. Stuffed *golubtsy* with a garlicky sour cream sauce; lamb braised in *tkemali*, tarragon, and wine; pan-seared beef-stuffed *blinchiki* still hot from the stove; and saffron-flecked pilaf studded with dried fruit fill out the already brimming spread. It's not until a couple of hours later, when everyone has had their third helping and can barely get up from their seats, when we've laughed, cried, and bickered some more, that the worry of whether we made enough food is allayed. We are content, which means we are ready for dessert.

For some, this meal may seem like a random mishmash of cuisines. But for my family—and the tens of million people worldwide that make up the Soviet diaspora—it represents a familiar weaving of collective and national identities. With links to Russia, Georgia, Armenia, Ukraine, and beyond, my family—like so many families—operated in a world of cultural cross-pollination during the USSR. And we have continued to do so long after its collapse. Our culinary diversity, no surprise, reflects that experience. To fully understand how we got here, though, it pays to go back in time.

My great-grandfather Matthew was a successful farmer in central Russia in the 1920s. A little too wealthy and influential for Stalin and his gang, he was marked to have his lands confiscated and to be sent to Siberia. Whether it was luck or the Divine, the night before he was to be paid a visit by the Bolsheviks, his neighbor tipped him off. He fit what he could into a wagon and set off with his wife and six children. After a couple months on the road, with a detour in Turkmenistan, they landed in Tbilisi, the capital city of Georgia. My mom's father, Ivan, was only seven at the time.

For most of the Soviet Union's history, borders between the republics functioned less as barriers than as dashed lines. Decades of both forced displacement and voluntary internal migration saw families scattered throughout the regions—if they were lucky, some, like mine, ended up in burgeoning capital cities like Tbilisi. It had mild weather, sunny people, plenty of opportunities for work, and, compared to more austere parts of the Soviet Union, a relative abundance of goods. When my mom was born in 1959, Tbilisi was a melting pot, where customs, language, and food were exchanged.

Russian served as the lingua franca at school and work, where my mother and her ten other siblings mixed with Georgians, Armenians, Kurds, Azeris, and Uzbeks, among other ethnic groups. Most of my mom's childhood was plagued by standing in line for hours at a time for tomatoes or bread and subsisting on watered-down soups and *suhariki* (croutons). But by the time she was in her late teens, rations had lessened, and feeding a large family became less of a conundrum. Out in the workforce or married into new, slightly wealthier families, my mother and aunts, with their newfound time and resources, began to approach cooking with joy.

Standard Soviet fare was ever present: *kotleti* (cutlets), beef Stroganoff, and *kompot* (fruit beverage). You could count on these dishes—heavy on the canned goods, but short on ingredients—to appear in every local canteen and home from Moscow to Tashkent. But over time Georgian *badrijani* (eggplant rolls) and *khinkali* (soup dumplings), Uzbek *plov* (pilaf), and Armenian *dolma* (stuffed grape leaves) won a place at my family's table, too, next to Russian buckwheat kasha and pirozhki. Learning from their co-workers, neighbors, and new relatives, they even began to add a bit of Georgian flair to their repertoire: a little *adjika* (chili paste) worked into their chicken marinade for instance, or cilantro and raw garlic stirred into their goulash or cabbage rolls.

They had become, as the author Anya von Bremzen would say, masters of the art of Soviet cooking. And it wouldn't be long until the food that sustained them in the USSR would also be what carried them through when it came time to leave that life behind.

In 1990, my mom married my father, an Armenian whose family had also resettled in Tbilisi by way of Baku.

By then, between the growing political unrest and economic instability under Mikhail Gorbachev, the writing was on the wall. Life in Soviet Georgia was becoming untenable, so they began the maddening process of emigrating. After two frustrating years of waiting on documents and a month of screening and medical exams in Moscow (not to mention the fall of the Soviet Union), on September 26, 1992, with a suitcase in one hand and a little wooden basket carrying me, a newborn, in the other, my parents boarded their flight to America. They were officially refugees.

Within a few years, no one on either side of my family was left in Georgia. Some, like my parents, left the region entirely, emigrating to the US, Canada, Israel—any country that would have them. Others resettled in Kherson, Ukraine (where my grandfather had retired, and where I was born), while the rest made their way up to Moscow. Almost seventy years after my great-grandfather arrived in Tbilisi, our family found itself displaced again.

When we landed in Rhode Island, my aunt Natasha and uncle Enver were already waiting for us, and soon after, three of my mom's sisters and their families joined. We had each other, but most important, we were able to find and connect with other newly arrived immigrant families as well, many of them through the "Russian" church. Comprising refugees from all over the former Soviet Union, the church wasn't just Russian though. The founding families represented Estonia, Latvia, Georgia, Moldova, and Ukraine. Representation from all the former republics continued to grow as the congregation did, and while we acknowledged and respected each other's differing backgrounds, we also felt a deep kinship—banding together over faith, our new immigrant label, a common language, and, crucially, a love and appreciation for each other's food.

Church potlucks were a smorgasbord of Soviet favorites, Eastern bloc hits, and regional favorites (although the occasional pig in a blanket did make an appearance). We would feast on *zakuski* (small bites) and plov at each other's weddings. At cookouts, we enjoyed *shashlyk* (shish kebabs) cooked over an open flame and gossiped over the crack and pop of *semechki* (sunflower seeds). At dinner parties we'd swap recipes for Armenian *gata* (flaky pastries) or *medovik* (honey cake) at the end of the evening. In short, it was a little Soviet microcosm, but with Jesus and Paul replacing Marx and Lenin.

◆ ◆ ◆ ◆

In high school, I remember resenting the way we cooked. "Why can't we ever branch out? Why do we always stick to the same things? Why are we so boring?" I would pick up cookbooks and issues of *Gourmet* and *Saveur* at the library and pore over them—the recipes enticing, yet inaccessible, since we lacked the pantry to prepare them. I took any holiday or special occasion as an excuse to cook up something new, my family gamely obliging (even though they themselves didn't feel the need to venture into unfamiliar territory).

But as happens to all immigrant kids who leave their home only to miss their family's food, I eventually found my way back to my mom's kitchen in my early college years—but this time with curiosity rather than frustration. At first, it was to learn and write down recipes, making sure they wouldn't be lost with that generation. We never had a box of index cards or binders fastidiously organized by letter or meal type, no cookbooks I could crack open. Instructions primarily lived inside my mom's and aunts' heads, everything done by feel or by eye, *na glaz*. So it was my job to punctuate every step with questions over technique or backstory. (*Hold on! Let me write that down!*)

Over time, my recipes gained headnotes filled with stories and memories recounted during these cooking sessions. I learned that chicken soup with homemade *lapsha* (noodles) was my grandmother's favorite food and the last thing she requested before she died. How my mom learned to cook Georgian food working as a secretary at an engineering institute: During their lunch breaks, her Georgian co-workers would fry up potatoes, dole out their beloved cheese-filled *khachapuri* and vegetable-walnut *pkhali*, and pour glasses of a neon-green tarragon soda called *tarhun*. I gained an appreciation for the Soviet Union's obsession with sweetened

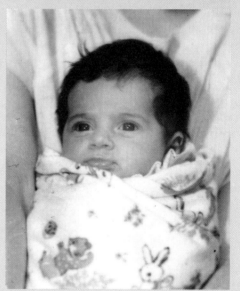

condensed milk—pouring it over their *blinchiki* and kefir-based pancakes known as *oladushki*, beating it into buttercreams, stirring it into tea, or dipping bread or wafers into it (*if* they were lucky to get their hands on a can, that is).

These recollections made me realize that my own upbringing within the Soviet diaspora was worth exploring. Devouring bowls of *varenyky* (dumplings) with my Ukrainian friends as we sat on the floor watching the Soviet cartoon *Cheburashka* on TV; learning how to make Uzbek *plov* at my friend Sasha's house; going to the Eastern European market to pick up the essentials: *kolbasa*, smoked mackerel, *ikra*—caviar both of the sea and eggplant varieties—jars of *tkemali* (sour plum sauce) and *adjika*, a box of bird's milk chocolate, and maybe a *Kyivskyi torte*.

Inspired, I started a food blog. I pitched newspapers and started to teach cooking classes. I hosted dinners, participated in bake sales, and ran fundraisers, all featuring the food of my family and our wider community. Preserving and showcasing our foodways left me feeling deeply connected: to my ancestors, who gave me their DNA; to my mother and aunts, who passed down their recipes; to a homeland that I've only ever experienced secondhand; and to my immigrant community, whose own experiences reflect and parallel my own. It also led me to this moment. In Russian, *chesnok* means "garlic" and is the origin of my last name. The same humble allium happens to be a cornerstone ingredient of Georgian cuisine. Taken together, *Chesnok*, the book, becomes a tribute to my roots in both Eastern Europe and the Caucasus.

Chesnok—its recipes, anecdotes, and essays—doesn't represent only my family's culinary heritage. It's an invitation to sit at, and experience, the breadth and nuance of the post-Soviet table, as well as the spirit of warmth and generosity at its heart. My aim is not to perpetuate a simplistic monolith of the Soviet legacy, but to speak to a diaspora of people who still live with and navigate its complexities and contradictions. Here I work to share the traditions and rituals that link us, while also celebrating that which makes us unique—to understand not only the way we cook, but why.

FROM UPPER LEFT CORNER, CLOCKWISE: Family Portrait in Tbilisi, Oct. 1969; A year after we moved to RI, Dec. 1993; Immigration photo of me at 2 months, Kherson, Aug. 1992; Me and Dedushka Vanya at his RI apartment, 1996; Church photo in RI, New Year, 1999.

AN EVOLVING IDENTITY

Historically, the label "Russian" was used as a catch-all for the whole of the Soviet diaspora. Not just by those outside our community, but also within. When speaking with Americans, it's always been easiest to just leave it at "I'm Russian," because who has time to get into geopolitics?

Within the Soviet diaspora, we've always had an acute awareness of each other's ethnicities. "От куда вы?"—*Where are you from?*—is often the first question asked when meeting another Russian-speaker. It's the lens through which we see and place each other in our world. Historically, though, once that initial check was established, no one dwelled on who came from where, because we were brought together by larger forces at play: our shared language, history, and trauma. So, over time, we've allowed the label "Russian" to be used to lump us all together. We shopped at the local Russian store, visited the Russian neighborhoods in Brooklyn's Brighton Beach borough, and ate at Russian restaurants. If you looked a little closer, though, you'd see that "Russian" never really painted the full picture.

Five to ten years ago, I probably would've also called this food (and this book) Russian—with an asterisk. The explanation for the symbol buried somewhere in the intro. But Russia's recent war on Ukraine no longer provides us the luxury of that simplification. We have become too self-aware of our differences; our national identities taking precedence over our collective one.

Given recent events and the reckoning of self-identity that came with it, I use the term "post-Soviet" to describe this book and, more increasingly, myself. Some have argued that this term is problematic—that it perpetuates Russian imperialism towards former Soviet republics. Used in reference to Russia's neighbors striving to maintain their sovereignty today, this is true. But used in the context of a diaspora that wouldn't have existed if it wasn't for the Soviet Union and its collapse—it allows me to speak to the breadth of this specific group of people and their food-ways without having one culture or cuisine co-opt the others. Post-Soviet is the most accurate and concise descriptor I can provide, and the most transparent one.

What Does That Mean for the Recipes in This Book?

Given my family's background—with our ties to both Eastern Europe and the Caucasus—you'll find a blend of foods from both regions (with a particular bent to the dishes and flavors of the latter) and a touch of Central Asia as well. It's by no means a comprehensive culinary guide to all the former republics or ethnic groups of the USSR (and the collective Soviet repertoire for that matter), nor is it a deep dive into any one cuisine. It's a reflection of our particular experience as immigrants who came from the country of Georgia; our tastes and preferences; and all the places and people who have left their touch on the way we cooked before we came to America, and afterwards.

So, yes, you'll find the cabbage, potatoes, meat, and mayo of the Soviet era. (Which, hey, before you knock it, try my family's Olivier Salad on page 118 and get back to me.) But also, the pillowy stuffed pies and briny ferments from Russia; hearty yet vibrant braises and walnut- and garlic-flecked salads of Georgia; the famous pilafs from Azerbaijan and Uzbekistan; and the glistening ruffled dumplings and melt-in-your-mouth farmer-cheese-stuffed crepes of Ukraine. The stories that fill out the book help place these dishes in the larger scope of post-Soviet culture.

It's also important to note the recipes here do not aim to reinvent the wheel; they're not Russian-*ish* or Georgian with a twist. They are traditional dishes, done exceptionally well, that my family has relied on time and time again to knit us together and remind us of the home we left behind. They may have been carried over from the old country, shared with us by those in our diaspora community, or based on our travels and my research into regional cuisines beyond our roots. If I've taken license to change or update a recipe, it's either to make it more streamlined or accessible to the wider public—or to show my own journey in cooking these foods.

What About the Recipe Titles?

The names of the recipes in the book reflect how we refer to them in my family, be it in Russian, Ukrainian, or Georgian, and so forth. Most of the time, this nomenclature is straightforward and will correlate with how they're referred to in their native countries and the diaspora at large. Sometimes, it's fuzzier. I do this because I want to emphasize that the foodways of our region don't always perfectly reflect borders. When this happens, I will point it out and give alternative names in pertinent languages.

Deciphering Cuisines

A clarification that Georgia is not another Slavic country (or state, for that matter) usually turns into a wider discussion on the differences between food of the Caucasus and that of Eastern Europe. In general, Eastern European cuisine is characterized by its love of sour in the form of cultured dairy, ferments, and pickles; smoked seafood and cured meat; whole grains such as rye, buckwheat, millet, and barley; and foraged berries, mushrooms, and greens. You'll find hearty soups, stews, and braises; pitch-dark breads, dumplings of all shapes and forms; a plethora of yeasted enriched doughs, and an impressive French-inflected pastry repertoire. You won't find many spices used outside of black pepper and paprika, but dill, hot mustard, and horseradish all provide necessary zip.

While there is plenty of preserving that happens in the Caucasus, the emphasis in the kitchen is more on the fresh and vibrant. It's known for its abundant uses of herbs and greens; nightshades such as tomatoes, eggplants, and peppers; nuts (especially walnuts); fresh cheese and yogurt; sunflower oil; and sour fruit such as plums, pomegranates, and grapes in both sweet and savory applications. You'll come across richly flavored legumes, stuffed vegetables, filled dumplings, flatbreads such as lavash and kayak-shaped *shotis puri*, skewered grilled meat and roasted poultry, and for all but the Georgians, rice (they, instead, prefer cornmeal). Fruit is often the dessert of choice, whether it's fresh, juiced and dried into fruit leathers, or simmered down into spectacular *murabba*, preserves. What pastries there are tend to be rustic, often filled with nuts or dried fruit. Georgian cuisine is made furthermore distinct by its use of blue fenugreek and ground marigold, which, combined with ground coriander, make up their main spice blend *khmeli suneli*.

Having roots in both areas, I can safely say that a common through line between the two is a way with hospitality and knowing just how to bestow upon guests an abundance of food and drink.

INGREDIENTS AND
OTHER NOTES

In the Soviet Union (and even today in many Eastern European countries), baking recipes were measured in 100-gram, 150-gram, and 250-gram faceted glasses. Of course, oftentimes a recipe would call for just "a glass," leaving you then guessing what size glass they were referring to. Smaller amounts would be measured in either "tea" spoons or "table" spoons (the kind you eat with), further specified with or without a mound. As a result, many housewives ended up using whatever glass or spoon they had in their kitchens and adding enough of an ingredient until it looked "right." All that to say, there were a *lot* of inconsistencies—my mom laughs that it was always a toss-up whether her bakes would work out or not.

Thankfully, these days we have digital scales that eliminate any guessing games and will set you up for cooking and baking with success (especially if these recipes are new to you). Once you realize how much a scale streamlines prep and cleaning, not to mention allays anxiety around mismeasuring, it'll quickly become indispensable.

Quantities here are generous, so when I say something serves 4, it really does. That's because all our cooking is done to feed larger groups or to last us a few days so we're not stuck in the kitchen each night. If this poses a problem, for many of the soups, stews, dumplings, and pastries, whatever you don't eat can be frozen. Or use it as an excuse to invite some friends over for dinner!

You can get many of the items below at your local Eastern European store. Otherwise, Suneli Valley (sunelivalley.com) sells fresh, high-quality Georgian spices and sauces. Kalustyan's (foodsofnations.com) is also a great resource. I've included additional sources when applicable.

ADJIKA: This chili paste hails from the Georgian regions of Abkhazia and Samegrelo. Usually red, although sometimes green, it is a preparation of hot and sweet peppers, garlic, herbs, and spices, such as coriander, ground marigold, and blue fenugreek—every cook has their own "special" blend. It's often sold as a paste or relish, but dried spice blends are also common. Avoid jarred *adjika* that has tomato in the ingredient list, which is a sign that it'll be closer to a mild roasted red pepper spread and not what you want. Use adjika as an accompaniment to grilled meats or in marinades, or swirl it into soups, stews, or even yogurt to make a spicy dip. Suneli Valley and Marneuli are my favorite brands for adjika paste, and the former also makes a great dried spice blend. Portuguese jarred hot chopped peppers (not to be confused with red pepper flakes) make a great adjika substitute.

ANAHEIM PEPPERS: These smoky, medium-hot light-green peppers add just the right balance of savory bite and sweetness to our sauces and soups.

EGGS: All eggs are large with an average weight of 50 to 55 grams.

EGG NOODLES: Finely cut egg noodles, or *vermishel* as we call them, can usually be found in the kosher section of regular grocery stores. Also sold as *Fadennudeln* under German brands in the Eastern European store. Wider-cut noodles, such as pappardelle, are best with beef stews like goulash or beef Stroganoff.

FLOUR: All the recipes were tested with Gold Medal bleached all-purpose flour. In this book, a cup of flour weighs 130 grams. If you don't have a kitchen scale, use the spoon-and-sweep method. This is also how I measure my sugars, cocoa powder, and other dry ingredients.

GEORGIAN HERBS/SPICES: In addition to the following herbs/spices with their own entries—*khmeli suneli*, *kviteli kvavili*, and *utskho suneli*—there are also these: *Kondari* is dried summer savory that is used to flavor meats, vegetables, and beans. *Ombalo* is dried pennyroyal mint that you'll often find in the sour plum sauce *tkemali*. Svanetian salt is a spiced salt blend from the mountainous region of Svaneti. I love sprinkling it on my fried eggs, tossing it with vegetables or potatoes before roasting, or rubbing it onto grilled or roasted pork—chicken would also be good!

GHERKINS: A smaller variety of pickled cucumber that has a crunchy, bumpy texture. We always keep a jar around for snacking and *zakuski* (small bites), as well as for Olivier and vinegret salads. Make sure to get the kosher dill whole variety, never sweet. Claussen and Vlasic brands are our preference.

HERBS: Maybe it's from our time in Georgia, but herbs in my family are typically added by the fistful, not by tablespoons. As such, for many of the recipes, herb quantity is written in terms of bunches, not clamshells. I've found an average "large" bunch to be about 65 grams, or 2¼ ounces. Otherwise, just eyeball it and don't get too bogged down on being exact—a little too much or too little parsley will not make a huge difference!

As for prepping herbs, you'll notice that for cilantro, unlike other herbs, I typically call for all of it, stems and all. That's because stalks carry the most flavor—it starts to dilute as you get closer to the leaves. As for other herbs, such as parsley and dill, I'll usually weigh or eyeball what I need, remove the hardier, woody stems, and work with the remaining leaves and tender stems.

To ensure your soft herbs such as dill, parsley, and cilantro last for as long as possible, once they're well rinsed, remove any excess liquid in a salad spinner. Lay

them out in an even single layer on a clean kitchen towel or a few layers of paper towel. If you have time, let them air dry for an hour or two. Then wrap them up in a paper towel or clean kitchen towel and store in a produce bag or ziplock in the crisper drawer of your refrigerator.

KEFIR: A fermented dairy (often cow's milk) product, kefir has a smoothie-like consistency that hits just the right balance of sweet, tart, and tangy. Not only do we love to drink it for its healthful properties, but we employ it in the kitchen as well. We use it to tenderize yeasted and pastry doughs, as a base for a cold soup, or to inoculate milk to culture other dairy products, such as *tvorog* (farmer cheese) or *ryazhenka* (cultured baked milk). Look for the full-fat or whole-milk kind.

KHMELI SUNELI: This translates to "dry spices." What garam masala is to Northern Indian cooking, *khmeli suneli* is to Georgian cuisine. Every home cook has their own blend. In its most basic form, it contains ground coriander, blue fenugreek, and ground marigold, but might also include dried parsley, basil, dill, tarragon, summer savory, bay leaf, and mint. Feel free to substitute for the same quantity of a 50/50 blend of ground coriander and blue fenugreek whenever a recipe calls for this blend.

KVITELI KVAVILI (GROUND MARIGOLD): This earthy spice, whose name translates to "yellow flower," is the dried and ground petals of the *Tagetes patula* marigold (*not* the kind you'd get at the florist). It's used to bring warmth both in color and flavor to dishes. You will be hard-pressed to find a substitute for it.

MATSONI: This is Georgian yogurt (see page 107 for more details). You can make your own using cultures from Cultures for Health (culturesforhealth.com).

MAYONNAISE: What would Soviet cuisine be without it? Hellmann's (or Best Foods on the West Coast) is our pick.

PICKLED HERRING: Don't confuse this with Scandinavian pickled herring in vinegar! You're looking for pickled herring in oil with salt—that's it. Serve it on its own, seasoned with a little vinegar and thin coins of onion, or in the iconic layered salad called Herring Under a Fur Coat (page 128).

SALT: All the recipes were tested with Diamond Crystal kosher salt, which weighs in at 9.7 grams per tablespoon (my microscale and I agree to disagree with the box, which says 8.4 grams). Where I can, I've provided salt measurements, but they are starting points because my salt preferences may be different than yours (unless you, too, are a salt fiend). Gram amounts are included where it really counts (mainly in the ferments and preserves chapter), so even if you're working with a different salt, you can go by weight if you have a scale. If you use Morton kosher or fine sea salt, start by adding half of the salt amount called for and adjust from there.

SMETANA: This is cultured sour cream. In its original Slavic form—super thick, tart, and so creamy it's almost sweet—it's more like French crème fraîche than the anemic stuff you'll find in US grocery stores. Because of its high butterfat content, it stands up to heat well and is less likely to curdle. Add a dollop to flavor and round out dishes like beef Stroganoff, to brighten soups, or to lend a creamy note to fresh salads. If you can't make it to an Eastern European store to get some, we like either Nancy's Probiotic or Darigold sour cream.

SUNFLOWER OIL: We rely on both refined and unrefined in our kitchen. The former is our go-to neutral cooking oil (a light olive oil or safflower oil would make fine substitutes). The latter is liquid sunshine in a bottle. Minimally processed, the golden-hued oil lends a very fragrant, nutty flavor. Use it as a finishing oil for salads and vegetables. The best comes from Ukraine or, if you're lucky enough to get your hands on some, from the eastern Georgia region of Kakheti.

SWEETENED CONDENSED MILK: How many times has one of my aunts or uncles launched into a story about finding a ruble on the ground and rushing to spend it on a can of sweetened condensed milk—only to get a major spanking when they got home for squandering the money? Today, they're a little less desperate when it comes to the sticky, sweet stuff, but I swear their tone turns reverent any-time conversation steers toward this one-time Soviet delicacy. We use it to enhance our buttercreams, fill cookies, and to top our breakfast items.

TKEMALI: The name for both the sour plum and sauce made from it (see page 182 for a recipe and more details). If not making your own, Suneli Valley makes a great one. At the Eastern European store, I like Golden Fleece brand.

TVOROG: This is farmer cheese (see page 55 for a recipe and for more details). If not making your own, you'll find the best at your local Eastern European shop (we love the Fresh Made Amish brand). It's dry and crumbly, making it versatile for cooking and baking.

UTSKHO SUNELI (BLUE FENUGREEK): The seeds of this plant are dried and ground into a powder. *Utskho suneli* translates to "foreign spice," speaking to the fact that it was most likely brought over from India. The spice has a complex, mildly bitter, and nutty profile that is less astringent than regular Indian fenugreek (which I would not recommend as a substitute).

VANILLIN: This synthetic powder is all bakers in the Soviet Union had access to for vanilla flavoring. It's potent, so only a little is needed—my mom would dip the handle of a spoon into a jar and measure out enough to cover only the very tip. When I got into baking in high school, I was shocked that she would use something so inferior when we had access to *real* vanilla extract. These days, I've come around and use it out of nostalgia, mainly in my buttercreams—it's the only way to give them that nostalgic taste I grew up with. It's a bit harder to find, so vanilla sugar in packets (such as Dr. Oetker brand) has become a popular alternative and is sold in many American grocery stores.

NA GLAZ

It's a particular kind of hell trying to wrangle a recipe out of my mom over the phone. Any question about an amount or a cooking time is generally met with the same response: "I do it by eye." Or, as she would say in Russian, "*Na glaz.*"

"Add flour, *na glaz.*"

"Just watch it. You'll know *na glaz* when it's done."

"Depends on the size of the bunch. Add half of it and then add more if needed, *na glaz.*"

Or my personal favorite: "No, I don't remember the measurements. Everything is *na glaz.*"

Around the point that she starts to contradict herself or offer up an arbitrary item like her orange mug with the flowers as a measuring unit is when I deem enough hair pulling is enough, and I hang up the phone. The notes down in front of me are a jumble of Russian and English approximations.

But I take the paper into the kitchen with me, and I begin to chop, stir, or knead anyway. Because what I've realized, over time, is that when I hit a gap or a question in the recipe, a funny thing happens. Images—my memory—take over. Cake batter thick as sour cream, slowly falling in ribbons from the whisk. Pale eggshell-white dumpling dough, smooth as a baby's bottom, springing right back when pressed with a finger. A burbling, filled-to-the-brim pot of borsch with just, *just* enough crimson red broth to suspend the shredded vegetables, but no more.

I embrace and trust my intuition to propel me forward. An intuition, in my case, cultivated from a lifetime of watching, helping, hanging out, and simply passing through my mom's and aunts' kitchens. In other words, I begin to cook *na glaz.*

CHAPTER ONE

BREAKFAST

RYAZHENKA

CULTURED BAKED MILK

Whenever I go to the Eastern European market, I skip over the kefir and instead grab a bottle of *ryazhenka*. Like kefir, this Ukrainian cultured drink (also known as *varenets* in Russia) is cool, tangy, and refreshing; but because the milk is first baked, it's custard-like with notes of dulce de leche. In the weeks after my son was born, I got into the habit of making it at home—a quiet little luxury I'd sip on to keep me awake and fueled during those around-the-clock nursing sessions.

To make it, milk is first cooked in a low oven until its sugars and proteins have caramelized and browned. During the process, the milk also develops a thin crust that comes to life in the oven, puffing and sputtering as the circulating air lifts it up and down. For many, this baked milk, stirred into coffee or sipped on its own, is an end goal in and of itself. But if you take it one step further and culture it, you get ryazhenka. Have it as a snack, dessert, or with breakfast; plain or with berries or jam. You can bake with it, too, swapping it in recipes that call for plain yogurt or kefir.

··

8 cups (1.9 kg) organic whole milk (avoid ultra-pasteurized)
⅓ cup (80 g) live-culture sour cream or plain kefir, at room temperature

MAKES ABOUT 1½ QUARTS (1.5 KG)

Position a rack in the center of the oven and preheat the oven to 300°F (150°C).

In a nonreactive, heavy-bottomed, ovenproof pot, bring the milk to a boil over medium heat. Stir occasionally to keep the milk from forming a skin, and as it comes to a boil, stir more frequently and do not walk away; otherwise your milk might burn at the bottom or foam up and spill over the sides of the pot. As soon as it starts to boil, remove from the heat.

Transfer the pot to the oven and bake, uncovered, until the milk smells like dulce de leche, is pale brown, and has a thin, very dark-brown crust on top, 2 to 3 hours, depending on how deep of a caramelized flavor you like.

Remove from the oven. Use a slotted spoon to break through the crust and carefully pull it back to allow the steam to escape without burning your hand. Fully remove the crust and set it aside on a plate. (At this point you can allow the milk to fully cool and then refrigerate it, along with the crust, for 2 to 3 days before proceeding with the fermentation.)

Allow the milk to cool, uncovered, at room temperature until the milk reaches 110°F (44°C), or it feels like warm bath water when you dip a clean pinky into it. Start checking after about 45 minutes. If you refrigerated the milk, you'll have to heat it to this temperature before continuing.

When ready, ladle some milk into a small cup and stir in the sour cream until smooth and combined. Pour back into the milk and whisk to combine. Either keep the milk in the pot or divide it into sterilized jars; top the surface with torn or cut pieces of the browned crust if desired.

Cover with a lid and lightly seal if using jars. Set in a warm place (see Finding the Warm Spot, page 38) free of drafts and leave undisturbed for 8 to 12 hours. It's ready when it is thick and

set (it will continue to thicken once chilled) and comes away from the sides when you tilt the jars.

Refrigerate until thoroughly chilled, 6 to 8 hours. The ryazhenka should be thick enough to eat with a spoon; if you'd rather it be more of a drinking consistency, stir the ryazhenka vigorously until it thins out. Store in airtight jars in the refrigerator for up to 3 weeks.

Note: *Start this project about 5 hours before you plan to go to sleep so that the ryazhenka can culture overnight and be ready in the morning when you wake up (see Sterilizing Jars + Streamlined Canning, page 176).*

VARIATION
Slow Cooker or Instant Pot Method: *Bake the boiled milk on low in a slow cooker or on the slow-cooker setting in the Instant Pot for 8 to 10 hours until the top is a caramel brown. Proceed with the rest of the recipe as directed.*

FINDING THE WARM SPOT

If you've ever struggled to find a warm place for fermenting, especially in the winter, here's what I like to do: Turn the oven light on and preheat the oven to the lowest temperature. When ready to transfer the covered pot or jars into the oven for culturing, turn the oven off (but keep the light on!).

If you can't use the oven, lay two small insulating blankets or towels on the dining table or other flat surface and put a kitchen towel over the top. Place the covered pot or jars in the middle. Wrap the blankets up and over the vessels, making an insulated cocoon to sustain the ferment's warmth and allow it to slowly culture. Place in the warmest spot in your house.

At room temperature, fermenting dairy can take 24 to 48 hours, so if yours isn't ready after the designated time in the recipe, allow it to keep sitting. Provided that your culture was indeed alive and you added it at the right temperature, the milk will eventually thicken.

APPLE OLADUSHKI

KEFIR PANCAKES

Oladushki are like American pancakes but better—slightly chewy on the inside, while the exterior, reminiscent of a freshly fried fritter, is golden and crispy—thanks to the plenty of oil they're pan-fried in! My mom always adds diced apple, which provides a nice textural contrast and hint of sweet and tart. You can of course omit the fruit, gently folding the dry ingredients until no traces of flour remain (think of this recipe like a muffin or quick bread, where it's better to undermix the batter). You can serve them with the same toppings as American pancakes, but we also always eat them with sour cream. They are best within the first couple of hours they're made, but you can revive oladushki with a reheat in a toaster oven.

• •

1⅔ cups (215 g) all-purpose flour
½ teaspoon baking soda
1 cup (240 g) full-fat plain kefir, warmed
1 egg
2 tablespoons granulated sugar
1 teaspoon vanilla extract
¾ teaspoon kosher salt
1 medium apple, cored and cut into small cubes
Neutral oil, such as sunflower or safflower oil, for the skillet
Powdered sugar, for dusting

MAKES 10 PANCAKES

In a small bowl, whisk together the flour and baking soda. Set aside.

In a second, larger bowl, whisk together the kefir, egg, granulated sugar, vanilla, and salt. Sift in the flour mixture and use a silicone spatula to gently fold it in until three-quarters of the way combined—you should still see floury lumps. Add the apple and gently fold until just incorporated and no traces of flour remain. It's important not to overmix here, otherwise your oladushki will come out gummy. Cover the bowl with a large plate and set aside for 20 minutes to allow the baking soda to activate. After this point, make sure not to stir the batter!

When ready to cook the oladushki, line a large plate with paper towels and set near the stove. Pour enough oil into a large nonstick skillet to cover the bottom of the pan. Set the pan over a smidge lower than medium heat and heat until the oil is very hot and shimmering.

Working in batches of 4, drop about ¼ cup (60 ml) of batter into the oil and use the back of a spoon to flatten the batter into even rounds—they will expand and double in size as they cook. The oladushki should quietly sizzle, not sputter or crackle, so adjust the heat as needed if they are browning too quickly (as they typically do on the first round). Cook until the bottom is golden and the interior has had some time to set up, 3 to 5 minutes. Use two forks to carefully flip the oladushki over. Cover the skillet with a lid and cook until the other side is golden and the interior is fully set, another 3 to 5 minutes. Transfer to the paper-towel-lined plate.

Cook the remaining batches, adding more oil to the pan as necessary, until no batter remains. Dust with powdered sugar and serve immediately.

SYRNIKI

FARMER CHEESE PANCAKES

At their best, *syrniki* are light, airy, and melt-in-your-mouth chubby pucks of tangy farmer cheese encased in a golden, crisp exterior. At their worst, they're pasty, rubbery, or have totally oozed into a puddle when pan-frying. The key to avoiding disappointing syrniki is, well, the *syr* (cheese). It's very important to use farmer cheese that is crumbly or on the drier side. Add a little egg, a little flour (rice flour produces the lightest pancakes), some sugar, and salt, and you're well on your way to this beloved breakfast treat. Use a gentle hand when flipping the delicate cakes.

Serve syrniki with the obligatory dollop of sour cream and something sweet to garnish: Jam or a fruit compote, fresh berries, honey, or syrup will all do.

....

1 pound (450 g) dry crumbly farmer cheese,
    homemade (page 55) or store-bought
1 egg yolk
2 tablespoons granulated sugar
½ teaspoon kosher salt
½ teaspoon vanilla extract
3 tablespoons (30 g) white rice flour or a
    combination of half semolina and half all-
    purpose flour
2 tablespoons neutral oil, such as sunflower or
    safflower, plus more as needed
Powdered sugar, for dusting

MAKES 8 PANCAKES

In a medium bowl, use the back of a spoon to mash the farmer cheese against the walls of the bowl until it's smooth and finely textured. For extra light syrniki, work it through a fine-mesh sieve.

To the farmer cheese, add the egg yolk, granulated sugar, salt, and vanilla. Using a spoon, mix thoroughly to combine. Add the flour and mix to incorporate. At this point, you can cover and refrigerate the mixture overnight.

Generously flour a work surface, as well as a large plate. Divide the mixture into 8 equal portions. Working with one piece at a time, dust with flour and gently roll it into a ball between lightly floured hands, then place it on the floured work surface. Lightly press down to form a puck and use your hands to shape the synrik into a 2½-inch (6.5 cm) disc. You can also use the flat edge of a knife to tap on the top and sides of the puck to smooth them out. Set the synrik on the flour-dusted plate and form the other syrniki. (If making ahead, freeze the syrniki for up to 2 months. See note below.)

Line a plate with paper towels and set near the stove. In a large nonstick skillet, heat the oil over medium heat until it shimmers. Working in two batches (you want to make sure you have plenty of room to flip them), cook the syrniki until golden brown on the bottom, 2 to 3 minutes. Use a rubber spatula to carefully flip and cook the second side just until golden, another 1 to 2 minutes. Transfer to the paper-towel-lined plate. Cook the second batch, adding more oil if needed to keep the pan well-greased.

Dust with powdered sugar and serve immediately. The syrniki are best as soon as they're made.

Note: *Cook frozen syrniki straight from frozen over medium-low heat, covered, allowing for a couple of extra minutes on each side.*

GRENKI

SAVORY FRENCH TOAST

Grenki are toast and eggs all in one. The key is not to overthink it and approach it as more of a concept than a strict recipe: The end goal being something you just throw together without measuring cups or spoons. My grandmother would fry these up for my mom and her ten (!) siblings, which they would then pair with strong sweetened black tea for breakfast or with chicken soup for lunch or dinner (the eggy, spongy interior is great for sopping up anything warm and brothy).

To make it a bit more substantial, once the second side is browning, generously sprinkle some Swiss or Cheddar cheese on top (and maybe add a slice of ham if you have it around) and cook until the bottom is crisp and golden brown and the cheese is melted.

· ·

2 eggs
Generous ¼ teaspoon kosher salt
Generous ¼ teaspoon freshly ground black pepper
¼ to ⅓ cup (60 to 80 g) whole milk, depending on
    how eggy you want it
Unsalted butter, for cooking
4 to 6 slices day-old white bread (a crusty artisan
    loaf also will work!), cut into thick slices

SERVES 2

In a shallow dish, beat together the eggs, salt, and pepper until smooth and combined. Whisk in the milk to incorporate. Set aside.

In a large nonstick skillet, melt a knob of butter over low heat. When the butter has melted and starts to foam, increase the heat so that it starts to sizzle.

Place a slice of bread in the egg mixture and soak for a few seconds. Flip and let the other side soak—continue to flip and soak one or two more times until the bread is evenly saturated, but not mushy.

Shake off any excess egg and place in the pan with the sizzling butter. If your pan is large enough, add a second piece of soaked bread to the pan. Cook until the bottom turns golden brown, about 2 minutes.

Flip and cook, adding more butter if needed to evenly coat the pan, another 2 minutes. The toast is done when you press on the center and it springs right back. If it doesn't, keep cooking, flipping the slices from time to time, until done.

Transfer to a serving plate and repeat with remaining slices. Serve immediately while still hot.

SCRAMBLED EGGS WITH TOMATOES

These scrambled eggs that my mom made for me are so easy that they became one of the first dishes I learned how to cook on my own as a child. They are fast, simple, and comforting and make a great anytime-of-the-day meal. Make sure you toast some bread while the eggs come together so you can use it to mop up all the juices. Best when made with peak tomatoes, but can also be made year-round using a good hothouse varietal—just make sure it's ripe!

....

2 eggs
¼ teaspoon kosher salt, plus more as needed
1 teaspoon unsalted butter or ghee
1 small firm-ripe tomato, cored and chopped
Granulated sugar
Freshly ground black pepper

SERVES 1 (OR MORE; SCALE AS NEEDED)

In a small bowl, lightly beat the eggs with the salt until smooth and combined. Set aside.

Heat an 8-inch (20 cm) nonstick skillet over medium heat until hot. Add the butter and once it has melted and starts to sizzle, add the chopped tomato, its juices, and a generous pinch of salt and sugar. Cook, stirring occasionally, until the tomatoes totally collapse and are no longer distinct, 4 to 5 minutes. Season with a few grinds of black pepper. Pour in the eggs. Allow to set for 30 seconds without stirring. Then, using a wooden spoon or spatula, begin pushing the eggs from the outside to the center of the pan. Tilt the pan so that any runny egg can flow into and fill the gaps. Pause, allowing the raw egg to set up a bit, and then repeat.

Continue stirring in this manner until the eggs are about 70% cooked. At this point, I usually remove the pan from the heat and continue stirring and breaking up large clumps until the eggs are just slightly underdone. If you like your eggs a bit harder, continue to cook them until you're happy with where they're at.

Transfer eggs to a serving plate and eat immediately.

MANNAYA KASHA

SEMOLINA PORRIDGE

No one who grew up in the Soviet Union (or their eventual offspring) escaped childhood without being fed a bowl of *mannaya kasha*. My own memories of *manka*, as it's affectionately known, begin with battles in the high chair: my mom attempting to coax me into one more bite while I cried and pulled away. Later, there was Aunt Dina from church—her little old face perpetually scrunched up in a grimace—who would stand over me at breakfast during summer camp and not let me leave until I finished my bowl. Yet, despite these traumatic experiences, given enough time, I have grown nostalgic for manka. When done right, it's supremely comforting and, dare I say, delicious.

The key is not to skimp on the good stuff (i.e., butter, milk, and sugar); to combine it first with cold water before heating it up so that it doesn't turn lumpy; and to serve it hot, as soon as it comes together. The result is a smooth, creamy porridge that—I mean it—even the pickiest eater will love. I recently started to prepare it for my toddler son, who, to my amazement, gobbles it all up. Maybe there's hope for mannaya kasha yet!

••

½ cup (120 g) water
2 tablespoons fine semolina or 3 tablespoons cream
    of wheat
Pinch of kosher salt
½ cup (120 g) whole milk
1 tablespoon granulated sugar, plus more to taste
1 tablespoon unsalted butter

SERVES 1

In a small saucepan, whisk together the water, semolina, and salt until smooth and combined. Set over medium-low heat and cook, whisking constantly, until the mixture has thickened and starts to simmer, about 3 minutes.

Gradually pour in the milk. Adjust the heat to maintain a gentle simmer and cook, whisking constantly, until the porridge is creamy and thick, 2 to 3 minutes. It will thicken as it cools, so if you like your porridge on the thinner side, add more water or milk to thin it out. Stir in the sugar and butter. Once the butter has melted, taste and add more sugar if desired.

Serve immediately as is or with another pat of butter, fresh fruit, syrup, or your favorite preserves.

Note: *You can make this with either fine semolina or, as we did when we moved to the States, cream of wheat. If using the latter, just make sure not to get instant. At the Eastern European store, fine semolina is sold as* mannaya krupa.

MILLET PORRIDGE WITH PUMPKIN

Porridge (*kasha*) in all its forms was considered extremely nutritious for children and, as such was often served at day cares and schools throughout the Soviet Union. This pumpkin millet variation was often on the menu. Slowly simmered in milk, the millet collapses into a creamy, slightly earthy porridge with just a hint of chew; the pumpkin lends a warm, inviting sun-gold hue. Traditionally you stir in granulated sugar or honey at the end to taste, but honestly, it's so good and just sweet enough from the pumpkin and dairy, that I find it doesn't need much more in that department.

....

1 cup (200 g) millet
2 cups (480 g) water, plus more for soaking
    and rinsing
½ teaspoon kosher salt, plus more to taste
2 cups (480 g) whole milk, or more as needed
1 pound (450 g) pumpkin or winter squash,
    peeled and cut into ½-inch (1.3 cm) cubes
¼ cup (55 g) unsalted butter
Granulated sugar or honey (optional)

SERVES 4, WITH LEFTOVERS

In a medium bowl, combine the millet and enough water to fully submerge. Soak for 6 to 8 hours or overnight. (If you forgot this step, pour enough boiling water over the millet to cover and let it sit for 10 minutes before proceeding.)

Drain the millet. Place it in a medium pot (which you'll use for cooking) and add enough water to submerge. Swish it around, drain, and repeat again.

Return the millet to the pot. Add the 2 cups (480 g) water and salt. Bring to a boil over medium-high heat. Cover, reduce the heat to maintain a gentle simmer, and cook for 15 minutes. The water will mostly, but not fully, evaporate.

Stir in the milk and pumpkin. Bring to a simmer again and cook, stirring occasionally to prevent the porridge from sticking, until the porridge is thick, creamy, and has lost its bitter edge, 30 to 35 minutes. If the porridge starts to get too thick at any point, stir in more milk or water to loosen it up.

Stir in the butter and cook for another minute or two. Remove from the heat. Taste and add more salt if desired. Cover and let sit for 10 to 15 minutes before serving. If desired, serve topped with a sweetener.

Store in an airtight container in the refrigerator for up to 5 days or in the freezer for up to 2 months. To reheat, scoop your desired amount into a small saucepan, add a generous splash of water or coconut milk per cup of porridge being reheated, and bring to a gentle simmer, stirring occasionally, so that the porridge is heated through. Stir and serve.

Note: *My Aunt Natasha also makes a vegan version: Omit the butter and swap out the cow's milk for 1¾ cups (420 g) canned full-fat coconut milk and ¼ cup (60 g) water.*

BLINCHIKI

SLAVIC-STYLE CREPES

Quick *blinchiki*—thin melt-in-your-mouth crepes—often began with a request on Saturday mornings. Happy to oblige, my mom would thin some Bisquick batter with milk and start churning them out. As a *blinchik* landed in the stack, she'd hold a stick of butter like a glue stick and swipe it across the crepe's surface to give it a glossy, rich finish. Impatient, I'd swipe one, fold it and roll it up like a carpet, and dunk it into copious amounts of sour cream and Aunt Jemima syrup, and then repeat. That is, until I found myself splayed out on the couch in a carb coma, unable to move.

Nowadays we make the batter from scratch and opt for real maple syrup. I'll put out berries, preserves, honey, Nutella, and even sweetened condensed milk to fill out the spread. The sour cream is still a must. As for my restraint? Well, I'm still working on it.

....

3 eggs
2 cups (480 g) whole milk, warmed or at
    room temperature
1½ cups (195 g) all-purpose flour
3 tablespoons (45 g) neutral oil
2 tablespoons granulated sugar
¾ teaspoon kosher salt
1 cup (240 g) boiling water
Cold butter, for frying and coating

MAKES ABOUT 24 CREPES

In a blender, combine the eggs, milk, flour, oil, sugar, and salt and blend until the batter is completely smooth and lump free, 20 to 30 seconds. With the blender running, add the boiling water all at once and mix to combine. The batter should be a bit thinner than heavy cream. Allow the batter to rest for 30 minutes at room temperature. (Or refrigerate in an airtight container for up to 2 days.)

When ready to cook the blinchiki, have a large plate and cold stick of butter at the ready. Heat a 10-inch (25 cm) nonstick skillet over medium to medium-high heat (see Note). Use the stick of butter to swipe a thin layer over the bottom of the pan and then mop up any excess with a paper towel.

Give the batter a good stir. With the pan at an angle, ladle a scant ¼ cup (60 ml) of the batter into the pan while simultaneously tilting the pan in a circular motion. You want the batter to spread into a very thin, round layer over the bottom of the pan. Shake the pan back and forth to spread the batter to any spots it didn't reach. Work quickly and don't despair if your first blinchik comes out less than ideal—we have a saying in Russian: "первый блин—комом," meaning the first blin is always lumpy. It'll take a few tries to get the amount of batter and the swirl right.

Cook until the edges begin to brown and start to come away from the pan slightly, the bottom is lightly golden and lacy, and the top looks set, about 1 minute. Use your fingers or spatula to loosen the edge closest to you and quickly flip. Cook until the bottom is set and golden in patches, 10 to 15 seconds. Turn out onto the large plate (the bottom should be facing up now) and swipe butter all over to give it a nice glossy finish. Repeat the process, stacking and buttering the cooked blinchiki as they're done, until no more batter remains. Serve immediately. Store well wrapped in the refrigerator for 2 to 3 days.

Note: *I've found that you get different types of blinchiki depending on the heat of your pan. If you want a lacy blinchik, you'll want to cook at a higher heat. If you want blinchik that's closer to a traditional crepe (and/or you're planning on filling them), cook over medium heat.*

BLINCHIKI WITH BEEF

We love blinchiki plain, and we love them even more filled and pan-fried until golden and crisp or baked until even more tender. I suggest making a full recipe of Blinchiki (page 48)—you'll have some left over that are perfect for breakfast or snacking. You can also double the filling if you're cooking for a big crowd or want to stash some away in the freezer for another day.

This savory filling, while nothing fancy, is a Slavic favorite. There's something about the slightly sweet *blinchik* paired with the juicy beef and onion that is particularly beguiling. While they're best hot off the stove served for lunch or light supper, the little parcels also travel well, making them wonderful for road trips and beach days.

••

A generous splash of water, chicken broth, or beef broth
1 pound (450 g) ground beef (85/15)
1 tablespoon extra-virgin olive oil or neutral oil, plus more for frying
1 medium yellow onion, finely diced
1 tablespoon unsalted butter
A few sprigs parsley or dill, finely chopped (optional)
Kosher salt and freshly ground black pepper
12 Blinchiki (page 48)

MAKES 12 FILLED BLINCHIKI

Heat a large nonstick skillet over medium-low heat. Pour in the water and then add the ground beef. Using a wooden spoon, break up the beef into smaller pieces. Reduce the heat to low, cover, and cook, stirring occasionally, until the beef is tender and cooked through, 6 to 8 minutes. Use a slotted spoon to scoop the beef into a medium bowl and set aside. Pour out and discard any of the meat juices and wipe the pan clean.

Set the skillet over medium heat and heat the oil until shimmering. Add the onion and cook, stirring occasionally, until it's soft, translucent, and has lost its raw edge, 8 to 10 minutes. Remove from the heat. Stir in the cooked meat and butter and once combined, stir in the parsley or dill (if using). Taste and season with salt and pepper. Allow to cool before proceeding. (The filling can be stored in an airtight container in the refrigerator for 1 to 2 days.)

Spoon about ¼ cup (35 g) of the meat mixture onto the bottom third of a blinchik. Bring the bottom edge over the filling to cover. Fold the left and right sides over the filling and then tightly roll up the blinchik, like a burrito. Set aside and continue until you have filled all your blinchiki. (You can make them ahead to this point and store the filled blinchiki in the refrigerator for 3 to 4 days from the day the meat was cooked; or in the freezer for 2 to 3 months.)

When ready to serve, add enough oil to evenly cover the bottom of a large nonstick skillet and heat over medium heat until hot. Working in batches of 4 or 5, lower the blinchiki into the oil away from you. Cook until the bottom is golden and crisp, 2 to 3 minutes. If they're browning too quickly, reduce the heat. Flip, reduce the heat to medium-low, and cook until golden and warmed through, 3 to 5 minutes. Transfer to a serving plate and cook the remaining blinchiki.

BLINCHIKI WITH FARMER CHEESE

These are what you might know as Jewish blintzes. Serve with sour cream on the side and a spoonful of fruit compote (such as Sour Cherry Compote, page 195)—preserves or fresh fruit would also be welcome.

1 pound (450 g) farmer cheese, homemade (page 55) or store-bought
1 egg yolk
3 tablespoons (35 g) granulated sugar
½ teaspoon kosher salt
¼ teaspoon vanilla extract (optional)
12 Blinchiki (page 48)
Olive oil or neutral oil, such as sunflower or safflower, for frying
Powdered sugar, for dusting

MAKES 12 FILLED BLINCHIKI

SLAVIC CREPE GLOSSARY

Bliny (*sing.* **blin**): These are made with a leavened batter that can be cooked into chubby pucks or, as they more often do in Russia and Ukraine, thin pan-size crepes.

Blinchiki (*sing.* **blinchik**): *Blinchiki* are made with a "quick" unleavened batter that is cooked and eaten like French crepes. The word also describes the filled, rolled, and pan-fried blinchiki.

Nalysnyky (*sing.* **nalysnyk**): Ukrainian term for blinchiki that are filled with *tvorog* (farmer cheese) and then pan-fried or baked.

In a medium bowl, mash the farmer cheese with the back of a spoon against the wall of the bowl to break up the curds until it's finely textured. Add the egg yolk, granulated sugar, salt, and vanilla (if using) and mix until smooth and combined. (Alternatively, you can process everything together in the bowl using an immersion blender.)

Spoon 3 tablespoons (50 g) of the cheese mixture onto the bottom third of a blinchik. Bring the bottom edge over the filling to cover. Fold the left and right sides over the filling and then tightly roll up the blinchik, like a burrito. Set aside and continue until you have filled all your blinchiki. (You can make them ahead to this point and store the filled blinchiki in the refrigerator for 3 to 4 days or in the freezer for 2 to 3 months.)

When ready to serve, add enough oil to evenly cover the bottom of a large nonstick skillet and heat over medium heat until hot. Working in batches of 4 or 5, lower the blinchiki into the oil away from you. Cook until the bottom is golden and crisp, 2 to 3 minutes. If they're browning too quickly, reduce the heat. Flip, reduce the heat to medium-low, and cook until golden and warmed through, 3 to 5 minutes. Transfer to a serving plate and cook the remaining blinchiki.

Dust with powdered sugar and serve immediately.

BAKED NALYSNYKY
WITH FARMER CHEESE

In Odessa, huge platters of these baked *Nalysnyky* filled with sweetened *tvorog* are made for weddings and other special occasions. My friend Yana's grandmother, Babushka Galya, would often bake up enough to fit an entire hotel pan and bring them to church potlucks. Doused in butter, slightly sweet and tangy, the Nalysnyky melt in your mouth and it's easy to eat an entire plate if you aren't careful. She graciously shared her recipe with me and I share it with you here, albeit with some changes. I hope these would make her proud!

••

½ cup (115 g) melted unsalted butter, for the baking
    dish and brushing the blinchiki
1½ pounds (680 g) farmer cheese, homemade
    (page 55) or store-bought
1 egg
Generous ¼ cup (60 g) granulated sugar
¾ teaspoon kosher salt
Generous ¼ teaspoon vanilla extract (optional)
18 Blinchiki (page 48)

SERVES 6 TO 8

Preheat the oven to 325°F (160°C). Generously brush an 8 x 11-inch (20 x 28 cm) baking dish (or other 2½-quart / 2.4 L baking dish) with melted butter.

In a medium bowl, mash the farmer cheese with the back of a spoon against the wall of the bowl to break up the curds until it's finely textured. Add the egg, sugar, salt, and vanilla (if using) and mix until smooth and combined. Set aside. (Alternatively, you can process everything together in the bowl using an immersion blender.)

Take the stack of blinchiki and flip them onto a cutting board so that the more browned side is facing up.

Working with one blinchik at a time, evenly spread a thin layer of the farmer cheese mixture on top, leaving a slight border around the edges and right down the middle so that the filling doesn't leak out when baking. Fold the blinchik 1½ inches (4 cm) over itself, then continue to roll the blinchik up like a carpet. Cut in half. Transfer the two pieces to the prepared pan, seam side down and cut side facing in toward the center. Repeat, nestling the filled blinchiki into an even layer.

Generously brush the blinchiki with melted butter. Repeat with remaining blinchiki to create two more layers, generously brush each layer with butter. (The assembled blinchiki can be made and stored in the refrigerator up to a day in advance. Add 5 to 10 minutes to the baking time.)

Generously brush the blinchiki with half of the remaining melted butter. Repeat with the remaining blinchiki to create a second layer, generously brush with the rest of the butter. Evenly sprinkle the blinchiki with some sugar. Cover tightly with foil.

Bake until the blinchiki are soft, tender, and completely heated through, 35 to 40 minutes. Serve ideally while still hot or warm, but room temperature also works.

Leftovers can be stored in the refrigerator for 3 to 4 days.

Note: *When making the blinchiki for this recipe, cook them for only a couple seconds on the second side to keep them tender.*

TVOROG

FARMER CHEESE

I always marveled at how my Aunt Olga could set out a pot of milk to warm overnight, and by late morning the next day have cheese. What she was conjuring was, in fact, a simple curd cheese called *tvorog*. A bit drier than ricotta with a sharper, tangier edge, tvorog is a workhorse in the Slavic kitchen. It's turned into everything from Syrniki (page 41) and Easter *paskha*, cheesecakes of different shapes and sizes, as well as into a filling for Vatrushki (page 82), pirozhki (page 76), and Blinchiki (page 48), among other delectables. It's also great fresh, blended with herbs and green onions and spread on toast as a snack or—my personal favorite—topped with a dollop of sour cream or yogurt and a generous dousing of sugar or honey for breakfast or dessert.

When I asked my aunt to walk me through her process, she, like most women of her generation, didn't bother with exact temperatures or amounts—it was all by look and feel. After some trial and error, I've woven some technical details into her method to set you up for success. You'll get enough tvorog to make any recipe in the book that calls for it, and then some.

••

1 gallon (3.8 kg) organic whole milk (avoid ultra-pasteurized)
½ cup (120 g) organic whole-milk yogurt or kefir, at room temperature

MAKES ABOUT 2 POUNDS (910 G)

In a large, heavy-bottomed, nonreactive pot, heat the milk over medium heat, stirring frequently to make sure it doesn't burn at the bottom, until it reaches 110°F (44°C), or it feels like warm bath water when you dip a clean pinky into it.

In a small bowl, stir together the yogurt with a few ladles of the warmed milk. Stir back into the milk. Cover the pot and place somewhere warm (see Finding the Warm Spot, page 38),

undisturbed, for 8 to 12 hours. The cultured milk is ready when it's the consistency of thin yogurt, comes away from the sides of the wall when you tilt the pot, and tastes slightly tangy.

Place the pot, uncovered, over low heat. Do not stir at this point! Instead, gently shake the pot from time to time to circulate the milk and keep it from burning on the bottom. As it warms, you'll start to see large cracks in the surface as the dairy separates into curds (white cottage-cheese-like clumps) and whey (yellowish liquid). Continue to heat, giving it a couple of gentle stirs from time to time, until you have small distinct curds that have completely separated from the whey. Remove from the heat and let cool for 1 hour.

Meanwhile, set a colander over a large bowl and line it with a couple layers of cheesecloth or a clean muslin towel.

Pour the cooled curds and whey into the cheesecloth (you might have to do this in batches if your colander isn't large enough, waiting for the whey to drain off a bit before pouring again). Drain for at least 2 to 3 hours and up to 8 or 10 hours at room temperature (see Note). For a dry, crumbled tvorog, place a plate over the tvorog and set a heavy weight over it while it drains. Transfer to an airtight container. (Store the tvorog in the refrigerator for up to 2 weeks and in the freezer for up to 2 months.)

Note: *Do not toss the whey! If your tvorog ends up too dry, you can stir some of the whey back into it until the desired consistency is achieved. Other uses for whey: Swap it for the liquid in yeasted doughs, such as for pirozhki, khachapuri, or blinchiki. You can also use it to marinate meat, ferment vegetables, make caramel, or add a protein boost to oatmeal, smoothies, or soup.*

CHAPTER TWO

DUMPLINGS, PASTRIES, AND BREADS

VARENYKY

UKRAINIAN DUMPLINGS

Whenever I make *varenyky*, I'm reminded of the first time I tried them: It was summertime, the AC was blasting, and I was sitting on my friend Ruta's bedroom floor, watching old videos of the Soviet cartoon *Cheburashka* with her and her siblings. Her mom brought us lunch—*tvorog*-filled dumplings smothered in sour cream and generously dusted with sugar—and as I tucked in, I was lovestruck. The soft, tender dough, the bright, slightly salty cheese, the granular sweet hit from the sugar melding with tangy sour cream. It was like eating tiny, sumptuous pillows of joy and comfort. I quickly learned, as I shuffled into the kitchen for a second helping, that one bowl is never enough when it comes to varenyky.

I still have a soft spot for those sweet varenyky, but I've come to appreciate them in all their forms. Unlike *pelmeni*, dumplings with a bit more of a snap to their dough and made with meat filling, varenyky are more tender and are typically prepared with vegetables, fruit, or cheese. Like any dumpling endeavor, however, varenyky demand your time and patience—but I don't think I need to convince you that the effort will be worth it. Varenyky are also good boiled and then pan-fried in butter until golden.

••

DOUGH
3 cups (390 g) all-purpose flour (see note page 61),
    plus more for rolling
1 tablespoon kosher salt
¾ cup plus 1 tablespoon (195 g) boiling water
3 tablespoons (45 g) neutral oil

FILLING (CHOOSE ONE)
Herbed Mushroom and Potato Filling (recipe
    follows)
Farmer Cheese Filling (recipe follows)

TO FINISH
Kosher salt
1 to 2 tablespoons unsalted butter
Sour cream, for serving
For sweet dumplings: 1 to 2 tablespoons granulated
    sugar or Sour Cherry Compote (page 195) or
    other preserves

MAKES ABOUT 40 DUMPLINGS

Make the dough: In a large bowl, mix together the flour and salt. Make a well in the center and add the boiling water and oil. Using a large spoon, gradually incorporate the flour by knocking it from the inside edges of the well into the wet ingredients. At first the dough will be crumbly. Switch to your hands and bring the dough together and knead it into one mass.

Scrape the dough out onto a clean work surface and continue to knead until it's mostly smooth, feels soft with a bit of resistance, and slowly springs back when you poke it, 10 to 12 minutes. Wrap in plastic wrap or an old produce bag and allow to rest at room temperature for at least 30 minutes and up to 2 hours.

Make the filling: Make either the savory or sweet filling and allow to come to room temperature before proceeding.

Assemble the varenyky: After its rest, the dough should be smooth as a baby's bottom and very pliable. Generously dust a baking sheet with flour. Divide the dough in half and leave one half covered under a slightly damp cloth while you work with the other.

On a lightly floured surface, roll out the dough into a 15-inch (38 cm) round (or as close as you can get) about ⅟₁₆ inch (2 mm) thick. Use a 3¼-inch (8 cm) cookie cutter or the rim of a wide glass to stamp out rounds of dough. You should get about 15. Any leftover dough scraps can be brought together, placed under the damp cloth, and rerolled at the very end after it's had time to rest again.

Fill each round with about 2 teaspoons of filling. Fold the round into a half-moon and pinch the edges to seal. You can leave the varenyky this way, or pleat the edges.

To pleat the edges, starting at one corner, fold a triangle of dough from the edge down over itself. Pinch to seal, extending that part a bit as you press on it. Fold down a second triangle right next to the first. Press down to seal and repeat, working

your way around the edge. Tuck the last triangle underneath itself.

Transfer the shaped dumplings to the prepared baking sheet and cover with a damp kitchen towel to prevent them from drying out. Repeat with the remaining dough and filling. At this point, the dumplings can be cooked or frozen (place the baking sheet directly into the freezer and then transfer to an airtight bag once they're frozen).

Finish the varenyky: Bring a large pot of well-salted water to a nice, gentle boil. You don't want it too vigorous or the dough will rip apart and develop holes. Drag a large spoon around the pot until it creates a whirlpool.

Working in batches, add the dumplings into the center of the whirl. Once they've floated to the top, 2 to 3 minutes, cook them for 1 minute more. Stir occasionally with a spoon to make sure the dumplings don't stick to the bottom of the pot. Use a slotted spoon or spider strainer to fish out the dumplings, shaking off any water, and spoon directly into a large bowl.

Add some of the butter, depending on how many dumplings you've cooked, and gently stir together to make sure the melted butter evenly coats the dumplings. Dish out among serving bowls and serve with sour cream. If making sweet varenyky, generously dust with sugar or spoon the sour cherry preserves or compote over the dumplings before dolloping with sour cream. Eat immediately!!

FLOUR FOR DUMPLINGS

For the varenyky and the following dumpling recipes, I used a Gold Medal bleached all-purpose flour that clocks in at about 10.5% protein. Depending on the all-purpose or plain flour you use, you might have to adjust the water or flour to fine-tune the dough. If the dough feels tacky or sticky, dust it with more flour. If, after a few minutes of kneading, the dough feels dry or there is still a lot of flour leftover, then add a ½ teaspoon of water onto the dough or dry bits and knead to incorporate. Repeat as needed. A lot of this comes with practice, so go by feel and don't get nervous!

HERBED POTATO AND MUSHROOM VARENYKY FILLING

Some of Eastern Europe's best flavors all in one savory, delectable dumpling. For an even *more* classic take, omit the mushrooms and dill and add a handful of good melty cheese like Cheddar or Gruyère instead.

. . . .

1 pound (450 g) Yukon Gold potatoes, peeled and quartered
Kosher salt
½ pound (225 g) cremini mushrooms, finely diced
3 tablespoons (45 g) unsalted butter
1 small yellow onion, finely diced
½ cup (15 g) dill, finely chopped
¼ teaspoon hot or sweet paprika, plus more to taste
Freshly ground black pepper

MAKES ENOUGH FILLING FOR 40 DUMPLINGS

Place the potatoes in a medium saucepan or pot and fill with enough cold water to cover and generously salt. Bring to a boil. Reduce the heat and simmer, uncovered, until they can be pierced easily with a fork, 15 to 20 minutes. Drain and transfer to a medium bowl.

Meanwhile, heat a large nonstick skillet over medium-high heat. Add the mushrooms and dry-sauté, stirring occasionally, until the liquid the mushrooms release has mostly evaporated, 6 to 8 minutes.

Reduce the heat to medium and add the butter, onion, and a generous pinch of salt. Cook until the edges of the onion begin to brown and the mushrooms take on color, 10 to 12 minutes. Remove from the heat.

Mash the potatoes with a fork or potato masher. Add the mushroom mixture, dill, and paprika, and mix to combine. Taste and season with salt and pepper to taste and more paprika if needed. Allow to cool to room temp before filling the dumplings.

FARMER CHEESE VARENYKY FILLING

Tangy, salty, and just slightly sweet, all these dumplings need is some sour cream or vinegar. For a sweeter turn, top them with a dusting of sugar or a spoonful or two of sour cherry preserves or compote (page 195).

. . . .

1 pound (450 g) dry crumbled farmer cheese, homemade (page 55) or store-bought
4 teaspoons granulated sugar (optional)
1 teaspoon kosher salt

MAKES ENOUGH FILLING FOR 40 DUMPLINGS

In a medium bowl, mix together the farmer cheese, sugar (if using), and salt until combined. Can be used cold or at room temperature.

PELMENI

SIBERIAN DUMPLINGS

Come across a chest freezer in the Eastern European store and it will almost always be filled to the brim with frozen Siberian dumplings called *pelmeni*. Sometimes they'll be professionally packaged with a label, but more times than not, they're packed into large ziplock bags—a little paper slipped inside reveals the type. Most people rely on these store-bought dumplings to get their pelmeni fix. But what if your local pelmeni aren't very good? What if you don't have access to an Eastern European store? What if... you just have a lot of time on your hands to fill? In that case, I've got just the recipe for you. The process, while time-consuming, is quite cathartic and transports me to Siberia, where the winters are so cold that uncooked pelmeni are stashed outside in banks of snow or unheated barns and sheds. Now how's that for a freezer?

Yes, this recipe makes a lot of pelmeni, but considering that a family of four can easily put away fifty dumplings in a sitting—then the yield becomes quite reasonable. To break up the process, you can make the filling a day in advance. Pelmeni are often tossed in melted butter and then topped with sour cream and a few grinds of black pepper. Equally delicious is simmering the dumplings in Mama's Bouillon (page 90) and serving them together as a simple soup.

··

DOUGH
3½ cups (455 g) all-purpose flour (see note page 61), plus more for dusting
1 tablespoon kosher salt
¾ cup plus 1 tablespoon (195 g) very warm tap water
1 egg, beaten
1 tablespoon sunflower oil

FILLING
1½ medium yellow onions, quartered
12 ounces (340 g) ground beef (80/20 or 85/15)
12 ounces (340 g) ground pork
4 teaspoons kosher salt
Generous 1 teaspoon freshly ground black pepper
⅓ cup (80 g) ice water

TO FINISH
Kosher salt
1 to 2 tablespoons unsalted butter
Freshly ground black pepper (optional)
Sour cream, Russian-style hot mustard, or white vinegar (optional)

MAKES ABOUT 100 DUMPLINGS

Make the dough: In a large bowl, mix together the flour and salt. Make a well in the center and add the water, egg, and oil. Using a large spoon, gradually incorporate the flour by knocking it from the inside edges of the well and into the wet ingredients. Once the spoon becomes cumbersome to work with, switch over to your hands and mix until it becomes one large, shaggy mass.

Turn out the dough onto a work surface and continue to knead for 5 to 7 minutes. At first the dough will be rough and uneven, but by the end it will be mostly smooth, elastic, and spring right back when you press it. Wrap it in plastic wrap or an old produce bag and allow it to rest at room temperature for 30 to 45 minutes.

Make the filling: In a food processor, process the onions until pureed. Transfer to a large bowl. (You can also finely grate the onions by hand.) Add the beef, pork, salt, and pepper. Mix, squeezing the meat through your fingers, until evenly combined. Drizzle in the water, a bit at a time, and mix until fully incorporated.

Holding the bowl in place with one hand, start to knead the meat with the other by scooping the meat from the bottom with a closed hand, folding it over the top, and flattening it back it down with the heel of your hand.

Don't be afraid to get aggressive! You want to properly work it here, which will result in a juicy filling with a pleasant, bouncy bite.

Continue to knead this way for a couple more minutes until the fat is evenly integrated and the meat is properly "agitated"—you're looking for a nice fat-smeared sheen and a tacky feel to the meat.

To test for seasoning, take a teaspoon of meat, set it on a plate, and microwave on high for 15 seconds. Taste and add more salt and black pepper if needed.

Refrigerate until ready to assemble, up to 1 day.

Assemble the pelmeni: After its rest, the dough should be smooth as a baby's bottom and very pliable. Generously dust a baking sheet with flour. Take one-quarter of the dough and leave the rest covered under a slightly damp cloth while you work.

On a work surface, roll out the dough into a rope about the thickness of your finger. If your dough is slipping on the work surface when rolling, dip your finger in water and use it to lightly wet the surface—this should create some traction. Cut the rope into ¾-inch (2 cm) nuggets—you should get around 25. Sprinkle flour over the pieces and gently toss them so they're evenly coated. Stand the pieces upright, gently reshape them if needed so that they're round, and then press down into their centers with your thumb to flatten them (They should look like red blood cells, or donuts without a hole). Roll each piece out into a 2-inch (5 cm) round, dusting with more flour as needed to prevent the dough from sticking.

Fill each round of dough with 1 to 1½ teaspoons of filling. Fold the round into a half-moon and pinch the edges to seal. Then take the two pointed corners and pull them down toward each other until the corners are overlapping and there's no gap in the middle.

Think of an old babushka taking the two corners of her head scarf and snugly tying them together below her chin.

Tightly pinch to seal. Then go over the edges again, pinching to flatten and smooth them out.

Transfer the shaped dumplings to the prepared baking sheet and cover with a damp kitchen towel to prevent them from drying out. Repeat with the remaining dough and filling. (At this point, the dumplings can be cooked or frozen. To freeze, place the baking sheet directly into the freezer and then transfer to an airtight bag once they're frozen.)

Finish the pelmeni: When ready to cook, bring a large pot of well-salted water to a nice, gentle boil. You don't want it too vigorous or the dough will rip apart and develop holes. Drag a large spoon around the pot until it creates a whirlpool.

Working in batches, quickly add the dumplings into the center of the whirl. Once they've floated to the top, 2 to 3 minutes, cook them for 3 minutes more. Turn the heat down to a lively simmer after the water comes to a boil again—this will make bursting less likely. Stir occasionally with a spoon to make sure the dumplings don't stick to the bottom of the pot. Use a slotted spoon or spider strainer to fish out the dumplings, shaking off any water, and spoon directly into a large bowl.

Add some of the butter, depending on how many dumplings you've cooked, and gently stir together to make sure the melted butter evenly coats the dumplings. Dish out among serving bowls and serve with garnish of choice (my personal pick is sour cream and black pepper). Eat immediately!!

KHINKALI

GEORGIAN SOUP DUMPLINGS

The Georgian Military Highway is an epic route that cuts through the Caucasus to connect Tbilisi to the North Ossetia town of Vladikavkaz. One minute you're driving through a narrow gorge: Snowcapped peaks and green-carpeted ridges loom on either side, herds of sheep and bales of hay dot the verdant slopes, and the Aragvi River, never far, rushes by. The next—you're ascending those mountains by way of precarious curves and switchbacks, holding on for dear life until the steep road hits its peak at Jvari Pass, around 8,000 feet.

At some point on the mountain road, at the stunning convergence of the two Aragvi Rivers, the Black and the White, sits Pasanauri. A popular country retreat for city folk in Soviet times, the quaint town is still a destination. Its visitors, however, make the journey not to gaze at the waters but to eat the town's famed *khinkali*: large, juicy, meat-filled soup dumplings characterized by their many pleats and little topknot known as *kudi* (hat).

Some claim it's the special quality of the river water, and others say it's the local flour that make the dumplings so toothsome. It may also be the lush backdrop of the mountains and the sound of the Aragvi, just across the road from where you're seated at a restaurant. Whatever it is, the town's khinkali—with their taut, glistening skins and brothy interior—are truly memorable.

I've had many khinkali in my life, but since my first trip back to Georgia as an adult in 2015, I've been on a quest to re-create one that would be deemed Pasanauri-worthy. A plate of my own soup dumplings doesn't come with a dazzling mountain setting, but it will certainly inspire some trip-planning.

Khinkali are typically served with a dusting of freshly cracked black pepper and a sense of urgency—these are best eaten as soon as they come out of the pot. A true Georgian would scoff at a dollop of sour cream on the side, but it's how my Slavic dairy-loving family eats them, so take the suggestion or leave it. You can serve khinkali with a salad and easily call it a meal; although in Georgia it's often just one part of a *supra*, a multi-dish feast.

This recipe can easily be scaled and lends itself well to a khinkali-making party. Cook however many you think you'll eat and freeze the rest for when the next dumpling craving strikes. Any leftover cooked khinkali can be revitalized the next day with a light pan-fry in butter.

....

DOUGH
3¾ cups (490 g) all-purpose flour (see note
page 61), plus more for dusting
1 tablespoon kosher salt
1 cup (240 g) ice-cold water
1 tablespoon sunflower oil

FILLING
1 medium yellow onion, sliced into eighths
1 cup (35 g) roughly chopped cilantro leaves
and stems
2 tablespoons roughly chopped parsley leaves
and tender stems
½ pound (225 g) ground beef (85/15)
½ pound (225 g) ground pork
2 teaspoons kosher salt, plus more to taste
1 teaspoon red pepper flakes
¾ teaspoon ground cumin
⅔ cup (160 g) cold water

TO FINISH
Kosher salt
Freshly ground black pepper
Sour cream (optional)

MAKES 16 TO 18 DUMPLINGS

Make the dough: In a large bowl, whisk together the flour and salt. Make a well in the center and add the water and oil. Using a large spoon, gradually incorporate the flour by knocking it from the inside edges of the well and into the wet ingredients. Once the spoon becomes cumbersome to work with, switch over to your hands and mix until it becomes one large, shaggy mass.

Turn out the dough onto a work surface and continue to knead the dough, incorporating any last bits of flour and dough, for 10 to 15 minutes. At first it will be rough and uneven, but by the end it will be a bit smoother (it will look slightly pockmarked), elastic, and will spring right back when you press it. If, after a few minutes of kneading, the dough is still dry or has unincorporated bits, add a teaspoon of water (or more as needed) onto the dough and knead to incorporate. Wrap the dough in plastic wrap or an old produce bag. Refrigerate for at least 45 minutes and up to 2 hours.

Make the filling: In a food processor, combine the onion, cilantro, and parsley and process until very finely chopped. Transfer to a large bowl. Add the beef, pork, salt, pepper flakes, and cumin. Mix, squeezing the meat through your fingers, until evenly combined. Drizzle in the water, a bit at a time, and mix in until fully incorporated.

Adding water here is important because it keeps the filling moist and juicy during the cooking process. It, in turn, soaks up the flavor and fat of the meat and becomes the wondrous broth the dumplings are known for.

Holding the bowl in place with one hand, start to knead the meat with the other, scooping the meat from the bottom with a closed hand, folding it over the top, and flattening it back it down with the heel of your hand.

Don't be afraid to get aggressive! You want to properly work it here, which will result in a juicy filling with a pleasant, bouncy bite.

Continue to knead this way for a couple more minutes until the fat is evenly integrated and the meat is properly "agitated"—you're looking for a nice fat-smeared sheen and a tacky feel to the meat.

To test for seasoning, take a teaspoon of meat, set it on a plate, and microwave on high for 15 seconds. Taste and add more salt, pepper flakes, and cumin if needed.

Refrigerate for 15 to 20 minutes and up to 1 day.

Assemble the khinkali: After its rest, the dough should be smooth as a baby's bottom and very pliable. Generously dust a baking sheet with flour. Divide the dough in half and leave one half wrapped and refrigerated while you work with the other.

On a lightly floured work surface, roll out the dough into a 10-inch (25 cm) round about ¼ inch (6 mm) thick. You want the dough on the thicker side because you'll be rolling it out again once you cut it into rounds.

Use a 3-inch (7.5 cm) cookie cutter or wide glass to stamp out rounds from the dough. You should get 7. Any leftover dough scraps can be brought together, wrapped in plastic with the remaining dough, and rerolled at the very end after it's had time to rest again.

Roll out the rounds until 5 ½ to 6 inches (14 to 15.25 cm) in diameter.

Give your meat a good mix with a spoon to incorporate any liquid that's been released. Then place about 2 tablespoons of filling in the center of each round. Using your thumb and pointer finger, pick up the edge at 12 o'clock and bring it in toward the center. Grab the edge at 11 o'clock with your other hand and bring it over to 12 to fold the dough and form a pleat. Pinch the pleat in place. Moving in a counterclockwise direction and always working over the center (the hand that started at 12 o'clock should ideally never move), fold and pinch as you go, allowing each pleat to slightly overlap the previous one. If at any point the meat seems to be sliding out, grab the unpleated edge, pull up, and shake the meat back into the center of your little "beggar's purse." Continue until the filling is completely encased. The magic number of pleats is nineteen—anything less is considered amateur—but I say 12 or 13 are more than enough. As long as the top is tightly closed (you don't want any juices leaking out!), that's all that matters.

Firmly pinch the topknot to tightly seal. Use a paring knife to trim the top for a clean-cut edge (or don't and keep it rustic). Transfer the dumplings to the flour-dusted baking sheet and repeat with the remaining dough and filling. (At this point, the dumplings can be cooked or frozen. To freeze, place the baking sheet directly into the freezer and then transfer to an airtight bag once they're frozen.)

Finish the khinkali: When ready to cook, bring a large pot of well-salted water to a boil. Working in batches of 8 (or less if your pot is smaller), lower each khinkali into the pot, dangling it a bit in the water to help the dough set before letting go. Give the khinkali a very gentle stir with a wooden spoon so that they don't stick to the bottom or to each other. Cook for 8 minutes (11 to 13 minutes if cooking from frozen).

Remove with a slotted spoon, shaking off any water, and spoon directly onto a serving platter. (If I'm feeding a crowd, I usually get another batch immediately going while the first round is being tucked into.)

Garnish with several cracks of black pepper. Bring the plate of khinkali to the table, warning diners to wait a few minutes before digging in to avoid scalding broth. Serve with sour cream on the side, if you dare.

HOW TO EAT KHINKALI

Put down that fork and knife—you won't be needing them here. The whole art to eating Georgian *khinkali* is to never allow the broth to escape anywhere except for into your mouth. The topknot or *kudi*—typically not eaten—will serve as your handle for holding the dumpling, as well as your way of keeping count of how many you've consumed. So choose the tastiest-looking khinkali and pick it up by its topknot with your fingers. Puncture the top part of the khinkali with a bite and knock back your head and slurp: A stream of unctuous broth will hit your palate. Then, when you're confident no more soup is left, take another bite to reveal juicy, tender meat. Continue to devour the dumpling until all that's left is the doughy handle. Repeat until your plate is littered with kudi. The person with the most, wins.

IMERULI KHACHAPURI

GEORGIAN CHEESE BREAD

While boat-shaped Adjaruli *khachapuri* gets all the attention, Imeruli khachapuri is, by far, the one most often consumed in Georgia. A melt-in-your-mouth flat round of dough encasing a melty, gooey cheese filling that is perfectly balanced with tangy, briny curds. It's so popular that Georgian economists have even created a Khachapuri Index—using the cost of its ingredients and resources to gauge inflation and the strength of the economy. It's our favorite at home, too. We'll serve it for lunch or dinner as part of a larger spread, as a snack, and even as leftovers for breakfast. Khachapuri all day, baby.

· ·

DOUGH
1 cup (240 g) whole milk, lukewarm
½ cup (120 g) sour cream, at room temperature
2 tablespoons sunflower oil, plus more for greasing
1¼ teaspoons instant yeast
1 teaspoon sugar
3¼ cups (425 g) all-purpose flour, plus more for
    dusting
1½ teaspoons kosher salt

FILLING
1 pound (450 g) low-moisture whole-milk
    mozzarella, shredded, at room temperature
5 ounces (140 g) feta cheese, grated, at room
    temperature
5 ounces (140 g) whole-milk ricotta cheese, at room
    temperature
1 egg, at room temperature
1 teaspoon all-purpose flour

A cold stick of unsalted butter

MAKES FOUR 8- TO 10-INCH (20 TO
25 CM) ROUNDS

Make the dough: In a large bowl, whisk together the milk, sour cream, 1 tablespoon of the oil, yeast, and sugar to combine. Switch over to a wooden spoon and gradually begin to add the flour, along with the salt, a bit at a time, mixing to incorporate after each addition. Once the spoon becomes cumbersome to work with, switch over to your hands and knead until all the flour has been incorporated and you have a cohesive dough. The dough will be shaggy and slightly sticky. Resist the urge to add more flour! Cover with a clean kitchen towel and allow the dough to rest for 15 minutes.

Transfer the dough to a lightly greased surface. Pour a little of the remaining 1 tablespoon oil on your hands and begin to knead the oil into the dough. If needed, use a dough or bench scraper to release the dough when it sticks to the surface so you can keep kneading. Once no oil remains, continue to knead for 4 to 5 minutes. By the end, the dough will still be tacky, but when handled with greased hands it will be soft and supple with a satiny sheen. When you pull on it, it will feel strong but will still tear after 3 to 4 seconds.

With lightly greased hands, form the dough into a ball and transfer to an oiled bowl. Cover the bowl with a slightly damp kitchen towel and set aside to proof in a warm place for 1 hour.

Turn the dough by taking one edge and gently stretching it up and over toward the center. Repeat until you've stretched all the edges.

Cover again and proof for another 1 hour. Turn the dough again.

Turn the dough out onto a lightly floured surface. Pat the dough into a rectangle and cut the dough into 4 equal portions (about 200 g each). Form into even balls and place on a generously floured surface, cover with the kitchen towel, and let rest until the balls are soft and slightly puffy, 15 to 30 minutes.

Make the filling: In a medium bowl, stir together the mozzarella, feta, ricotta, egg, and flour until thoroughly combined. Divide into 4 sturdy balls and set aside.

Assemble the khachapuri: Take one piece of dough, keeping the others covered, and pat it out gently with your fingers into a 6-inch (15 cm) round with the center a little thicker than the edges. Place one ball of filling in the middle. Carefully grab two opposite sides of the dough, bring them up over the filling, and pinch them together. Hold them securely together with one hand as you bring up the remaining edges over the filling, pleating as you go and pinching the ends together tightly at the top to secure like a drawstring purse.

Gently start flattening out the filled dough with your fingers. Sprinkle a little flour and flip it over. Continue to flatten the dough with your fingers and palms (you can also use a rolling pin), gently working from the center out to the edges to spread the filling out evenly, until you have a 9- to 10-inch (23 to 25 cm) round. If there are any tears, try to lightly pinch the dough together or nip a piece of dough from one of the other balls and patch up the hole.

Heat a 12-inch (30 cm) nonstick skillet over medium heat. Once hot, carefully transfer the khachapuri to the pan. If you have space in the pan to do so, press down on the outer edge of the khachapuri to further widen the round. Cook until the bottom begins to firm up and brown spots develop all over, 4 to 5 minutes. Carefully flip over and glide the stick of butter over the top like a glue stick to coat the khachapuri evenly. Cook for another few minutes until the bottom is browned—if the khachapuri begins to inflate, pierce it with the end of a sharp knife to release steam. Flip the khachapuri over onto a serving plate—the unbuttered side should be facing up—and give the second side a light coating of butter. Repeat the process with the remaining pieces of dough, stacking the khachapuri on top of each other as they come out of the pan.

Let cool a bit for the cheese to set before cutting the stack into eighths. Serve immediately. (Store well wrapped at room temperature for 1 day and then in the refrigerator for 2 to 3 more days.)

PENOVANI KHACHAPURI

GEORGIAN FLAKY CHEESE BREAD

This sheet-pan version of *penovani khachapuri*—usually sold as a compact, handheld street food—is made with shatteringly crisp puff pastry and is a nonnegotiable at our big family parties. As the platter hits the table, a bit of a flurry ensues over who gets the corners (or, as we call them, *popuchki*—"little butts"). Thankfully there's always enough pieces to go around, corner or no corner, and eventually everyone gets their fill. It's impossible to get tired of this khachapuri, so don't be surprised if it becomes a staple in your family, too.

••

Unsalted butter, for greasing
All-purpose flour, for dusting
One (17.3-ounce / 490 g) box frozen puff pastry, thawed but chilled
1 pound (450 g) low-moisture whole-milk mozzarella cheese, shredded
5 ounces (140 g) feta cheese, grated
5 ounces (140 g) whole-milk ricotta cheese
1 egg, lightly beaten with a pinch of kosher salt

SERVES 8 TO 10

Preheat the oven to 375°F (190°C). Lightly grease a 10 × 15-inch (25 × 38 cm) jelly-roll pan or an 11 × 17-inch (28 × 43 cm) glass baking dish or something similar in size. These sizes will give you the best pastry-to-cheese ratio.

On a lightly floured surface, roll out one puff pastry sheet slightly larger than the size of your pan and transfer it to the pan. Sprinkle the mozzarella in an even layer over the dough, leaving a thin border all around. Evenly crumble the feta cheese over the top. Dollop the ricotta in small spoonfuls all over in an even layer.

Roll out the second piece of dough to the size of your pan and lay it over the cheese. Pinch the edges of the pastry layers together to tightly seal like you really mean it—I go over my pinches a couple of times to make sure there aren't any gaps. We don't want any precious cheese oozing out! Then roll the edges up and over the pie and pinch and flatten all over again. Generously brush the pastry with the beaten egg, making sure you get the edges, too. Poke the top of the pastry, save for the edges, all over with a fork—you can't have too many pokes.

Bake the pie until crisp and golden brown and the bottom is firm, 30 to 35 minutes.

Let cool a bit for the cheese to set before cutting into squares and serving.

TREUGOLNIKI

BEEF TURNOVERS

My mom prepared these savory triangular pastries for parties and I'd eat one after another, neglecting the rest of the food. I couldn't get enough, and neither could our guests—by the end of the night, only flaky crumbs remained.

....

All-purpose flour, for dusting
One (17.3-ounce / 490 g) box frozen puff pastry,
    thawed but chilled
Beef Treugolniki Filling (recipe follows)
Egg wash: 1 egg, lightly beaten with a pinch of
    kosher salt

MAKES 18 TURNOVERS

Line two baking sheets with parchment paper.

On a lightly floured surface, roll one puff pastry sheet into a 12-inch (30 cm) square. Cut into 9 squares and very lightly brush the edges of each with egg wash. Place a generous 2 tablespoons of filling into the center of each. Fold each square in half to form a triangle and pinch the edges together tightly to seal, then crimp with a fork. Transfer the pastries to the prepared baking sheet and refrigerate while you repeat the process with the remaining pastry.

Refrigerate the assembled pastries to firm up the dough, 20 to 30 minutes. (Or keep covered in the fridge for 2 hours or freeze for up to 2 months. Just add a few extra minutes to the baking time.)

When ready to bake, position racks in the top and bottom thirds of the oven and preheat the oven to 375°F (190°C).

Remove the pastries from the refrigerator and generously brush each pastry with egg wash. Use a fork to prick small vents into the pastries.

Bake the pastries until they are puffed up, golden brown, and firm to the touch, 22 to 27 minutes, switching racks and rotating the pans front to back halfway through.

Serve warm or at room temperature.

BEEF TREUGOLNIKI FILLING

Slowly simmering beef and then grinding it up, while very old-school, results in a filling that is tender and flavorful. Use it to fill Blinchiki (page 48), Pirozhki (page 76), and as the base for Navy-Style Pasta (page 144). For a quicker version, use the sautéed beef filling on page 50.

....

1 pound (450 g) marbled beef, such as round, chuck,
    or shank, excess fat or silver skin trimmed
Kosher salt
2 tablespoons sunflower or extra-virgin olive oil
1 medium yellow onion, finely diced
Freshly ground black pepper

MAKES ENOUGH TO FILL 18 TURNOVERS

Place the beef in a medium pot and fill with enough water to cover by 2 inches (5 cm). Add 1 teaspoon salt and bring to a simmer over medium-high heat. Skim any scum that floats to the surface, then cover and adjust the heat to maintain a gentle simmer. Cook until the beef is very tender, 2 to 3 hours.

Remove the beef from the pot (reserve the broth) and allow to cool completely. Remove any cartilage or bone, then run the beef through a meat grinder fitted with the large grinding plate. Alternatively, shred the beef into pieces and very finely chop with a food processor.

In a large sauté pan, heat the oil over medium heat. Add the onion and a pinch of salt and cook until the onion is soft, translucent, and has lost its raw edge, about 10 minutes.

Stir in the beef and 1 cup (240 g) of the reserved broth. If the meat still seems a bit dry, add more broth. Taste and season with salt and pepper. Reduce the heat to medium-low and cook for 2 to 3 more minutes to allow flavors to meld. Remove from the heat and allow to cool completely.

MASTER DOUGH

FOR PIROZHKI, PIROG, AND VATRUSHKI

It's hard to imagine a food more characteristically Slavic than pie. In Russia and Ukraine, for instance, entertaining is so enmeshed with enveloping a filling in dough that the word for "pie" (*pirog/pyrig*) finds its root in the word "feast" (*pir/pyr*). I now realize that our family, exposed to such an array of cultures, was exceptionally lucky. If we weren't eating Georgian *khachapuri*, Uzbek *samsa*, or Crimean *chebureki*, then we were enjoying a pirog in some shape or form.

This master dough is low on sugar so it lends itself to both sweet and savory preparations and can be used to make either a large-format pirog or smaller pies such as oval-shaped *pirozhki* or open-faced *vatrushki*. I've matched fillings with the type of pie we usually pair with them, but know they are all interchangeable, so once you get the hang of it, I encourage you to experiment and make your own pie traditions!

••

¾ cup (185 g) plain whole kefir, at room
    temperature or slightly warmed
⅓ cup (80 g) whole milk, lukewarm
1 egg, at room temperature
1 egg yolk, at room temperature
4 tablespoons (55 g) sunflower oil, plus more
    for greasing
1 tablespoon granulated sugar
1½ teaspoons instant yeast
1½ teaspoons kosher salt
3¼ cups (425 g) all-purpose flour, plus more
    as needed

**MAKES ENOUGH FOR 20 PIROZHKI,
10 VATRUSHKI, OR 1 LARGE PIROG**

In a large bowl, whisk together the kefir, milk, egg, egg yolk, 2 tablespoons of the oil, sugar, yeast, and salt until combined. Switch over to a wooden spoon and gradually begin to add the flour a bit at a time, stirring to incorporate before adding more. Once the spoon becomes cumbersome to work with, switch over to your hands and continue mixing until all the flour has been incorporated and you have a cohesive dough. The dough will be slightly shaggy and sticky—resist the urge to add more flour! Cover and allow to sit for 15 minutes.

Transfer the dough to a lightly greased surface. Pour a little of the remaining oil on your hands and begin to knead the oil into the dough. Repeat until the full 2 tablespoons have been incorporated. If needed, use a dough or bench scraper to release the dough when it sticks to the counter so you can keep kneading. Once no oil remains, continue to knead for 4 to 5 minutes. By the end, the dough will still be tacky, but when handled with greased hands it will be soft and supple, with a satiny sheen. When you pull on it, it will feel strong but will still tear after 3 to 4 seconds.

With lightly greased hands, form the dough into a ball and transfer to an oiled bowl. Cover the bowl with a slightly damp kitchen towel and set aside to proof in a warm place for 1 hour.

I proof my dough in the oven using the proof setting or, if your oven doesn't have one, with the oven light on. Turn on the oven light or proof setting before starting to mix the dough to bring the oven up to temp.

Turn the dough by taking one edge and gently stretching it up and over toward the center. Repeat until you've stretched all the edges. Cover again and proof for another 1 hour, for a total of 2 hours. Turn the dough again. (This can be done 1 day in advance; see Note.)

The dough is now ready to be divided and shaped according to the recipe.

Note: *You can make the dough 1 day in advance: After the dough has proofed for 1 hour and been turned, cover the surface with plastic wrap and refrigerate for at least 8 hours and up to 24 hours. When ready to assemble, turn the dough and go right into dividing and shaping. The dough will have to come to room temperature before proceeding with the rest of the recipe.*

PIROZHKI

SLAVIC STUFFED BUNS

For many, these plump, pillowy stuffed buns are synonymous with babushkas—of which there are two kinds. The first are the babushkas who invite you into their warm, sunny kitchens with a smile and the smell of freshly steeped tea and apple-filled *pirozhki* baking in the oven. The second you'll find perched in a street-corner kiosk, a greasy smell of fried meat and dough wafting in the air. As she slips a hot *pirozhok* into old newspaper wrapping and hands it to you, this babushka is more likely to give you a disapproving grimace than a grin.

Thankfully, having access to a babushka is not essential to enjoying *pirozhki*. The dough is straightforward to make (my mom would even use Pillsbury biscuit dough as a shortcut back in the day) and the filling can be prepared in advance. The decision to bake or pan-fry depends on what you're stuffing them with. Fillings that are smooth and homogeneous (such as potato or farmer cheese) I find are best fried. Those that are chunky (e.g., cabbage or apple) can go either way. But use your discretion. Just know that there is nothing like a still-hot pirozhok (however they're prepared), so don't wait too long before taking a bite.

• •

Pirozhki Filling (pages 78–79)
Master Dough (page 75)
All-purpose flour, for dusting
Egg wash: 1 egg, lightly beaten with a pinch
    of kosher salt (if baking)
Stick of cold unsalted butter (if baking)
Sunflower oil (if frying)

MAKES 20 BUNS

Form the pirozhki: Line two baking sheets with parchment paper. Make sure the filling is at room temperature.

Transfer the proofed and turned dough onto a lightly floured surface. The dough should be supple and pliable and shouldn't be sticky at this point. If it is, generously flour the dough and surface as needed. Divide the dough into 20 equal portions (about 40 g each).

Working with one piece at a time, fold the edges of the dough toward the center and pinch them together to create a ball. Place the ball on a work surface, seam side down, and cup it, making sure the edge of your hand is lightly touching the work surface. Start rolling the dough, pressing down slightly, in tight circles against the work surface. The goal is for the dough to "catch" and to use that friction to make the surface of the ball taut. Set aside and repeat the process with the remaining pieces, making sure to cover the balls with a slightly damp, lightweight kitchen towel. Allow the balls to rest so that the gluten in the dough relaxes and the balls puff up a bit, 10 to 15 minutes (if the dough came from the fridge, they will have to come fully to room temperature before proceeding).

Assemble the pirozhki: Lightly flour a work surface. Working in batches of 5, starting with the first balls you rolled, turn a ball over so that the seam side is facing you. Gently pat each piece of dough into a 3-inch (7.5 cm) round. Add about 2 tablespoons of filling to the center of each round. Bring two sides up and over the center and pinch the edges very tightly together to seal. Working toward one end of each pie, pinch the edges together to seal one side, then the other side, to create an oblong, boat shape. Flip the bun so that it's seam side down and gently flatten with your hand. Repeat with the rest of the dough.

For baked pull-apart style buns: Place the buns about ¼ inch (6 mm) apart from each other on the baking sheet. For baked or fried individual buns: Set them at least a pinky's distance apart from each other. Keep them covered with a slightly damp kitchen towel or old produce bag while you fill and form the rest of the pirozhki. Once done, let the buns rest in a warm place, covered, until soft and puffy and the dough springs back slowly when pressed with a finger (the divot shouldn't completely fill back in), 20 to 30 minutes.

To bake the pirozhki: Preheat the oven to 350°F (180°C). Gently brush the buns with the egg wash, making sure to get the undersides, too. Bake until the buns are golden and firm, 25 to 30 minutes. As soon as the pirozhki come out of the oven, hold a cold stick of butter like a glue stick and glide it over the tops and edges—the heat of the buns will instantly melt it. Cover the buns with a clean kitchen towel to capture steam and soften the exterior as the buns cool.

To fry the pirozhki: Line a plate with paper towels and set near the stove. Pour ¾ inch (2 cm) of oil into a skillet or sauté pan and heat the oil over medium heat until the oil is hot and shimmering. To test, dip the end of a wooden spoon or chopstick into the oil—if the oil starts to sizzle around the stick, the oil is hot enough. Working in batches of 3 to 4 at a time, carefully lower the pirozhki into the oil away from you and cook until golden brown on both sides, 2 to 3 minutes on each side. Transfer to the paper-towel-lined plate while you finish frying the rest of the pirozhki.

Serve the pirozhki while still hot or warm. Any leftovers can be covered and stored at room temperature for a day, after which you can transfer to the refrigerator and keep for another day or two.

POTATO, CRÈME FRAÎCHE, AND LEEK PIROZHKI FILLING

This filling, along with the following two, is traditional, but with a bit of a twist. You can also swap out yellow onions for the leeks, and sour cream for the crème fraîche. Keep in mind the filling must be room temperature before assembly.

....

1½ pounds (680 g) Yukon Gold potatoes, peeled and quartered
Kosher salt
3 tablespoons (45 g) unsalted butter
2 medium leeks, dark-green tops trimmed off, halved lengthwise and thinly sliced crosswise
⅓ cup (80 g) crème fraîche or smetana, plus more to taste
3 tablespoons (45 g) whole milk or reserved water from cooking potatoes, plus more as needed
Pinch of freshly grated nutmeg
Freshly ground black pepper

MAKES ENOUGH FOR 20 BUNS

Place the potatoes in a medium saucepan or pot and fill with enough cold water to fully cover. Generously season the water with salt and bring to a boil. Reduce the heat and simmer, uncovered, until they can be pierced easily with a fork, 15 to 20 minutes. Drain, reserving a few tablespoons of the cooking water if not using milk.

Meanwhile, in a medium sauté pan, melt the butter over medium heat. Add the leeks and cook until they soften and begin to brown on the edges, 6 to 8 minutes. Remove from the heat. Add the potatoes and mash with a fork or potato masher to break up the potatoes. Add the crème fraîche, milk (or reserved potato water), nutmeg, and pepper to taste. Continue to mix until you have stiff, chunky mashed potatoes. If the mixture seems a bit dry, add more milk. If it needs more creaminess or tang, add crème fraîche. Taste and season with salt, pepper, and, if needed, nutmeg. Cool to room temperature before proceeding.

HERBED FARMER CHEESE PIROZHKI FILLING

Bright with a kick of heat, this savory farmer cheese filling lends itself especially well to fried pirozhki. Keep in mind the filling must be room temperature before assembly.

· ·

1¼ pounds (565 g) farmer cheese, preferably
    dry and crumbly
1 egg, beaten
1 cup (30 g) dill, finely chopped
1 cup (30 g) parsley, finely chopped
⅓ cup (10 g) tarragon leaves, finely chopped
1¼ teaspoons red pepper flakes
Kosher salt

MAKES ENOUGH FOR 20 BUNS

In a medium bowl, mix together the cheese, egg, herbs, pepper flakes, and a big pinch of salt until an herb-flecked paste forms. Taste and season with more salt if needed.

For other filling ideas, try out the meat filling from either Treugolniki (page 74) or Blinchiki with Beef (page 50); the filling from Pirog with Cabbage, Carrots, and Egg (page 80); the potato, mushroom, and onion varenyky filling (page 62); and the sweetened farmer cheese vatrushki filling (page 83).

BROWN BUTTER AND APPLE PIROZHKI FILLING

I like to use a combination of apples (such as Granny Smith, Pink Lady, and McIntosh) to add a variety of flavors and textures to the filling. Keep in mind the filling must be room temperature before assembly.

· ·

½ cup (75 g) golden raisins
2½ tablespoons (40 g) rum
3 tablespoons (45 g) unsalted butter
3 medium apples (about 1½ pounds / 680 g), cut
    into ⅜-inch (1 cm) cubes
Grated zest of ½ lemon, plus more to taste
2 tablespoons granulated sugar, plus more to taste
½ teaspoon ground cinnamon, plus more to taste
½ teaspoon vanilla extract
Kosher salt

MAKES ENOUGH FOR 20 BUNS

In a small saucepan, heat the raisins and rum over medium heat until the rum begins to simmer. Set aside for at least 30 minutes and up to a few hours, tossing occasionally, to allow raisins to rehydrate and absorb the rum.

In a medium skillet, melt the butter over medium heat. Continue to cook until the butter has browned—you'll see brown specks beginning to form at the bottom of the pan, the butter will stop foaming, and it will have a nutty aroma when you smell it. Add the apples. Increase the heat to high and toss to coat them completely in the browned butter. Cook, stirring constantly, until they lose their raw edge but still have some bite, 3 to 4 minutes. Remove from the heat. Mix in the rum-soaked raisins, lemon zest, sugar, cinnamon, vanilla, and a generous pinch of salt. Taste and season with more sugar, zest, spice, or salt if needed. Let cool completely before using.

PIROG WITH CABBAGE, CARROTS, AND EGG

This "slab" pie is great for bigger groups and potlucks, and a piece or two of it on the go makes for a satisfying snack. The cabbage-and-egg filling is beloved throughout the diaspora. You can also make the *pirog* in a 10 × 15-inch (25 × 38 cm) jelly-roll pan. Just avoid pans that are narrow on the bottom.

·····································

FILLING
2 tablespoons sunflower oil or extra-virgin olive oil
1 large yellow onion, thinly sliced
3 medium carrots, coarsely grated
Kosher salt
2 tablespoons red wine vinegar
½ medium head green cabbage, outer leaves
    removed, cored and thinly sliced
1 small bunch of green onions, thinly sliced
½ large bunch of dill, finely chopped
Freshly ground black pepper
4 hard-boiled eggs, peeled and cut into medium dice

PIROG
Sunflower oil, for the baking dish
Master Dough (page 75)
All-purpose flour, for dusting
Egg wash: 1 egg, lightly beaten with a pinch of
    kosher salt
Stick of cold unsalted butter, for finishing

MAKES ONE 9 × 13-INCH (23 × 33 CM) PIE

Make the filling: In a large skillet or saucepan, heat the oil over medium heat. Add the onions, carrots, and a generous pinch of salt and cook until the vegetables begin to soften, 8 to 10 minutes.

Add the vinegar and deglaze the pan, scraping up the browned bits from the bottom of the pan. Stir in the cabbage and another pinch of salt and cook, stirring often, until the cabbage cooks down and softens but still has some crunch, 10 to 12 minutes.

Remove from the heat and stir in the green onions and dill. Taste and add salt and black pepper until generously seasoned. Cool completely before stirring in the chopped eggs. At this point, the filling can be refrigerated for 1 to 2 days. Make sure it is room temperature before filling the pie.

Assemble and bake the pirog: Lightly grease a 9 × 13-inch (23 × 33 cm) baking dish or pan with oil. Set aside.

Transfer the proofed and turned dough onto a lightly floured surface. The dough should be supple and pliable and shouldn't be sticky at this point. If it is, generously flour the dough and surface as needed. Divide the dough into 2 pieces: one piece should be 500 g, and the other will be approximately 300 g.

Set the larger piece of dough on a lightly floured surface (keep the other piece covered for now) and dust the top with flour, as well as the rolling pin. Roll out the dough into an 11 × 15-inch (28 × 38 cm) rectangle. As you work, focus on rolling out the edges a bit thinner than the center and periodically lifting the dough up from the surface and sprinkling with more flour as needed so it doesn't stick. Slip your hands and forearms underneath the dough and carefully transfer it into the prepared baking dish. Stretch and move the dough so that it evenly lines the bottom. Lift the sides up so that they're propped up against the walls of the pan.

Spoon the filling onto the dough and spread it out into an even layer. At this point, the filling should prop the edges up for you. Roll out the second piece of dough into a 9 × 13-inch (23 × 33 cm) rectangle and carefully transfer it to the pan. Stretch and move the dough as needed so it evenly covers the pirog. Pinch the edges of the two layers together to seal tightly. Cover with a slightly damp kitchen towel or old produce bag

and allow to rest, in a warm place, until soft and puffy and the dough springs back slowly when pressed (the divot shouldn't completely fill back in), 25 to 35 minutes.

Meanwhile, preheat the oven to 350°F (180°C).

Before baking, check to see if any of the edges have come undone and pinch to seal again. Gently brush the top with the egg wash. Use a paring knife to cut a ½-inch (1.3 cm) hole into the dough in the center and four 2-inch (5 cm) slits around it to allow steam to escape.

Bake until the pirog is golden and firm on top, 40 to 45 minutes. Transfer to a wire rack. Hold

a cold stick of butter like a glue stick and glide it all over the top—the heat of the pirog will instantly melt it. Cover it with a clean kitchen towel to catch the steam and soften the edges as the pirog cools.

After 30 minutes, run a butter knife or offset spatula along the edges of the pirog and turn it out onto a large platter or cooling rack. Invert it back onto the wire rack and allow it to finish cooling. Serve the pirog while still warm or at room temperature. Well-wrapped, the pirog can be kept at room temperature for 1 day, after which it should be refrigerated for up to 3 or 4 days.

VATRUSHKI

FARMER CHEESE-STUFFED BUNS

These little open-faced pies filled with sweetened farmer cheese are our version of morning buns. As with other *pirozhki*, these are best washed down with tea while still warm or within a few hours of baking.

....

VATRUSHKI
Master Dough (page 75)
All-purpose flour, for dusting
Egg wash: 1 egg, lightly beaten with a pinch of
*   kosher salt*
Farmer Cheese Vatrushki Filling (recipe follows)

STREUSEL (OPTIONAL)
3 tablespoons (35 g) granulated sugar
3 tablespoons (25 g) all-purpose flour
1½ tablespoons unsalted butter, at room
*   temperature, torn into small pieces*

MAKES 10 HAND-SIZE BUNS

Assemble the vatrushki: Line a baking sheet with parchment paper. Set aside.

Transfer the proofed and turned dough onto a lightly floured surface. The dough should be supple, pliable, and shouldn't be sticky at this point. If it is, generously flour the dough and surface as needed. Divide the dough into 10 equal portions (about 80 g each).

Working with one piece at a time, fold the edges of the dough toward the center and pinch them together to create a ball. Place the ball on a work surface, seam side down, and cup it, making sure the edge of your hand is lightly touching the work surface. Start rolling the dough, pressing down slightly, in tight circles against the work surface. The goal is for the dough to "catch" and to use that friction to make the surface of the

ball taut. Repeat the process with the remaining pieces. Place the balls on the prepared pan in a row of 3, alternating with a row of 2, spacing them about 1½ inches (4 cm) apart. Lightly cover with plastic wrap or an old produce bag and allow to rest in a warm place until soft and puffy and the dough springs back slowly when pressed (the divot shouldn't completely fill back in), 30 to 40 minutes.

Meanwhile, position a rack in the center of the oven and preheat the oven to 350°F (180°C).

Make the streusel (if desired): In a small bowl, whisk together the sugar and flour. Add the butter and use your fingers to work the butter into the dry ingredients until it resembles wet sand. Set aside.

Finish the vatrushki: Generously flour the bottom of a glass 2⅜ inches (6 cm) across and use it to press down on the center of each round to the very bottom to make an indent. Reflour the glass as needed. Use your fingers to shape the indent if the dough springs back.

Brush the dough rounds with the egg wash. Divide the filling among the 10 rounds and use the back of a spoon to press the filling into the indentation and even it out. Sprinkle the rounds evenly with the streusel, if desired.

Bake the vatrushki until the filling is puffed and edges are golden, 25 to 30 minutes, rotating the pan front to back halfway through.

The vatrushki are best the day they're baked, but can be kept refrigerated for up to 2 days and rewarmed as needed.

FARMER CHEESE
VATRUSHKI FILLING

Farmer cheese gets the cheesecake treatment in this bright, citrus-scented filling. Keep in mind the filling must be room temperature before assembly. You could also use the mixture to fill pan-friend blinchiki (page 51) or baked nalysnyky (page 52).

. . . .

1 pound (450 g) farmer cheese, homemade (page 55)
*   or store-bought*
3 tablespoons (45 g) sour cream
1 egg yolk
¼ cup (50 g) granulated sugar
1½ teaspoons grated lemon zest
1 teaspoon grated orange zest
½ teaspoon vanilla extract
Pinch of kosher salt

MAKES ENOUGH FOR 10 BUNS

In a medium bowl, mash the farmer cheese with the back of a spoon against the wall of the bowl to break up the curds until it's smooth and finely textured. Add the sour cream, egg yolk, sugar, lemon zest, orange zest, vanilla, and salt and mix until smooth and combined. (Alternatively, you can process everything together in the bowl using an immersion blender.)

JAZZING UP VATRUSHKI

- Stir a handful of golden raisins (could be soaked first in rum if you like!) into the cheese.

- Top the filled buns with fresh berries (just avoid strawberry) or sour cherries before baking.

- Skip the cheese filling completely and swap in thick jam or preserves!

KULICH

EASTER BREAD

If panettone and brioche had a love child, it would be *kulich*, a traditional Slavic Orthodox Easter bread that is also known as *paska* in Ukraine. The tall, domed bread signifies life, the warmth and arrival of spring, and of course indulgence, as it is enjoyed at a festive table that decisively breaks the Lenten fast. According to my mom, my grandfather would mix the dough in a huge tub (he had eleven children, don't forget) by hand and would completely soak through his undershirt by the time he finished. Unfortunately, a family recipe was never passed down, but after years of testing various methods, my mom and I have finally landed on one we're happy with. Don't worry, there's no sweating involved!

We used to bake off our breads in old Folger coffee cans that we'd save, but they're made of plastic now, so special forms it is. As for decorating, you can go all out with a marshmallow glaze, sprinkles, and such—or keep it simple with a dusting of powdered sugar. A big, piped *XB* (for "Christ is Risen" in Slavic languages) is also common. Serve it on Easter day as part of a festive breakfast or brunch or for dessert.

···

MIX-INS
⅔ cup (105 g) golden raisins
⅔ cup (95 g) unsweetened dried cherries or
    cranberries or chopped apricots
⅓ cup (50 g) chopped candied orange or lemon
    (or more dried fruit plus 1 tablespoon orange
    or lemon zest)
2 tablespoons rum or a liqueur such as Maraschino
    or orange
1½ teaspoons vanilla extract
⅔ cup (160 g) water
¾ cup (150 g) granulated sugar

SPONGE
1 cup (120 g) water, lukewarm
1 cup (130 g) all-purpose flour
½ teaspoon instant yeast

DOUGH
3 to 3½ eggs (170 g)
7 to 8 egg yolks (120 g)
3 cups (390 g) higher-protein all-purpose flour,
    such as King Arthur (11.7% protein)
Rounded ½ cup (115 g) granulated sugar
1 tablespoon kosher salt
1½ teaspoons instant yeast
1 teaspoon crushed cardamom seeds (from about
    20 cardamom pods)
¾ teaspoon lightly packed freshly grated nutmeg
¾ cup (170 g) unsalted butter, cubed, at room
    temperature

GLAZE
Scant ⅓ cup (75 g) cold water
1¼ teaspoons unflavored gelatin powder
1 cup (120 g) powdered sugar
Sprinkles, for topping (optional)

**MAKES ABOUT 3¼ POUNDS (1.5 KG)
DOUGH, ENOUGH FOR 3 MEDIUM LOAVES**

Soak the mix-ins: The night before you want to mix the dough, in a medium bowl, combine the raisins, dried fruit, candied citrus or zest, rum, and vanilla. In a medium saucepan, bring the water and sugar to a boil, stirring to help fully dissolve the sugar. Remove from the heat and pour over the dried fruit. Allow to cool and sit at room temperature overnight.

Make the sponge: In a small bowl, mix together the water, flour, and yeast to combine. Let sit in a warm place until the sponge has roughly doubled in size and the top has bubbled and domed, 1½ to 2 hours.

Mix the dough: Drain the soaked mix-ins in a fine-mesh sieve and let sit in the sieve while you mix the dough.

In a stand mixer fitted with the dough hook, combine the sponge, whole eggs, egg yolks, flour, granulated sugar, salt, yeast, cardamom, and nutmeg. Mix on low for 1 to 1½ minutes until you have a cohesive yet shaggy dough. Increase the speed to medium and mix for 8 to 10 minutes for medium gluten development—when you pull on the dough, it should feel strong but still tear.

Now it's time to add the butter—it should be malleable and still hold together when pinched. With the mixer on medium speed, add the butter a cube at a time, waiting until the cube is mostly incorporated before adding more. This step will take 5 to 8 minutes. The dough should be supple, smooth, shiny, and should clear the walls of the bowl. When you pull on the dough, it should feel extendable.

Sprinkle the drained mix-ins in an even layer over the dough. Mix on low for 2 minutes, scraping down the bowl as needed if the dried fruit sticks to the sides of the wall, to evenly distribute. Remove the bowl from the stand mixer and wipe the dough hook clean with a wet hand.

Cover the bowl with a slightly damp kitchen towel and set aside in a warm place for 1 hour. Turn the dough by taking one edge and gently stretching it up and over toward the center. Repeat until you've stretched all the edges. Cover again and proof for another 1 hour. Turn the dough again.

Gently scrape the dough out of the bowl and onto a lightly floured surface. Pat the dough into a rectangle and divide it according to the forms you're working with (see Note). Working with one piece at a time and with a gentle touch, fold the top edge down halfway, then fold the bottom edge over it, so it's folded in thirds, like a letter. Fold the sides toward the center and flip the dough and form into a sort of ball. Place the ball, seam side down, into your form. Repeat with the remaining pieces.

If baking the same day, place the kulichi onto a baking sheet and cover loosely with plastic wrap. Set them in a warm place to proof for 1½ to 2 hours, or until the dough looks aerated and feels wobbly or jiggly when gently shaken. It will have risen almost to the top edge of the liner, and the dome will be peaking over it. If baking the next day, place the kulichi in the fridge overnight—the next day, set in a warm place, they will take a bit longer to proof.

To bake the kulichi: About 30 minutes before the kulichi are done proofing, position a rack in the center of the oven (there shouldn't be any racks above it) and preheat the oven to 340°F (170°C).

Bake the kulichi until the top is a very dark mahogany brown and the internal temperature reads 190°F (90°C); rotate the pan from front to back halfway through the baking time. For a medium-size mold, check between 25 and 30 minutes. Allow to cool completely before glazing.

Make the glaze: Before you make the glaze, make sure you have your kulichi and any sprinkles at the ready—the glaze sets up quickly once you stop mixing it and it begins to cool.

Pour half of the water into a small bowl. Sprinkle the gelatin evenly over the water and let bloom for 5 to 10 minutes—it will swell and become jelly-like. In a small saucepan, combine the powdered sugar and remaining water, stirring to dissolve the sugar. When it comes to a simmer, remove from the heat and transfer to the bowl of a stand mixer fitted with the whisk. Add the gelatin and stir until it's melted. Mix on medium speed until the glaze doubles in volume, is bright white and glossy, and starts to feel stiff, about 5 minutes. Working quickly, spoon the glaze over the tops of the kulichi, frost, and then top with sprinkles, if desired. Let set for at least 30 minutes before cutting into or packaging up.

Note: *You can bake in any paper panettone or kulich mold or metal can. For medium-size loaves, use forms that are about 5¼ inches (13.5 cm) wide and that will hold about 430 g of dough. For large-size loaves, use forms that are about 6¾ inches (17 cm) wide and that will hold about 700 g of dough. Any leftover dough can be baked in a small can or form.*

CHAPTER THREE

SOUPS

MAMA'S BOUILLON

This simple, quick, and lightly flavored broth represents one of the foundations of my mother's cooking. I love that the diminutive size of the Cornish hen makes it feel less of a to-do. Once made, you can keep going and make the Soup-Lapsha (page 93) or use it as a base for any of the other hot soups in this chapter. For a lower-sodium option, reduce or omit the salt, but I do find it really helps in flavoring the hen.

· ·

1 whole Cornish game hen (1½ to 2 pounds / 680 to
    905 g), thawed if frozen
3 to 3½ quarts (3 to 3.3 L) water
1 celery stalk, halved
1 large carrot, halved
1 small yellow onion, halved
1 small bunch of herb stems (optional), such as
    parsley and/or dill, tied together
1 tablespoon kosher salt

MAKES ABOUT 3 QUARTS (3 L) BROTH,
PLUS MEAT FROM THE BIRD

Place the hen in a 6- to 8-quart (6 to 7.5 L) pot and add 3 quarts (3 L) of the water. Add more water if necessary to ensure the hen is completely submerged. Bring to a simmer over medium-high heat. Skim and discard any scum that floats to the surface. Once all the scum is removed, add the celery, carrot, onion, herb stems (if using), and salt. Partially cover, adjust the heat to maintain a very gentle simmer, and cook, turning it over halfway through so that it cooks evenly, until the hen is fall-apart tender (the leg will easily pull away from the bird), about 45 minutes.

Remove from the heat and transfer the hen to a medium bowl (if not picking the meat right away, I recommend at least removing the skin while it's still warm and moist). Discard the vegetables and herbs. At this point, the broth can be strained and stored in an airtight container and refrigerated for 4 to 5 days or frozen for 2 to 3 months. Refrigerated, the chicken will last 3 to 4 days.

SOUP-LAPSHA

CHICKEN NOODLE SOUP

For most of my babushka Nadya's life, if she wanted to make this chicken soup, a favorite food of hers, she had to prepare the fine-cut noodles, *lapsha*, by hand. She'd start by clearing off the wooden table that was built specifically for the task by my *dedushka* (grandfather). After breaking into a sweat from kneading the pasta dough, she'd then use a long rolling pin (that he also made) and all her remaining arm muscle to roll the dough out until it was very thin. She'd fold the sheet, like a carpet, and then cut it along its length into loose coils. The strands would be separated and then hung and dried until they were ready for soup. It wasn't easy work, but that was just a fact of life back then.

Raising eleven children in Soviet Georgia eventually took a toll on Babushka Nadya, and the last years of her life were marked by a failing heart that left her largely bedridden. One day, a few weeks after being hospitalized for a massive heart attack, she turned to my mom and asked for a bowl of soup-lapsha. It was clear that she needed a dose of comfort. So my mom rushed home to grant the request. She remembers my babushka eating the soup with pure, unhindered pleasure and thanking my mom over and over again. *Spasibo, maya Larisachka, spasibo.* Later that night, my babushka was hit by a second heart attack in her sleep and passed away.

For me, a bowl of this chicken noodle soup is sustenance, yes, but it's also a story of love and heartbreak. We no longer make the lapsha by hand, but that doesn't make it any less nourishing.

•••

Poached Cornish game hen from Mama's Bouillon (page 90) or half a rotisserie chicken
3 quarts (3 L) Mama's Bouillon (page 90) or store-bought chicken broth
2 medium russet potatoes, peeled, quartered, and cut into matchsticks ¼ inch (6 mm) thick
2 medium carrots, peeled and cut into ¼-inch (6 mm) half-moons
2⅔ to 3 ounces (75 to 90 g) dried egg vermicelli or fine-cut egg noodles
Kosher salt
¾ cup (25 g) dill, finely chopped
4 to 5 sprigs parsley, finely chopped
2 green onions, white and light-green parts only, thinly sliced
½ teaspoon red pepper flakes, plus more for serving
Sour cream, for serving

SERVES 4 TO 6

Remove the skin from the bird and pick the meat off the bones. Set the meat aside and discard the skin and bones.

In a large pot, bring the broth to a boil over medium-high heat. Stir in the potatoes, carrots, vermicelli, and a generous pinch or two of salt. Partially cover, adjust the heat to maintain a steady simmer, and cook, stirring occasionally, until the potatoes and carrots are tender but still have a slight bite, 8 to 10 minutes.

Stir in the meat, dill, parsley, green onions, and pepper flakes. Taste and season with more salt if needed. Serve with a dollop of sour cream and more pepper flakes if desired. When we're sick, my mom will even press a fresh clove of garlic right into the bowl before eating. Store in the refrigerator for up to 5 days or in the freezer for up to 3 months.

BORSCH

I'm not going to beat around the bush—a good pot of borsch is a labor of love. Chopping, grating, slicing, boiling, and sautéing: You're exercising all your culinary chops here. But if you lean into the process and don't rush it, you'll be rewarded with something that will warm your belly, and soul, for days. Originally from Ukraine, this beet-and-cabbage soup has been adopted by every corner of the former Soviet Union. Indeed, I find borsch to be deeply personal, nostalgic, and for those reasons, divisive—the only best or "right" borsch is the one you grew up with. With the addition of a spicy Anaheim chili, red pepper flakes, and pungent cilantro along with the classic dill, my family's borsch has some serious Georgian flair.

Be warned, this makes a very large pot of borsch. If you're going to put in all that effort, you might as well enjoy it for a while. Invite some friends and family over and make an evening out of it (I like to serve it as a first course to Pelmeni, page 63) or freeze what you don't eat.

••

2¼ to 2½ pounds (1 to 1.15 kg) meaty beef shanks
3½ quarts (3.3 L) water
Kosher salt
3 medium russet potatoes, peeled and quartered
3 tablespoons (45 g) sunflower oil or extra-virgin olive oil
1 large yellow onion, diced
2 large carrots, peeled and coarsely grated
1 large Anaheim chili, halved, seeded, and thinly sliced crosswise
3 tablespoons (50 g) tomato paste
1 large tomato, cored and chopped
3 medium beets, peeled and coarsely grated
½ medium head green cabbage, thinly shaved
½ teaspoon red pepper flakes, plus more to taste
1 large bunch of cilantro, finely chopped
1 large bunch of dill, finely chopped
Sour cream, for serving
Hearty bread, for serving

SERVES 8 TO 10

Place the beef shanks in a large (at least 8-quart / 7.5 L) pot. Add the water and 1 tablespoon kosher salt and bring to a simmer over medium-high heat. Skim any scum that floats to the surface. Once all the scum is removed, cover, adjust heat to maintain a gentle simmer, and cook until beef shanks are very tender and fall off the bone, 2½ to 3 hours.

Remove the shanks from the pot, reserving the broth. Allow the beef to cool completely, then pick the meat from the cartilage and bone and cut into bite-size cubes. Set aside. (The beef and broth can be prepared a day in advance.)

To the same pot, add the potatoes and more water, if needed, to keep them fully covered. Bring to a boil. Cover, adjust the heat to maintain a simmer, and cook until a knife inserted in the center of a potato meets little resistance, but the potato is still firm, 15 to 20 minutes. Transfer the potatoes to a bowl to cool. Do not toss out the cooking liquid, as this is your broth.

Meanwhile, in a large sauté pan, heat the oil over medium heat. Add the onion and a generous pinch of salt and cook until softened and translucent, 5 to 6 minutes.

Add the carrots, chili, and another pinch of salt. Cook this zazharka (see page 96), stirring frequently, until the vegetable edges soften and the onions begin to take on some golden color, 15 to 20 minutes. The vegetables should slowly caramelize and sweeten, not burn, but still have a bite, so make sure you stir often and reduce the heat if needed.

Stir in the tomato paste and a splash of water to help loosen it up and cook for another 2 to 3 minutes. Add the tomato and a pinch of salt and cook, allowing the tomato to break down, about 5 minutes.

Add three-quarters of the beets, a pinch of salt, and cook, another 15 minutes. The vegetables will meld, concentrate, and sweeten. If at any point the zazharka seems to be drying out, stir in a splash of water. Taste and season with more salt if needed so that the zazharka is well seasoned and flavorful.

Break the potatoes into bite-size pieces with a fork or the edge of a spoon. Return them to the pot of broth. Add the thinly sliced cabbage and remaining beets to the pot and bring to a simmer (you can cover with a lid to help speed this step up). Stir in the zazharka, cooked beef, and pepper flakes. Now, check the consistency of the soup. You want just enough liquid for the vegetables to be suspended in broth but not so much that they're swimming in it—this isn't chicken noodle soup. It might not need more water, but if it does, add a bit more water to thin the soup out. Taste and season with salt and, if desired, more pepper flakes (we like ours to have a bit of a kick!).

Bring to a gentle simmer again. Add the herbs and cook for another 2 to 3 minutes.

Serve with a generous dollop of sour cream and good hearty bread on the side. Stored in the refrigerator, the soup will last for 4 to 5 days, and will only get better as it sits.

Note: *This borsch can easily be made vegetarian. Omit the beef shanks, start with boiling the potatoes, and bump up the amount of oil to ¼ cup (55 g).*

ZAZHARKA

The base for our soups, our mirepoix if you will, is called a *zazharka*. It typically comprises onions and carrots, and sometimes peppers. The key to a good zazharka is cooking it slowly, so as to concentrate the sweetness of the vegetables without burning them. The other thing you'll notice is that we often cook our zazharka separately and add it to the broth after the meat, potatoes, or cabbage are done simmering. Not only is this multitasking, but it also helps the vegetables retain some toothsome texture and keeps their flavors bright. To make sure I maximize on its flavor: Once I've stirred the mirepoix to the soup, I ladle some of the broth into the now empty zazharka skillet, swirl it around to clean out the pan, and pour the liquid back into the pot.

GREEN BORSCH

Come spring, when the warming earth comes to life again, my mind turns to borsch—but not the one you're thinking of. Most people think of borsch as synonymous with beets, but in fact it's actually an umbrella term for a number of sour soups *without* beets. In this case, made with tender greens.

The main player in green borsch is sorrel or in Russian and Ukrainian, *shchavel*. Somewhere between a lettuce and an herb, this small edible green has an intense lemony tang that cuts through and brightens this light, yet hearty soup. Ideally, you want slender, arrow-shaped broad-leaf or French sorrel. You can supplement or substitute it with spinach, stinging nettles, or a combination of both. To make up for the loss in sour zing, add the juice of 1 lemon at the end, until the soup is bright and puckering. We make this green version whenever sorrel is available (early spring to late summer) and save the red borsch for when cooler days arrive.

2 medium russet potatoes, peeled and quartered
2½ quarts (2.4 L) water
Kosher salt
2 tablespoons sunflower oil or extra-virgin olive oil
1 tablespoon unsalted butter
1 large yellow onion, chopped
2 medium carrots, peeled and cut into ¼-inch
    (6 mm) half-moons
1 large bunch of sorrel (8 ounces / 225 g), stems
    included, roughly chopped
Large handful of spinach (about 2 ounces / 55 g),
    roughly chopped
½ large bunch of dill, finely chopped
¼ large bunch of parsley, finely chopped
1 garlic clove, crushed through a press
2 eggs, lightly beaten
½ teaspoon red pepper flakes, plus more to taste
Sour cream, for serving
Hearty bread, for serving

SERVES 4 TO 6

Place the potatoes in a large pot and cover with the water. Add 1 tablespoon kosher salt and bring to a boil. Partially cover, reduce the heat to maintain a simmer, and cook until a knife inserted in the center meets little resistance, but the potato is still firm, 15 to 18 minutes. Transfer the potatoes to a bowl to cool. Do not toss out the cooking liquid, as this is your broth.

Meanwhile, in a large sauté pan, heat the oil and butter over medium heat. Add the onion, carrots, and a generous pinch of salt. Cook the zazharka (mirepoix), stirring frequently, until the vegetable edges soften and the onions begin to take on some golden color, 15 to 20 minutes. The vegetables should slowly caramelize and sweeten, not burn, but still have a bite, so make sure you stir often and reduce the heat if needed.

Break the potatoes into bite-size pieces with a fork or the edge of a spoon. Return them to the pot of broth. Stir in the zazharka. Bring to a simmer again and add the sorrel, spinach, herbs, and garlic. As soon as the borsch begins to simmer, about a minute or two, it's ready for the eggs.

Slowly pour in the beaten eggs in a circular motion, gently stirring the borsch with your other hand. Let the soup stand for a few seconds to finish cooking the eggs. Remove from the heat.

Taste and season with the pepper flakes and salt to taste. Allow the borsch to sit for 30 minutes for the flavors to meld.

Give the soup a good, but gentle, stir before serving hot with a generous dollop of sour cream and hearty bread. As with most soups, it will taste better the next day. Store in the refrigerator for up to 4 days.

KHOLODNIK

COLD BEET SOUP

Cold fermented dairy, vegetables, and herbs make up the base of this soup as well as Okroshka (page 100), both popular and enjoyed throughout Eastern Europe. Tangy and refreshing, with a slight bit of heft, they're just the thing to turn to when temperatures rise and too much time at the stove feels daunting. This soup, featuring beets, is known as either *svekolnik* or *kholodnik* depending on where you're from. Some recipes have you use the water you boiled your beets in as the "stock" for your soup—a great option if you'd like a dairy-free version. But here, I use kefir. The beets turn the soup into an exquisite Barbie-pink shade and round out the tangy base with earthy sweetness.

· ·

½ pound (225 g) small red beets, scrubbed
½ pound (225 g) baby potatoes
5 eggs
Kosher salt
2 Persian (mini) cucumbers, finely grated
3 to 4 green onions, white and light-green
        parts thinly sliced, dark-green parts cut
        into thin strips
½ cup (15 g) dill, finely chopped
One (32-ounce / 950 ml) bottle plain full-fat kefir
⅓ cup (80 g) sour cream
Juice of 1 lemon, plus more to taste
1 cup (240 g) ice water (or reserved cooking liquid
        from beets)
Freshly ground black pepper

SERVES 4 TO 6

Place the beets in a medium pot and fill with enough water to cover. Bring to a boil, then reduce to a simmer, cover, and cook until fork-tender, 40 minutes to 1 hour, depending on the size of the beets. Scoop out the beets if you want to save the liquid to flavor the soup later, otherwise drain and allow to cool completely.

Meanwhile, add the potatoes and eggs (in that order) to a large pot and fill with enough water to cover. Generously salt the water. As soon as the water comes to a full boil, set a timer for 5 minutes. In the meantime, set up an ice bath in a medium bowl. Once the timer is up, scoop out the eggs, transfer them to the ice bath, and set aside to cool completely.

Cover the pot, adjust the heat to maintain a rolling boil, and cook the potatoes until a knife inserted in the center meets little resistance, but the potato is still firm (make sure you don't overcook them!), 7 to 10 minutes. Drain and allow to cool completely.

Peel the potatoes (if desired) and quarter them. Peel and dice 3 of the eggs. Peel and cut the beets into matchsticks ¼ inch (6 mm) thick or coarsely grate.

In a large pot, combine the potatoes, diced eggs, beets, cucumbers, the white and light-green parts of the green onions, and the dill. Add the kefir, sour cream, and half of the lemon juice and mix to combine. Begin to add the water or reserved beet liquid, stirring as you go, until you have a thin, almost drinkable consistency. I usually use the full amount, but if your kefir was on the thinner side, use a little less. Taste and season with salt and pepper. You want the soup to be tangy and bright, so add more lemon if needed.

Refrigerate until thoroughly chilled, about 1 hour. Before serving, add the dark-green parts of the green onions to ice water and allow to sit for a few minutes to "curl" up. Peel and halve the remaining 2 eggs.

Pour the soup into bowls and top with a halved egg. Garnish with green onion curls and a crack of black pepper before serving. Store in the refrigerator for up to 4 days.

Note: *While it's a bit prep-heavy, boiling your veggies and eggs ahead of time (say, in the cool of morning) makes assembly a breeze.*

OKROSHKA

COLD YOGURT SOUP

When I was growing up, our summer barbecues weren't complete without this chilled soup. It would be brought out at the last minute, ladled into mugs, and sipped on while we dug into everything else. Back then, I didn't get it (soupy yogurt with vegetables?!), but now I know better. When the hot, sweltering days set in, it's the cool, creamy tang of *okroshka* I crave.

• •

4 medium Persian (mini) cucumbers (about
    1 pound / 450 g total)
4 green onions, white and light-green parts only,
    thinly sliced
½ cup (15 g) dill, finely chopped
One (32-ounce / 900 g) container whole-milk
    Greek yogurt
⅓ cup (80 g) sour cream
1 tablespoon kosher salt, plus more to taste
½ teaspoon freshly ground black pepper, plus more
    to taste
Juice of 1 large lemon
2½ cups (360 g) ice water

SERVES 6 TO 8 AS AN APPETIZER

Finely grate the cucumbers into a large pot. Add the green onions, dill, yogurt, sour cream, salt, pepper, and half of the lemon juice and stir to combine. Add the water, stirring as you go, until you have a thin, drinkable consistency. Taste and season with more salt and pepper. You want the soup to be tangy and bright, so add more of the lemon juice if needed.

Refrigerate until thoroughly chilled, about 1 hour. Serve in mugs, sip, and enjoy. Store in the refrigerator for up to 4 days.

JUST ADD SOUR CREAM

It wasn't until I was finishing this book that I realized that every recipe in this chapter contains or recommends sour cream or, as we call it, *smetana* as a garnish. Consider it our version of lemon—except it adds not only necessary acidity and tang but also a rich creaminess to broths. I'll stir a finishing dollop into my broth and, to really gild the lily, smear a second over my toast. Don't knock it till you try it!

BROTHY SPLIT PEA, POTATO, AND HERB SOUP

To this day, it's a rare occurrence that a pot of soup isn't either simmering away on the stove or chilling in the fridge at my mother's house. In our culture, soup has always been considered extremely good for your *sistema* (overall health)—something *zhidkoe* (brothy) provides essential nourishment and hydration for optimal digestion. It was also historically a resourceful and economical method of cooking—soup managed to both stretch ingredients and feed a family for days. This not-your-typical split pea soup was a favorite in the rotation. A smaller amount of split peas keeps it on the brothier side; a bit of tomato paste, hot paprika, and turmeric build depth; and a handful of chopped herbs and garlic really brighten things up. You'll never make it any other way again!

• •

2½ quarts (2.4 L) Mama's Bouillon (page 90), store-bought chicken or vegetable broth, or water
½ pound (225 g) green or yellow split peas, rinsed
Kosher salt
2 tablespoons sunflower oil or extra-virgin olive oil
1 tablespoon unsalted butter
1 large yellow onion, chopped
2 large carrots, peeled and cut into ¼-inch (6 mm) half-moons
1½ tablespoons tomato paste
½ teaspoon hot or sweet paprika
½ teaspoon ground turmeric
2 medium russet potatoes, peeled, quartered, and cut into ⅛-inch (3 mm) matchsticks
3 to 4 garlic cloves, crushed through a press
½ large bunch of cilantro, finely chopped
4 to 5 sprigs parsley, finely chopped
½ teaspoon red pepper flakes, plus more to taste
Sour cream, for garnish
Crusty bread, for serving

SERVES 4 TO 6

In a large pot, bring the bouillon to a boil. Stir in the split peas and 1 tablespoon kosher salt. Cover, reduce the heat to a steady simmer, and cook until the split peas are almost cooked through but still have a slight bite, 45 minutes to 1 hour.

Meanwhile, in a large skillet, heat the oil and butter over medium heat. Add the onion, carrots, and a generous pinch of salt. Cook the zazharka (mirepoix), stirring frequently, until the vegetable edges soften and the onions begin to take on some color, 15 to 20 minutes. The vegetables should slowly caramelize and sweeten, not burn, but still have a bite, so make sure you stir often and reduce the heat if needed.

Stir in the tomato paste, a splash of water to loosen it up, the paprika, turmeric, and a generous pinch of salt. Cook for another 2 to 3 minutes. Taste and season with salt so that the zazharka is well seasoned and flavorful. Set aside.

Once the split peas are almost done, stir in the zazharka and potatoes. Cover, adjust the heat to maintain a steady simmer, and cook until the potatoes can be broken into with the edge of a spoon and the split peas are completely cooked through and falling apart, 10 to 12 minutes.

Stir in the garlic, cilantro, parsley, and pepper flakes and simmer for another 2 to 3 minutes. Remove from the heat. Taste and season with salt and, if desired, more pepper flakes.

Serve hot with a dollop of sour cream and crusty bread. Store in the refrigerator for up to 5 days.

Note: *If you have a leftover ham bone or shank, add it along with the peas to enrich and flavor the broth.*

MUSHROOM AND BUCKWHEAT CHICKEN SOUP

For those of you in the diaspora, you may not have had this exact recipe, but one bite and you'll agree that you *know* it. The flavors, ingredients, and heartiness will all be instantly familiar and nostalgic—and by virtue, nourishing in more ways than one.

....

1½ pounds (680 g) bone-in, skin-on chicken thighs
  (about 3 large)
2½ quarts (2.4 L) water
Kosher salt
1 pound (450 g) cremini mushrooms, cut into
  ¼-inch (6 mm) slices
3 tablespoons (45 g) sunflower oil or extra-virgin
  olive oil
1 large yellow onion, chopped
3 medium carrots, peeled and cut into ¼-inch
  (6 mm) half-moons
¾ teaspoon hot or sweet paprika
½ cup (100 g) roasted buckwheat groats (kasha)
2 medium russet potatoes, peeled, quartered, and
  cut into ⅛-inch (3 mm) matchsticks
½ teaspoon red pepper flakes, plus more to taste
½ large bunch of dill, finely chopped
¼ large bunch of cilantro, finely chopped
4 to 5 sprigs parsley, finely chopped
1 large garlic clove, crushed through a press
Sour cream, for garnish
Hearty bread, for serving

SERVES 4 TO 6

Place the chicken in a large pot and cover with the water. Add 1 tablespoon kosher salt and bring to a simmer over medium-high heat. Skim any scum that floats to the surface. Once all the scum is removed, partially cover, adjust the heat to maintain a gentle simmer, and cook until the thighs are tender, 40 to 45 minutes. Scoop out the thighs into a medium bowl. Once cool enough to handle, remove the skin and tear the chicken into bite-size pieces. Set the pot of broth and chicken aside. (The chicken and broth can be prepared a day in advance.)

Meanwhile, heat a 12-inch (30 cm) nonstick skillet or sauté pan over medium-high heat. Once the pan is hot, add the mushrooms and dry-sauté, stirring occasionally, until the liquid the mushrooms release has mostly evaporated and the pan starts to dry out, 6 to 8 minutes (this step might take a little longer if your pan is smaller). Remove the mushrooms from the pan, season with a generous pinch of salt, and set aside.

In the same pan, heat the oil over medium heat. Add the onion, carrots, and a generous pinch of salt. Cook the zazharka (mirepoix), stirring frequently, until the vegetable edges soften and the onions begin to take on some golden color, 15 to 20 minutes. The vegetables should slowly caramelize and sweeten, not burn, but still have a bite, so make sure you stir often and reduce the heat if needed.

Reduce the heat and stir in the mushrooms and the paprika and cook, allowing the flavors to meld, for another minute. Taste and season with salt so that the zazharka is well seasoned and flavorful. Set aside.

Bring the chicken broth to a boil. Stir in the buckwheat and a pinch of salt (if the broth needs it). Reduce the heat to maintain a simmer, cover, and cook for 10 minutes. Add the potatoes and cook until the potatoes can be broken into with the edge of a spoon and the buckwheat is tender, 10 to 12 minutes.

Stir in the zazharka, chicken, and pepper flakes. If the soup seems to be too thick at this point, thin it out with some water. Taste and season with salt and, if desired, more pepper flakes.

Bring to a gentle simmer. Add the herbs and garlic and cook for 2 to 3 minutes before removing from the heat. Serve with a generous dollop of sour cream and good hearty bread on the side. Store in the refrigerator for up to 5 days.

PEARLED BARLEY AND BEEF SOUP

Beef shank may be an economical cut, but after a few hours of simmering, it turns extremely tender and succulent. Added bonus: It produces a delectable broth that is also rich in collagen. The Georgian *adjika* (chili paste) here is added for a little color and kick of heat. Paired with our signature finish of fresh herbs and garlic, it adds a vibrant touch to what might otherwise be a run-of-the-mill soup.

....

2¼ to 2½ pounds (1 to 1.15 kg) meaty beef shanks
3½ quarts (3.3 L) water
Kosher salt
¾ cup (145 g) pearled barley, rinsed
2 medium russet potatoes, peeled, quartered, cut
    into ⅛-inch (3 mm) matchsticks
2 tablespoons sunflower oil or extra-virgin olive oil
1 large yellow onion, chopped
3 medium carrots, peeled and cut into ¼-inch
    (6 mm) half-moons
2 tablespoons tomato paste
1 to 1½ tablespoons adjika or hot chopped peppers
    (optional)
½ teaspoon red pepper flakes, plus more to taste
½ bunch of cilantro, finely chopped
¼ bunch of dill, finely chopped
4 to 5 sprigs parsley, finely chopped
1 large garlic clove, crushed through a press
Sour cream, for serving
Crusty bread, for serving

SERVES 4 TO 6

Place the beef shanks in an 8-quart (7.5 L) pot and cover with the water. Add 1 tablespoon kosher salt and bring to a simmer over medium-high heat. Skim any scum that floats to the surface. Once all the scum is removed, cover, adjust the heat to maintain a gentle simmer, and cook until the beef shanks are very tender and fall off the bone, 2½ to 3 hours.

Remove the shanks from the pot and allow to cool completely. Pick the meat from the cartilage and bone and cut into bite-size cubes. Set the meat aside. (The beef can be cooked and broth prepared 2 to 3 days in advance. Once chilled, you can skim the fat off the top of the broth before proceeding.)

Bring the broth to a boil again. Add the barley, cover, adjust the heat to maintain a rapid simmer, and cook for 20 minutes. Add the potatoes. Bring back to a simmer, cover, and cook until the potatoes can be broken into with the edge of a spoon and the barley is tender yet chewy, 10 to 15 minutes.

Meanwhile, in a large skillet, heat the oil over medium heat. Add the onion, carrots, and a generous pinch of salt. Cook the zazharka (mirepoix), stirring frequently, until the vegetable edges soften and the onions begin to take on some golden color, 15 to 20 minutes. The vegetables should slowly caramelize and sweeten, not burn, but still have a bite, so make sure you stir often and reduce the heat if needed.

Stir in the tomato paste, adjika (if using), and a splash of water to help loosen them up. Cook for another 2 to 3 minutes. Taste and season with salt so that the zazharka is well seasoned and flavorful. Set aside.

Once the barley and potatoes are done, stir in the zazharka, beef, and pepper flakes. Now, check the consistency of the soup. If it seems too thick and chunky, add a bit more water to thin the soup out. Taste and season with salt and, if desired, more pepper flakes (we like ours to have a bit of a kick!). Bring to a gentle simmer again.

Add the herbs and garlic and cook for another 2 to 3 minutes. Remove from the heat. Serve hot with a generous dollop of sour cream and crusty bread. Store in the refrigerator for up to 5 days.

MATSVNIS SUPI

HOT YOGURT AND RICE SOUP

Matsoni is Georgia's answer to yogurt. Thin and mildly tart, the fermented dairy is thought of as an "elixir" to long life, given its numerous associated gut-health benefits. Among its many applications in the kitchen, from being dolloped onto dolma and kneaded into *khachapuri* dough, my favorite might be in providing the base for this quick-to-prepare soup. Warming yet light, bright yet full of body, *matsvnis supi* (or matsoni soup) is the sort of dish that cradles the seasons. Indeed, I often remember my aunt Olga preparing it on cool, rainy days in the springtime and early summer—or whenever one of us was, quite literally, feeling under the weather. This soup may not be life-extending, but life-sustaining? Absolutely.

2 cups (480 g) plain whole-milk yogurt
½ cup (120 g) sour cream
1 egg
1½ quarts (1.4 L) water
½ cup (100 g) long-grain white rice
Kosher salt
1 tablespoon sunflower oil or extra-virgin olive oil
1 medium yellow onion, finely diced
¼ large bunch of dill, finely chopped
¼ large bunch of cilantro, finely chopped
1 large garlic clove, crushed through a press
Freshly ground black pepper

SERVES 4

In a medium bowl, whisk together the yogurt, sour cream, and egg to combine. Place the rice in another medium bowl. Cover with cool water and use your hand to gently agitate and swirl the rice, then drain. Repeat until the water is mostly clear.

In a medium pot, bring the water to a boil. Add the rinsed rice and 1½ teaspoons kosher salt. Cover, adjust the heat to maintain a low simmer, and cook until the rice is just shy of being done, 12 to 15 minutes.

Meanwhile, in a large skillet, heat the oil over medium heat. Add the onion and a generous pinch of salt and cook, stirring occasionally, until the onion starts to turn golden and brown at the edges, about 15 minutes. You want the onion to slowly soften and caramelize, so if it's starting to brown too quickly, reduce the heat.

Once the rice is done, reduce the heat to as low as it can go. Stir in the sautéed onion. Make sure the broth is not bubbling at this point. Whisking constantly, slowly pour in the yogurt/sour cream mixture and mix until fully incorporated.

Bump up the heat a bit to bring to a gentle simmer. Stir frequently to make sure the yogurt doesn't curdle as the soup warms up again. As soon as you see the first bubbles, add the herbs and garlic. Taste and season with salt and pepper. You want the soup to be tangy and bright—if not, stir in a little more yogurt.

Bring back to a gentle simmer, then remove from the heat. Allow the soup to sit for 10 to 15 minutes before serving. Any leftovers can be served cold or warmed up. Store in the refrigerator for up to 4 days.

Note: *Unless you make your own matsoni using store-bought cultures (see page 25), use the best-quality, tangiest plain yogurt you can find. Blending the dairy with egg and whisking it into the hot broth when it's no longer bubbling will help prevent it from curdling.*

CHAPTER FOUR

VEGETABLES AND SALADS

PKHALI TWO WAYS

GEORGIAN VEGETABLE PÂTÉ

After decades of throwing big, boisterous dinner parties together, our family is a fine-tuned machine when it comes to menu planning. That's because we often stick to the same cast of dishes, which are assigned to the same person each year. For instance, my mom is tasked with bringing, in addition to her beloved Ideal Torte (page 203), the *pkhali*. A kind of vegetable pâté, Georgian pkhali can be made cooked with vegetables or greens that are then mixed with a paste of walnuts, cilantro, garlic, and spices. You'll see at least two or three different kinds at a good table—ours always features spinach and beet. The Beet Pkhali here includes mayonnaise, which is not traditional but rather something my mom learned from a coworker; I think it adds richness and a welcome tang. Preparing pkhali is simple but best done in advance (perfect for entertaining purposes) to allow the raw garlic to mellow out. Pair pkhali with hearty, crusty bread or lavash—crackers or pita will also work in a pinch.

BEET PKHALI

2 pounds (900 g) medium-small beets, scrubbed
¾ cup (25 g) roughly chopped cilantro leaves
    and stems
4 garlic cloves, peeled but whole
⅔ cup (75 g) walnuts
½ small yellow onion, finely diced
¼ cup (60 g) mayonnaise
1 tablespoon kosher salt
1 teaspoon ground blue fenugreek
½ teaspoon ground marigold
¼ teaspoon cayenne pepper, plus more to taste
Pomegranate seeds, for garnish

SERVES 6 TO 8 AS AN APPETIZER

In a large pot, combine the beets with enough water to fully submerge. Bring to a boil, cover, and adjust the heat to maintain a steady rolling boil. Cook until the beets are fork-tender, 1 hour 15 minutes to 1½ hours, depending on size. Drain and set aside for 20 to 30 minutes, or until cool enough to handle. While the beets are still warm, hold a beet in one hand with a paper towel or clean kitchen towel, trim the top, and use the paper towel to rub the skin off—it should slip right off.

Grate the beets on the second to smallest holes of a box grater into a large bowl. Squeeze out the juice from the beets in one of two ways:

Squeeze the beets, a handful at a time, over a medium bowl, or wrap the beets in a large piece of cheesecloth or clean muslin cloth and wring out about 90% of the liquid. It's always amazing to see how much juice this produces! Return the squeezed beets to the large bowl and save the juice (my mom would always force me to drink this, claiming it was "good for the blood") or discard it.

In a food processor, combine the cilantro and garlic and process until finely chopped. Add the walnuts and pulse until finely chopped. Add this to the beets in the large bowl. Add the onion, mayonnaise, salt, blue fenugreek, marigold, and cayenne, and mix until fully incorporated. Taste and season with more cayenne if needed—you're looking for a nice kick. Cover and refrigerate for 4 to 6 hours or ideally overnight.

To serve, heap about half of the pkhali onto a small plate. Using a fork, press it down to form a flat puck about 1 inch (2.5 cm) high. Use the back of a spoon or knife to smooth out the edges. With the tines of a fork, make a crisscross pattern on the top and garnish with pomegranate seeds. Depending on how hungry your crowd is, repeat with the other half of the pkhali as needed, or store in the fridge for up to 4 days.

SPINACH PKHALI

Kosher salt
2 pounds (900 g) fresh mature spinach, rinsed
  (avoid baby spinach, which will turn gummy)
1⅓ cups (150 g) walnuts
Generous ¾ cup (30 g) roughly chopped cilantro
3 garlic cloves, peeled but whole
¼ small yellow onion, minced
2 tablespoons red wine vinegar
1 teaspoon ground blue fenugreek
½ teaspoon ground marigold
¼ teaspoon cayenne pepper, plus more to taste
Pomegranate seeds, for garnish

SERVES 6 TO 8 AS AN APPETIZER

Bring a large pot of salted water to a boil. Add the spinach a huge handful at a time. It won't seem like it will all fit, but keep pushing the spinach down into the water with a wooden spoon after each addition, and it will. Cook until the spinach is tender and bright green, 1 to 2 minutes. Drain and allow to cool completely.

Squeeze out the liquid from the spinach in one of two ways: Squeeze the spinach, a handful at a time, over the sink (or a small bowl if you want to save it!), or wrap the spinach in a large piece of cheesecloth or clean muslin cloth and wring out 90% of the liquid.

Roughly chop the wrung-out spinach. Pulse a few times in a food processor until the spinach is finely chopped. (Alternatively, very finely chop the spinach by hand.) Transfer to a large bowl.

In the same food processor, combine the walnuts, cilantro, and garlic and process until a paste forms. Transfer to the bowl with the spinach. Add the onion, vinegar, 1 tablespoon of salt, blue fenugreek, marigold, and cayenne, and mix until everything is fully incorporated. Taste and season with salt or more cayenne—you're looking for a kick of heat and bright sharpness from the vinegar. The garlic will be potent as well, but it'll mellow as the pkhali sits. Cover and refrigerate for 4 to 6 hours or ideally overnight.

To serve, heap about half of the pkhali onto a small plate. Using a fork, press it down to form a flat puck about 1 inch (2.5 cm) high. Use the back of a spoon or knife to smooth out the edges. With the tines of a fork, make a crisscross pattern on the top and garnish with pomegranate seeds. Depending on how hungry your crowd is, repeat with the other half of the pkhali as needed, or store in the fridge for up to 4 days.

SETTING THE TABLE

Our celebratory meals are always family-style and are divided into two sets: hot and cold. Anything that could be served at room temperature, what we would typically call *zakuski* (small bites), is pre-set (we'll even plate duplicates of each *zakuska* so that there's one at each end and no one misses out). They consist of spreads and pâtés, pickles and ferments, platters of fresh herbs or salads, cheese and salami, smoked fish and caviar, breads, and so on. Salty or crunchy—anything to whet the appetite. For groups who imbibe, zakuski are absolutely essential—there's no such thing as drinking without eating. The prerequisite toasting can go on for hours, so it's important to keep bellies full.

Once we're seated, then the entrée-style dishes come out (and *khachapuri*, of course), ready to be doled out while still steaming hot. Plates mounded high, we dig in. Dinner can last a few hours, long after the last helping is taken. We'll eventually break, some of us helping with cleanup, others moving to the couch—before coming back together for *chai*, teatime.

BADRIJANI

FRIED EGGPLANT ROLLS

One consequence of growing up in a melting pot is that you absorb and use multiple languages without it even registering. Take eggplant, for instance. I've heard this nightshade referred to as *badrijani* in Georgian, *baklazhany* in Russian, and sometimes *sinenkie* (meaning, both in Ukrainian and Russian, "little blues," which I just love). Oftentimes all by the same person. In their native country of Georgia, these eggplant rolls are typically stuffed with a spiced walnut paste and referred to as *badrijani nigvzit*. While I fully embrace the traditional filling, I find myself preparing them more often the way my mom was taught by an old Georgian co-worker, with a cilantro aioli of sorts. It serves less as a textural contrast and more as a carrier of flavor; infusing the slick, custardy eggplant with garlic, spice, and heat. I have converted many an eggplant hater with these rolls and would even be so bold as to call them transcendent—a new term to add to the word bank.

·····························

2 large globe eggplants (3 to 3½ pounds / 1.4 to
    1.6 kg total), peeled in alternating stripes, and
    cut lengthwise into planks ¼ to ⅜ inch (6 to
    9 mm) thick
Kosher salt
½ large bunch of cilantro, roughly chopped
2 garlic cloves, peeled but whole
¾ cup (180 g) mayonnaise
1 tablespoon water
Generous ¾ teaspoon khmeli suneli
¼ teaspoon cayenne pepper, plus more to taste
¼ cup (55 g) sunflower oil, plus more as needed
Pomegranate seeds, for garnish
Crusty bread, for serving

MAKES 24 ROLLS; SERVES 6 TO 8 AS AN
APPETIZER

Sprinkle each eggplant slice with a pinch of salt on both sides and transfer to a colander set over a bowl. Let stand for at least 30 minutes while you make the filling.

In a food processor, combine the cilantro and garlic and process until finely chopped. Add the mayonnaise, water, khmeli suneli, cayenne, and ½ teaspoon salt and process until smooth and creamy. The filling should be bright, punchy, and a tad salty. Set aside.

Working in batches, stack 4 or 5 eggplant slices on top of each other and use your hands to squeeze any excess liquid. Pat each slice dry.

Line a large plate with paper towels and set near the stove. In a large nonstick skillet, heat the oil over medium heat until shimmering. Working in batches, fry the eggplant slices until lightly browned on the bottom, 3 to 4 minutes. Reduce the heat if the eggplant is browning too quickly. Use a fork to pierce the base of the eggplant and flip. Cook until the bottom is lightly browned and the eggplant is fork-tender, another 2 to 3 minutes. As they are done, pick up the eggplant slices with the fork, shake them over the pan to remove any excess oil, and transfer to the paper-towel-lined plate. Repeat with the remaining slices, adding oil as needed.

While the fried eggplant slices are still warm, spread each slice generously with the filling and roll up, starting from the base. Transfer the rolls seam side down to a serving platter or storage container. Serve at room temperature, garnished with pomegranate seeds, and bread on the side.

Note: *When picking out eggplant, if the globe variety isn't available, look for varieties that are on the longer side, such as Japanese or Chinese, which will be more suitable for rolling. The recipe makes a lot of filling because I'd rather have too much than not enough to fill all the rolls. Use any remaining as a spread or dip, or a sauce to go with chicken or fish.*

GARLICKY CARROTS

My aunt Natasha would always delegate the tedious task of finely grating the carrots for this eighties-era *zakuska* (small bite) to her husband, my uncle Enver. He did it, but not without plenty of grumbling. I'll give him credit; the preparation is a bit tedious, but once seasoned and given time to rest, the carrots turn succulent from their own seasoned juices with a melt-in-your-mouth texture. It's the type of dish that doesn't immediately shout at you to try first, but once you have, you'll get why we put in the effort.

....

2 pounds (900 g) carrots, peeled and trimmed
½ cup (120 g) mayonnaise
4 garlic cloves, finely grated
2 teaspoons kosher salt, plus more to taste
1 teaspoon ground blue fenugreek (optional)
½ cup (15 g) cilantro, finely chopped (optional)

SERVES 6 AS AN APPETIZER

If using a food processor, have two large bowls ready. Using the grating disc, grate the carrots in the food processor and transfer to a bowl. Switch out the attachment for the blade. Working in batches, process the carrots until very finely chopped, scraping down the bowl as needed. Transfer each batch to the other bowl. (Alternatively, use the second to smallest holes on a box grater to grate the carrots into a large bowl.)

Add the mayonnaise, garlic, salt, blue fenugreek (if using), and cilantro (if using) and mix until thoroughly combined. Taste and season with more salt if needed. Refrigerate for at least a couple of hours, allowing the flavors to meld and for the carrots to release their juices, before serving chilled. Store in the refrigerator for up to 4 days.

Note: *Although using a food processor makes quick work of the carrots, prepping them by hand will give you the best texture.*

DOCTORED-UP MUSHROOMS

While mushrooms straight out of a can aren't very appealing, this quick marinade turns them into a tasty *zakuska* (small bite). Many marinate mushrooms from scratch, but my aunt Olga likes to use jarred or canned mushrooms (opyata, or nameko, mushrooms are our picks) to speed things along. Toss everything together and let them hang out in the fridge while you go about your day. It's as easy as that!

••

One (15-ounce / 425 g) can water-packed whole
    mushrooms, drained, rinsed, and halved,
    or one (18.7-ounce / 530 g) can marinated
    mushrooms, drained
¼ cup (20 g) thinly-sliced yellow onions
4 or 5 sprigs dill, finely chopped
2 or 3 sprigs parsley, finely chopped
1 garlic clove, minced
1½ tablespoons unrefined sunflower oil, plus
    more to taste
2 teaspoons white wine vinegar, plus more to taste
Kosher salt and freshly ground black pepper

SERVES 6 TO 8 AS AN APPETIZER

In a small bowl, toss together the mushrooms, onions, dill, parsley, garlic, oil, vinegar, and a big pinch or two of salt and pepper. Taste—the mushrooms should already be a lot more flavorful—and add more oil, vinegar, salt, and pepper until you're happy with them. Allow the mushrooms to marinate in the refrigerator for 4 to 6 hours or overnight before serving.

Note: *The Eastern European store will have marinated (yet still bland) jarred mushrooms; Asian markets tend to have a good selection of canned mushrooms.*

OLIVIER SALAD

RUSSIAN POTATO SALAD

When the Soviets did away with religion, New Year's Day replaced Christmas as the biggest holiday of the year. Families would decorate a New Year's tree (*novogodnyaya yolka*) and children would be visited by Grandfather Frost (*D'yed Moroz*) with presents. As for the celebratory dinner that evening, there was an unofficial menu that pretty much everyone adhered to. The table would be covered with a patchwork of small cold plates called *zakuski* (small bites) that were meant to sustain you through the evening as toasts were given and shots knocked back. The most famous and beloved, of course, being *olivye* (olivier) or *stolichnyi* (metropolitan) salat. A glorified potato salad originally dreamed up by nineteenth-century French chef Lucien Olivier for his famous restaurant in Moscow, it made its way to every corner of the USSR and beyond, where it became known simply as "Russian salad" in countries like Spain and Italy.

The Olivier of today is much less elaborate than it was in Lucien's time (his featured both grouse and crayfish), but when done right, is still delicious. Tangy pickles, dill and parsley, green onions, and not to mention a light touch with mayo, keep our family's take out of stodgy territory. When preparing it, just know that people have *opinions* when it comes to this salad—what should be included, what shouldn't. I, for one, do not add any cut-up hot dog or bologna, chicken, or apple to my salad. As for fresh or canned peas, I stand by the latter out of nostalgia. If you disagree, feel free to use my version as a rubric and adapt it accordingly to your personal preferences.

This recipe makes a generous amount (perfect for parties), but you won't have any trouble getting through a batch. As one recipe tester said, "I think this is the best Olivier I have made in my life."

....

5 medium Yukon Gold potatoes (1¼ pounds / 570 g)
4 medium carrots, peeled
4 eggs
Kosher salt
One (15-ounce / 425 g) can green peas, drained and rinsed
⅔ cup (115 g) diced gherkins or pickles
¾ cup to 1 cup (180 g to 240 g) mayonnaise, to taste
1 small bunch of green onions, white and light-green parts only, thinly sliced
½ large bunch of dill, finely chopped
3 to 4 sprigs parsley, finely chopped
2 teaspoons kosher salt, plus more to taste
1 generous teaspoon freshly ground black pepper, plus more to taste

SERVES 6 TO 8 AS A SIDE

Place the potatoes, carrots, and eggs (in that order) in a large pot and fill with enough water to cover the vegetables. Generously salt the water. Bring to a full boil. As soon as the water comes to a full boil, set a timer for 5 minutes. In the meantime, set up an ice bath in a medium bowl. Once the time is up, scoop out the eggs and transfer them to the ice bath. Set aside.

Cover the pot and adjust the heat to maintain a rolling boil. Cook the vegetables until a paring knife can slide through the center of the carrots with minimal resistance, another 10 to 15 minutes depending on thickness. Remove the carrots and add to the bowl with the eggs (it's okay if all the ice has melted).

Continue cooking the potatoes until a paring knife can also slide through, another 10 to 15 minutes. Drain and allow to cool completely before proceeding.

When ready to assemble, peel the potatoes and eggs. Cut the potatoes, carrots, and eggs into ⅜-inch (1 cm) dice. Add to a large bowl. Add the peas, pickles, mayonnaise, green onions, dill, parsley, salt, and pepper. Toss to evenly combine and coat the vegetables. Taste and add more salt and pepper if desired. Store in the refrigerator for up to 4 days.

VINEGRET SALAT

BEET, POTATO, AND SAUERKRAUT SALAD

This is a twist on the classic Russian potato salad: The mayo is replaced with unrefined sunflower oil and the gherkins for sauerkraut. The addition of beets, too, lends a lovely shade of pink. Serve it with herring or smoked mackerel, good rye bread, and some vodka and you're ready for a party.

....

5 medium red beets, scrubbed

4 medium Yukon Gold potatoes

3 large carrots, peeled

Kosher salt

3 tablespoons (45 g) unrefined sunflower oil, plus more to taste

2 cups (300 g) sauerkraut, homemade (page 185) or store-bought (see Note), squeezed to remove excess brine

One (15-ounce / 425 g) can green peas, drained and rinsed

½ small red onion, finely diced

½ large bunch of dill, finely chopped

¼ bunch of parsley, finely chopped

1 teaspoon finely ground black pepper, plus more to taste

SERVES 6 TO 8 AS A SIDE

Place the beets in a large pot and fill with enough water to cover. Bring to a boil, then reduce to a simmer, cover, and cook until fork-tender, 1 to 1½ hours. Drain and peel while still warm. Set aside to cool completely.

Meanwhile, place the potatoes and carrots in another large pot and fill with water to fully cover. Generously salt the water. Bring to a boil. Adjust heat to maintain a rolling boil, cover, and cook until a paring knife can slide through the center of the carrots with minimal resistance, 15 to 20 minutes depending on thickness. Remove the carrots and set aside.

Continue cooking the potatoes until a knife slips in easily, but the potato is still firm, another 10 to 15 minutes. Drain and allow to cool completely before proceeding.

When ready to assemble, dice the peeled beets into ⅜-inch (1 cm) cubes and transfer to a large bowl. Toss with 1 tablespoon of the oil to keep them from staining the other vegetables too much.

Peel the potatoes. Cut the potatoes and carrots into ½-inch (1.3 cm) cubes and add them to the beets. Add the sauerkraut, peas, red onion, dill, and parsley. Add the remaining 2 tablespoons oil, 2 teaspoons salt, and the pepper. Toss to evenly combine and coat the vegetables. Taste and add more salt, pepper, and oil if desired. Store in the refrigerator for up to 4 days.

Note: *The recipe is written using the sauerkraut I make at home and the kind sold in Eastern European markets. It's less assertive and mushy than the German-style you might be more familiar with. If using the latter, start with half the amount, taste, and add more until you're happy with how it tastes. You can also swap some or all of the sauerkraut for pickles and red kidney beans for the green peas.*

VESENNII SALAT

CABBAGE, CUCUMBER, AND RADISH SALAD

A mainstay of late-spring and summer meals (*vesennii* means "of spring"), this cabbage, cucumber, and radish salad—Slavic coleslaw if you will—is crunchy, cool, and creamy. It has just the right balance of heft and lightness to keep you coming back for seconds and thirds. Need I say more?

••

½ medium head green cabbage, thinly shaved
    or shredded
1 medium bunch of red radishes, tops removed, cut
    into thin matchsticks or half-moons
1 medium cucumber, peeled in alternating stripes,
    cut into thin half-moons
4 green onions, white and light-green parts only,
    thinly sliced
2 or 3 eggs, hard-boiled, peeled, and chopped
½ cup (15 g) dill, finely chopped
3 small garlic cloves, minced
⅓ cup (80 g) mayonnaise
3 tablespoons (45 g) sour cream
1½ teaspoons kosher salt, plus more to taste
¾ teaspoon freshly ground black pepper, plus more
    to taste

SERVES 6 TO 8 AS A SIDE

In a large bowl, toss all the ingredients together to evenly coat. Taste and season with more salt and pepper if needed and serve. (While the salad is best served as soon as you toss and season it, you can prep all the ingredients up to a day in advance before proceeding.) Store in the refrigerator for up to 3 days.

Note: *To make a vegan version, omit the eggs, mayo, and sour cream and dress the salad with unrefined sunflower oil instead.*

SALAT

TOMATO AND CUCUMBER SALAD

Tomatoes and cucumbers are a standard pairing throughout the former Soviet Union. In Georgia, cooks toss the duo in a zesty walnut dressing; in Russia and Ukraine they'll throw in a dollop of sour cream and go heavy on the dill; and in Uzbekistan, they drop the cucumber entirely, allowing the tomato to shine with thin slivers of onions.

In our family, *salat*, as we simply call it, is a bit of a kitchen-sink situation, but the basic formula remains constant: tomatoes and cucumbers, thinly sliced onions, loads of herbs, and a bit of raw garlic. The generous use of herbs really makes the salad sing, so add in whatever you have and don't skimp. We love to add Anaheim chili if it's around—bell pepper would also work. To finish, all it needs is a few glugs of unrefined sunflower oil (or extra-virgin olive oil) and, if desired, a sprinkling of red or white wine vinegar. In the winter months, we swap in hothouse varieties for their summer counterparts.

∙∙

2 large firm-ripe tomatoes, cored and cut into wedges
2 to 3 Persian (mini) cucumbers, sliced
1 small Anaheim chili, seeded and thinly sliced
1 small shallot, ¼ yellow or red onion, or 2 or 3 green
*   onions, thinly sliced*
1 large garlic clove, finely minced
3 or 4 sprigs cilantro, finely chopped
2 or 3 sprigs fresh basil, leaves picked and torn
*   (optional)*
2 or 3 sprigs dill, finely chopped
1 or 2 sprigs parsley, finely chopped
Unrefined sunflower oil or extra-virgin olive oil, for
*   finishing*
Red or white wine vinegar, for finishing (optional)
Kosher salt and freshly ground black pepper

SERVES 4 AS A SIDE

Place all the vegetables and herbs into a nice large serving bowl. Drizzle with two to three glugs of sunflower oil and a generous sprinkling of vinegar (if using). Add a couple big pinches of kosher salt and pepper. Toss to evenly coat. Taste and season accordingly, adding more salt and pepper as needed. Serve immediately.

VARIATION

Salati Nigvzit: *While our salad is already very Georgian influenced, we'll make it with walnuts when we want to mix it up. To prepare this variation, called* salati nigvzit *in Georgia, assemble the salad in the large bowl as directed, but omit the cilantro and garlic in the salad itself. Replace the vinegar with the juice of ½ lemon. Toss with the walnut dressing below.*

WALNUT DRESSING
¼ cup (30 g) toasted walnuts
1 large garlic clove, crushed and peeled
¼ teaspoon dried adjika, plus more to taste
½ teaspoon ground coriander
½ teaspoon ground blue fenugreek
Kosher salt
¾ cup (25 g) cilantro, roughly chopped
2 to 3 tablespoons water

In a large mortar and pestle, pound the walnuts, garlic, spices, and a big pinch of salt until they turn into a chunky paste. Add the cilantro a big pinch at a time and pound to incorporate before adding more. Do your best to mash it into as smooth a paste as possible. Add water, 1 tablespoon at a time, until you have the consistency of a thin pesto. Taste and season with more salt and spices accordingly.

Note: *Alternatively, you can blitz everything in the food processor and add the water slowly until the desired consistency is reached.*

VITAMIN SALAT

CABBAGE, BEET, AND APPLE SALAD

Chock-full of veggies—and vitamins!—with no mayo or dairy in sight, this healthful cabbage salad is sweet, tangy, and savory. At its most basic, it's just cabbage and carrots, but my aunt Natasha taught me this more elaborate version when I was in high school and I've never looked back. Vitamin Salat lasts for a couple of days, getting juicier with time, making all the effort of chopping and shredding worth it!

··

½ medium head green cabbage, thinly shaved or
    shredded
1 medium red beet, peeled and coarsely grated
2 medium carrots, peeled and coarsely grated
½ large tart apple, such as Granny Smith, cut into
    matchsticks
¼ small red onion, finely diced
⅓ cup (10 g) dill, finely chopped
¼ cup (7 g) parsley, finely chopped
3 tablespoons (45 g) unrefined sunflower oil or
    extra-virgin olive oil
2 tablespoons red wine vinegar or apple cider
    vinegar, plus more to taste
1½ teaspoons kosher salt, plus more to taste
½ teaspoon freshly ground black pepper, plus more
    to taste

SERVES 4 AS A SIDE

In a large bowl, toss all the ingredients together to evenly coat. Taste and season with more vinegar, salt, and pepper if needed and serve. Store in the refrigerator for up to 3 days.

ADJAPSANDALI

GEORGIAN RATATOUILLE

In the summers, as the heat of the sun abated and the workday concluded, my mother and I would drive over to our family's unofficial carpool lot, pile into my aunt's minivan, and head to the beach. By the time we arrived, the bikini-clad crowds had petered out and the beachside parking was free. We'd quickly unload, set up camp, and brave the murky, frigid waters.

Our appetites, whetted by our adrenaline-fueled plunge, eventually pulled us out of the water for a sunset dinner. Bundled in our towels, my cousins and I would huddle together and look on, like a hungry pack of wolves, as our mothers emptied food and drinks out of the coolers. Crunchy cucumber slivers and plump juicy tomato wedges comprised the first round of provisions. Briny squares of creamy feta and torn chunks of bread followed, and to bring it all together: *adjapsandali*. Generously mounded onto our bread with the cool ocean breeze imparting a salty kiss, the silky eggplant spread was fiery and absolutely moreish as the English would say.

Amid our rustic alfresco setting, adjapsandali felt luxurious, and it was. Time and generous glugs of oil work their magic to melt down eggplants, tomatoes, peppers, onions, and carrots until the mélange is jammy and confit-like. It resembles a French ratatouille, that is, until you stir in the fistfuls of cilantro and basil, hot chili, and garlic at the end. Some recipes will have you add potatoes or chunks of beef or lamb to fill it out, but I find that this simpler version is perfect as is. Make it when nightshades are at their peak and their natural sweetness can shine through.

· ·

4 medium eggplants (about 4 pounds / 1.8 kg total), peeled in alternating stripes, quartered lengthwise, and cut into pieces 1 inch (2.5 cm) thick
Kosher salt
3 large juicy, ripe tomatoes (about 2 pounds / 900 g total)

⅓ cup (75 g) sunflower oil, plus more as needed
2 large yellow onions, cut into medium dice
3 medium carrots, cut into ⅛-inch (6 mm) half-moons
2 bell peppers (preferably of various colors), cut into medium dice
1½ tablespoons tomato paste
Granulated sugar (optional)
1 to 2 serrano chilis, finely chopped along with seeds
4 garlic cloves, crushed through a press or minced
1 small bunch of cilantro (40 g), finely chopped
5 to 6 parsley sprigs, leaves picked and finely chopped
4 to 5 basil sprigs (preferably purple), leaves picked and chiffonade-cut
Crusty bread, for serving
Feta cheese, for serving

SERVES 6 TO 8 AS A SIDE

In a large bowl, toss the eggplant pieces with 1 tablespoon kosher salt and set aside while you prep the rest of the vegetables.

Peel the tomatoes (see box), chop them, and transfer to a colander set over a bowl and allow them to drain, stirring them from time to time to help encourage more liquid to drain.

In a large, wide, preferably shallow pot, heat the oil over medium heat. Add the onions, carrots, and a generous pinch of salt and cook until the onions start to take on color and the carrots have lost their raw edge, 12 to 15 minutes.

Stir in the bell peppers and another pinch of salt. Cook until the peppers have softened, 5 to 6 minutes. Add the tomato paste, a splash of water to loosen it up, and cook for another 2 to 3 minutes. Add the drained tomatoes and a pinch of salt. Set over low heat and let gently simmer, stirring periodically to keep the bottom from scorching, while you cook the eggplant.

Squeeze the eggplant in handfuls to release excess liquid. In a large wide skillet, heat 2 to 3 tablespoons oil over medium heat. Add enough eggplant pieces to cover the pan in an even generous layer. Partially cover the pan and cook until the bottoms have browned, about 5 minutes. Uncover, stir the eggplant, and continue to cook until the eggplant is evenly browned, fork-tender, and starts to look translucent, another 5 to 6 minutes.

Taste the tomato/onion mixture and season with salt. If you find the tomatoes to be too acidic, add a teaspoon or two of sugar to temper them. Once seasoned to your liking, gently fold in the first batch of cooked eggplant. From this point, be very gentle when stirring the vegetables—overmixing will result in mush.

Repeat browning the remaining eggplant pieces, generously adding more oil to the pan with each batch and gently folding them into the tomato mixture once finished cooking.

Meanwhile, the tomato/eggplant mixture should gently simmer in the background and be stirred from time to time. Once the last of the cooked eggplant is folded in, allow the vegetables to simmer for another 20 minutes. By this point the medley should be cooked down significantly and be jam-like. Taste and add more salt and/or sugar if needed.

Sprinkle the vegetables with half of the serrano chili, the garlic, cilantro, parsley, and basil in an even layer, then carefully stir them in. Cook, uncovered, for another 5 minutes and remove from the heat. Taste once more and season accordingly (and add more serrano if it doesn't have enough bite). Allow to cool completely before serving. Or better yet, refrigerate overnight and serve cold or at room temperature.

Best with some crusty bread and some feta on the side. Adjapsandali gets better with age and will keep in the refrigerator 5 to 7 days.

HOW TO PEEL TOMATOES

Bring a kettle of water to a boil. In the meantime, set up an ice bath. Score an X on the bottom of each tomato and place in a preferably deep, yet narrow heatproof bowl that will fit the tomatoes and enough water to submerge them. Pour the boiling water over the tomatoes to completely submerge and allow to sit for about 1 minute, or until the skins start to peel away from the tomatoes. Use a slotted spoon to transfer to the ice bath. The skins should slip off.

HERRING UNDER A FUR COAT

Donning a glamorous multihued *shuba* (fur coat) of grated vegetables, this herring knows how to make a splash. Like its Soviet sidekick Olivier Salad (page 118), the festive layered salad tends to make its debut at NYE dinners and is gracious enough to share the limelight with an array of other cold *zakuski* (small bites). I will be the first to admit that the concept of pickled fish with mayo and boiled, grated vegetables is a bit unusual, but it works. The potatoes and onions temper the fishiness of the herring; the beets and carrots lend a little vegetal sweetness. And the mayo—well, I'm obviously biased, but the mayo just makes everything taste better. If you like lox on your bagel with cream cheese, then you'll love this herring under a fur coat. Serve with good rye bread.

You can assemble the dish a day in advance, but wait to garnish it with the egg until serving since the beets dye everything pink as the salad sits. Also, you'll want salted herring fillets in oil from the Eastern European grocery store, not the pickled Scandi kind.

••

2 medium red beets, scrubbed
3 medium Yukon Gold potatoes
2 large carrots, peeled
2 eggs
Kosher salt
½ small red onion, finely diced
3 tablespoons (45 g) distilled white or apple
    cider vinegar
2 salted herring fillets packed in oil (about 100 g),
    finely chopped
¾ cup (180) mayonnaise
Dill sprigs, for garnish
Salmon roe caviar, for garnish (optional)

SERVES 6 TO 8 AS A SIDE

Place the beets in a medium pot and fill with enough water to cover. Bring to a boil, then reduce to a simmer, cover, and cook until fork-tender, 1 to 1½ hours. Drain and set aside for 20 to 30 minutes, or until cool enough to handle. While the beets are still warm, hold a beet in one hand with a paper towel or clean kitchen towel, trim the top, and use the paper towel to rub the skin off—it should slip right off. Set the beets aside to cool completely.

Meanwhile, place the potatoes, carrots, and eggs (in that order) in a large pot and fill with enough water to cover the vegetables. Generously salt the water. Bring to a full boil. As soon as the water comes to a full boil, set a timer for 5 minutes. During this time, set up an ice bath in a medium bowl. Once the time is up, scoop out the eggs and transfer them to the ice bath. Set aside.

Cover the pot and adjust the heat to maintain a rolling boil. Cook the vegetables until a paring knife or fork can slide through the center of the carrots easily, another 10 to 15 minutes depending on thickness. Remove the carrots and add to the bowl with the eggs (it's okay if all the ice has melted).

Continue cooking the potatoes until a knife slips in easily, but the potato is still firm, another 10 to 15 minutes. Drain and allow to cool completely before proceeding. (The boiled vegetables can be done a day or two in advance.)

When ready to assemble the dish, in a small bowl, toss the onion with the vinegar and let sit for 15 to 20 minutes.

Peel the potatoes, then carefully grate them on the largest holes of a box grater, making sure not to mash them. Set them aside. Rinse the grater and grate the carrots. Repeat the process with the beets, being careful not to get its color on the other vegetables.

Carefully arrange half of the grated potatoes in an even layer in a large clear glass bowl or, if you're feeling fancy, in the ring of a 9-inch (23 cm) springform pan set on a large serving plate. Add the herring in an even layer. Drain the onions and sprinkle them all over. Dollop half of the mayonnaise all over the herring/onion mixture and use the back of a spoon to smooth and even things out without pressing down too much. Top with the remaining potatoes and season with a pinch of salt. Repeat with a layer of carrots and then beets, making sure to season both layers with salt. Dollop the rest of the mayonnaise all over the beets and smooth it out with the spoon. (At this point you can refrigerate for up to 1 day.)

When ready to serve, peel and cut the eggs in half and remove the yolks from the whites. If you're still feeling fancy, using a spoon, press the whites through a fine sieve and garnish the top of the salad. Repeat with the yolks. You can also medium-grate or finely chop the eggs and top the salad that way, too. Garnish with sprigs of dill and/or bright-red salmon roe, if using. Remove the cake ring and serve immediately. Stored in the refrigerator, the salad will last for 2 to 3 days.

SOVIET HOME FRIES

These home fries, or *zharennaya kartoshka,* hold a special place in our hearts, right up next to borsch and Olivier Salad (page 118). Cut into matchsticks and shallow-fried in a skillet, some potatoes turn golden and crisp, others meltingly soft, and sometimes, the best bits stick together to create irresistible clusters of varying textures. Many a night has been saved thanks to a pan of zharennaya kartoshka, a pickle or some sauerkraut, and a couple of boiled *sosiski* (frankfurters) pulled from the freezer. But while the concept is simple, it does take some finesse to avoid soggy and/or burnt bottoms. Make sure you use the largest nonstick skillet you've got and cut the matchsticks as uniformly as you can. You can also stir in some browned thinly sliced onion toward the end of cooking or garnish with chopped parsley. Just be warned, whatever you serve them with will end up playing second fiddle—these potatoes always steal the show.

• •

2 to 2½ pounds (900 g to 1.14 kg) Yukon Gold or
    russet potatoes, scrubbed and peeled
Sunflower oil, light olive oil, or other neutral oil
    with a high smoke point, for frying
Kosher or sea salt

SERVES 2 TO 3 AS A SIDE

Cut the potatoes into matchsticks ⅜ inch (1 cm) thick—if working with large russet potatoes, halve them crosswise first. Rinse the matchsticks under cold water to remove excess starch and then use a paper towel or clean kitchen towel to blot the matchsticks on all sides until very, very dry. This ensures that the potatoes will brown and crisp up properly.

Line a large shallow bowl with paper towels and set near the stove. Add enough oil to a 12-inch (30 cm) nonstick skillet or sauté pan to generously cover the bottom of the pan. Heat the oil over medium-high heat until very hot and shimmering. To test, dip the end of a wooden spoon or chopstick in the oil—if the oil starts to sizzle around the stick, the oil is hot enough.

Once the oil is hot, sprinkle 2 generous pinches of salt evenly over the oil. Blot the matchsticks one more time before carefully lowering half of the potatoes a handful at a time into the oil. Use a spatula to help move them around and arrange them into as close to an even layer as possible— it's okay if some matchsticks are stacked here and there.

Cook, undisturbed, until the potatoes are crisp and golden brown on the bottom, 6 to 8 minutes. Adjust the heat as needed if the potatoes are browning too quickly. Flip and cook the other side, another 3 to 5 minutes.

Once both sides of the first batch of potatoes are browned, push them all to one side of the pan. Add half of the remaining matchsticks in an even layer on the now empty side. Then scoop up the browned potatoes and place them on top of the second batch of matchsticks to expose the other half of the pan. Add the rest of the matchsticks to the empty side and arrange in an even layer. Distribute the browned potatoes so that they are now sitting evenly atop the second batch of matchsticks on the bottom.

Cook until the potatoes are crisp and golden brown on the bottom, 6 to 8 minutes. Use the spatula to rearrange potatoes so that any uncooked sides are face down in the oil. Reduce the heat to medium and cook until the other side is browned, 6 to 8 minutes. Use a fork to check if the potatoes are tender and cooked through—it should meet with minimal resistance. If not, cover and continue cooking on medium-low heat, flipping the potatoes occasionally to encourage even browning, until the potatoes are done.

Using a slotted spatula or spoon, transfer the potatoes to the paper-towel-lined bowl (try to leave as much of the oil behind in the pan as possible). Sprinkle all over with salt to season and serve immediately. Store leftovers in the refrigerator for up to 3 days.

LECSÓ

STUFFED PEPPERS IN ZESTY TOMATO SAUCE

Lecsó or *lecho* is the traditional Hungarian method of stewing peppers with ripe tomatoes, onions, and paprika. There's no exact recipe—it's a rustic, end-of-the-summer dish that's meant to swoop in when you have an overflowing garden. These stuffed peppers are a play on lecsó that was popular in Georgia when my mom lived there. The hollowed-out vessels are filled with sautéed sweet carrots and cauliflower, then smothered in a spicy tomato-pepper sauce before being baked until wrinkled and charred in spots. They're delicious warm, but I find that they really shine when they're served chilled (which is also how we usually eat them).

••

STUFFED PEPPERS
6 to 8 bell peppers
Kosher salt
¼ cup (55 g) sunflower oil or extra-virgin olive oil
2 medium yellow onions, chopped
1 pound (450 g) carrots, peeled and shredded
½ medium head cauliflower, finely chopped
Freshly ground black pepper
2 medium firm-ripe tomatoes, sliced into rounds
    ¼ inch (6 mm) thick

LECSÓ SAUCE
2 tablespoons sunflower oil or extra-virgin olive oil
1 large yellow onion, chopped
1 Anaheim chili, seeded and chopped
Kosher salt
1 jalapeño, finely chopped along with seeds
2 tablespoons tomato paste
2 large juicy, ripe tomatoes, cored and chopped
½ teaspoon granulated sugar, plus more to taste

SERVES 6 TO 8 AS A SIDE

Make the stuffed peppers: Preheat the oven to 375°F (190°C). Find a medium baking dish where the peppers can fit snugly and sit upright.

Cut off the top one-third of the peppers and discard the seeds and ribs. Reserve the tops to use as "lids." Sprinkle the cavities of each bell pepper with a pinch or two of salt. Arrange the peppers snugly in the baking dish. Set aside.

In a large sauté pan, heat the oil over medium heat. Add the onions and a generous pinch of salt and cook until soft, translucent, and beginning to lose their raw edge, 8 to 10 minutes.

Add the carrots, cauliflower, and a couple pinches of salt and cook until the carrots and cauliflower have softened, 10 to 12 minutes.

Taste and season generously with black pepper and more salt if needed. Divide the carrot-onion mixture among the bell peppers, using your spoon to pack in the filling.

Make the lecsó sauce: In a sauté pan, heat the oil over medium heat. Add the onion, Anaheim chili, and a generous pinch of salt and cook until softened, 8 to 10 minutes.

Add the jalapeño (seeds and all), tomato paste, and a splash of water and cook for a couple more minutes. Stir in the tomatoes, a couple pinches of salt, and the sugar. Simmer, stirring occasionally, until the tomatoes have broken down into a chunky sauce, another 10 minutes. Taste and season with more salt or sugar if needed.

Spoon the sauce evenly over each pepper and spoon any extra in between the peppers. Top each pepper with a tomato slice and sprinkle each round with a bit of salt and black pepper. Put the "lids" back on. Add ¼ cup (60 g) water to the bottom of the dish and cover the dish tightly with foil. (At this point, the peppers can be well wrapped and refrigerated for 2 to 3 days before cooking.)

Bake the peppers for 45 minutes (or 1 hour if coming straight from the fridge). Remove the foil, spoon any juices over the lids, and continue baking until the peppers are soft when pierced with a knife, the skins are wrinkled, and the tops begin to blacken in spots, another 30 minutes.

Allow to cool. Serve while still warm, at room temperature, or better yet, when they're completely chilled through. Store leftovers in the refrigerator for up to 4 days.

CHAPTER FIVE

MEATS AND SEAFOOD

TABAKA-STYLE ADJIKA CHICKEN

When it comes to roasted chicken in my mom's house, I've only ever seen it done one way: spatchcocked, slathered in an *adjika*-spiced marinade, and cooked until the skin is crispy and the inside is juicy and succulent. While I've flirted with other recipes over the years, it's hers that I always come back to.

Traditionally, Georgian chicken *tabaka* is cooked under a heavy weight on the stovetop, but my mom keeps it simple and employs the slow, even (and cleaner) heat of the oven instead. As for adjika—that salty, intense chili condiment native to the western regions of Georgia—it lends the marinade both spice *and* heat. It comes in many forms (as a dried spice blend, thick paste, and as a saucy relish), so use whatever you can get your hands on. The other magical ingredient at play here is mayo, which not only carries and amplifies flavor, but also locks in the meat's juices to keep things super tender. I'm telling you, this recipe could win ribbons!

This marinade is our go-to for anytime we're preparing poultry, whether it's grilling wings, roasting thighs, or pan-searing breast. For what I consider a perfect meal, serve with Salat (page 123), Soviet Home Fries (page 131) or roasted potatoes, and Tkemali (page 182).

....

¼ cup (60 g) mayonnaise
¼ cup (15 g) finely chopped cilantro leaves
    and stems
3 tablespoons (50 g) adjika paste or relish, chopped
    red hot peppers, or chili garlic sauce (or
    1 tablespoon dried adjika)
2 tablespoons runny honey
3 to 4 garlic cloves, crushed through a press
    or minced
2 to 3 teaspoons kosher salt (see Note)
½ teaspoon freshly ground black pepper
1 whole chicken (4 to 5 pounds / 1.8 to 2.3 kg),
    patted dry

SERVES 4

In a large bowl, whisk together the mayonnaise, cilantro, adjika, honey, garlic, salt, and pepper until combined. (You can also blitz everything in a food processor until smooth.) You want it to be on the saltier side, so taste and season with more salt if needed. Set aside.

Set the chicken on a large cutting board, breast side down. Using sharp kitchen shears, remove the backbone by cutting down each side of the spine, starting from the tail end of the bird. Flip the chicken over so that it is skin side up and press down on the breastbone to flatten it. Trim any excess fat from around the cavity. Transfer to the large bowl with the marinade and rub it all over, making sure to get under the skin, too. Refrigerate for 4 to 6 hours, but preferably overnight; if short on time, 1 hour at room temperature will do.

When ready to cook, preheat the oven to 425°F (220°C). Line a baking sheet with foil.

Remove the chicken from the marinade, allowing any excess marinade to drip off and transfer to the prepared pan skin side up. Tuck the wings back behind the breast so they don't burn.

Roast for 20 minutes (the chicken should start taking on some color at this point). Reduce the oven temperature to 375°F (190°C) and roast until cooked through, or until the joint between the thighs and body registers at least 175°F (80°C) on an instant-read thermometer, another 15 to 25 minutes.

Let the chicken rest for 10 to 15 minutes before carving.

Note: *Taste your adjika and if it's on the saltier side (or if you're using a dried spice blend with salt in it), start with the smaller amount of salt and build from there.*

CHAKHOKHBILI

CHICKEN WITH TOMATO AND HERBS

Juicy, taut-skinned tomatoes ready to burst; heady, verdant heaps of basil, cilantro, and parsley; a generous pour (or two) of white wine; the lingering heat of chilis. *Chakhokhbili* is the sort of home-style cooking that stays with you, not least because it calls for all the best that summer has to offer. Instead of breaking down a whole bird, as is traditional, we swap in bone-in thighs and drumsticks instead. The fricassee-style dish benefits from some time on the stove to build flavor and depth, but the result is surprisingly light and fresh. Make sure to serve it with something to mop up the juices—mashed potatoes, polenta, pasta, or even just some hearty bread. We wait for August each year to make this, and I hope, upon trying, you will, too.

• •

4 bone-in, skin-on chicken thighs and 4 drumsticks (2½ to 3 pounds / 1.14 to 1.4 kg total), excess skin and fat trimmed, patted dry
Kosher salt and freshly ground black pepper
3 tablespoons (45 g) sunflower oil or extra-virgin olive oil
4 medium yellow onions, thinly sliced
5 garlic cloves, 3 thinly sliced, and 2 crushed through a press
2 teaspoons khmeli suneli (optional)
½ teaspoon red pepper flakes, plus more to taste
2½ pounds (1.14 kg) tomatoes (about 8 medium), peeled (see page 127), cored, and evenly chopped
½ cup (120 g) dry white wine
Granulated sugar (optional)
1 large bunch of cilantro, finely chopped
½ bunch of parsley, finely chopped
4 to 5 sprigs basil, leaves picked and chiffonade-cut

SERVES 4 TO 6

Generously season the chicken pieces all over with salt and pepper.

In a large Dutch oven or heavy-bottomed pot, heat the oil over medium-high heat. Working in two batches, add half of the chicken, skin side down. Reduce the heat to medium and cook, resisting the urge to move it around, until the skin is a deep golden brown, 8 to 10 minutes. You want the chicken to quietly sizzle but not sputter or crackle. You also want to keep the pan juices from burning. In both cases, reduce the heat as needed. Turn the pieces over and cook until lightly browned on the other side, another 3 to 4 minutes. Transfer the chicken to a plate or tray and set aside. Repeat with the remaining chicken.

To the same pot, add the onions and a generous pinch of salt. Cook over medium heat until the onions have collapsed, their juices are almost evaporated, and they begin to stick to the bottom of the pan and take on color, 12 to 15 minutes.

Add the sliced garlic, khmeli suneli, if using, and pepper flakes and cook for another minute or two. Add the tomatoes and white wine, reduce the heat to maintain a simmer, and cook, stirring occasionally, until the mixture starts to thicken a bit and the tomatoes completely fall apart, 12 to 15 minutes. When the tomato-onion mixture is done, taste. If the tomatoes are acidic, add a bit of sugar.

Nestle the chicken, skin-side up, back into the pan in a single layer and pour in any juices that have accumulated on the plate. Cover, adjust the heat to maintain a gentle simmer, and cook, undisturbed, until the chicken is cooked through and tender, 20 to 25 minutes, depending on the size of your chicken pieces.

Gently stir the herbs and pressed garlic into the sauce. Simmer, uncovered, for a few more minutes so that the garlic loses its raw edge. Taste and season with more salt, black pepper, and/or pepper flakes.

Note: *We typically make this with peeled tomatoes (my preference), but if you'd rather not, unpeeled will work as well.*

CHICKEN BAZHE

CHICKEN IN WALNUT SAUCE

One of the defining characteristics of Georgian cuisine is its impressive and deft employment of walnuts, the oldest-known cultivated food in the Caucasus region. Home cooks have turned the kernel into everything from pâtés and dressings to stews and desserts. One prime example of this ingenuity, and my personal favorite, is a velvety, fragrant walnut sauce called *bazhe*. To make it, walnuts are ground until almost sandy in texture, then flavored with a bouquet of spices, cilantro, and garlic, and finally, hydrated and thinned out. Bazhe is often served on the side, to be spooned over chicken, fish, grits, or vegetables. In this case, a cooked bird is fully submerged in it. Because it's so rich, both in flavor and calories, we often save bazhe for the holidays and pair it with hot, cheesy Mamalyga (page 173).

Industrious home cooks will painstakingly knead the spiced walnuts to extract a tawny-brown aromatic oil that they'll then drizzle over as a garnish. Store-bought walnut oil works in a pinch or omit it completely and scatter fresh pomegranate seeds over the top instead.

....

CHICKEN
1 whole chicken (3 to 4 pounds / 1.4 to 1.8 kg)
Water, for simmering
1 tablespoon kosher salt, plus more to taste

BAZHE SAUCE
2½ cups (300 g) walnuts
4 garlic cloves, peeled but whole
½ cup (20 g) roughly chopped cilantro leaves and
    stems
½ small yellow onion, roughly chopped
1½ tablespoons distilled white vinegar
Rounded 1½ teaspoons ground coriander
1 teaspoon ground blue fenugreek
1 teaspoon ground marigold
½ teaspoon cayenne pepper, plus more to taste
Kosher salt

Walnut oil or pomegranate seeds (optional),
    for garnish

SERVES 6 TO 8

Place the chicken in a large, preferably tall and narrow, stockpot and fill with enough water to completely submerge by 1 inch (2.5 cm). Add the salt and bring to a simmer over medium-high heat. Skim any scum that floats to the surface. Partially cover, adjust the heat to maintain a very gentle simmer, and cook, turning it halfway through so that it cooks evenly, until the chicken is fall-apart tender (the leg will come right off when pulled), 1½ to 2 hours.

Remove from the heat, transfer the chicken to a medium bowl, and allow to cool. Once cool enough to handle, remove the skin and pick the meat off the bones. Aim for slightly bigger than bite-size pieces, keeping large parts like drumsticks and wings with their bones intact. Set the meat aside and discard the bones and cartilage. Reserve the broth for the sauce. (Both can be made ahead and stored in separate airtight containers in the refrigerator for 3 to 4 days. The broth can be frozen for 2 to 3 months.)

Make the bazhe sauce: In a food processor, combine all the ingredients plus 2 teaspoons salt and process until a very thick paste forms.

Bring 2⅔ cups (640 g) of the broth to a boil. With the food processor running, slowly stream in the hot broth until fully incorporated. Continue to process for another full 2 minutes until the sauce is silky smooth and the consistency of a thin gravy. It might seem a little too thin, but it will thicken as the walnuts absorb the liquid and as it chills in the refrigerator. Taste: The sauce should have a pleasant kick of heat and be bright despite the richness of the nuts. Add more salt and cayenne if needed.

Finish the chicken bazhe: Place the chicken in a medium pot and pour the walnut sauce over it. Mix to fully coat. Refrigerate for a couple of hours or ideally overnight before serving. Serve cold or at room temperature, garnished with walnut oil or pomegranate seeds if desired.

BEEF STROGANOFF

Beef Stroganoff was originally invented at the turn of the nineteenth century, not in Russia but in France. Count Pavel Stroganov was spending the social season in Paris (as many Russians of noble birth did at that time), and while he admired all things French, he missed his native cuisine. So his chef added some Russian *smetana*, sour cream, to a basic French sauce and a culinary star was born. He named the dish after his employer, and beef Stroganoff went on to become an international success. Today, the dish may be just as well known in the US as it is in Russia—and seen as slightly retro or even pedestrian. But source a good cut of steak, don't overcook it, and you'll see that there's nothing mundane about this dish. Mushrooms aren't traditional, but I say keep them.

••

1½ tablespoons plus 1 teaspoon all-purpose flour, divided
1½ teaspoons kosher salt, plus more to taste
¾ teaspoon freshly ground black pepper, plus more to taste
1¼ pounds (570 g) boneless sirloin, strip, or rib-eye steak, excess fat removed, cut into ½-inch (1.3 cm) strips, patted dry
3½ tablespoons sunflower oil or light olive oil
6 ounces (170 g) cremini mushrooms, cut into ¼-inch (6 mm) slices
1 large yellow onion, thinly sliced
1½ tablespoons tomato paste
1¼ teaspoons paprika
Pinch of cayenne pepper
½ cup (120 g) dry white wine
1 cup (240 g) water
⅔ cup (165 g) sour cream
Buttered egg noodles or mashed potatoes, for serving
Handful of parsley chopped, for garnish

SERVES 4

In a small bowl, mix together the 1½ tablespoons flour, salt, and pepper. Lay the steak strips out on a baking sheet or large plate in an even layer and sprinkle the flour mixture all over. Toss the strips so that they're evenly coated and seasoned.

In a large sauté pan, heat 1 tablespoon of the oil over medium-high heat until very hot. Working in two batches, add the meat in a single layer and cook, undisturbed, for 1 minute. Toss the meat and continue to cook, stirring, until the meat is browned all over, about another minute. Transfer to a bowl or plate and repeating with the remaining meat.

In the now empty pan, add ½ tablespoon of the oil and heat over medium-high heat until very hot. Add the mushrooms, toss to coat, and then cook, undisturbed, until the bottom layer browns, 2 to 3 minutes. Continue to cook, stirring occasionally, until the mushrooms begin to brown, another 3 to 4 minutes.

Stir in the onions, the remaining 2 tablespoons oil, and a big pinch of salt. Cook, stirring occasionally, until the onions are nicely browned and start to look frizzled on the edges, 8 to 10 minutes.

Reduce the heat to medium. Stir in the tomato paste and a splash of water to loosen it up. Cook, stirring occasionally, for 2 to 3 minutes to deepen its flavor. Add the paprika, cayenne, and remaining 1 teaspoon flour, stir to evenly incorporate, and cook for 2 to 3 minutes. Add the wine and allow it to cook down until it's thick and saucy and clings to the onions and mushrooms. Add the water and bring to a simmer.

Stir in the beef and all its juices and gently simmer for 1½ to 2 minutes to warm it through and allow the sauce to slightly thicken. Reduce to the lowest heat or remove from the heat if needed so that the sauce doesn't bubble. Add the sour cream and stir to incorporate. Taste and season with more salt and black pepper if needed.

Serve spooned over egg noodles or mashed potatoes and garnish with parsley.

GOULASH

As a Soviet satellite state for decades, Hungary left its own impression on Eastern bloc countries, particularly in the culinary realm. Along with paprika and *lecsó* sauce, Hungarian goulash wedged itself into the Soviet repertoire and never left. Maybe part of why it was so wholeheartedly embraced was because it took what readily available meat there was—tough, poor-quality cuts—stewed it long enough until it was edible, and then smothered it in a paprika-laced sauce that flavored and, more important, disguised it. The irony is that what diners thought was goulash (a hearty meat-and-vegetable soup) was, and still is, actually closer to Hungarian *pörkölt* (slowly braised meat in a thick gravy). Whatever you decide to call it, this recipe, with its succulent, tender chunks of beef, full-bodied sauce, and lively herb-garlic finish, is leagues away from the Soviet canteen version it started as.

••

2¾ pounds (1.25 kg) boneless beef chuck roast, fat trimmed, cut into 1- to 1½-inch (2.5 cm to 4 cm) chunks, patted dry
Kosher salt
4 tablespoons (55 g) sunflower oil or light olive oil
1 large yellow onion, finely diced
2 medium carrots, peeled and finely diced
1½ teaspoons sweet paprika
Generous ½ teaspoon red pepper flakes, plus more as needed
2 tablespoons tomato paste
¼ cup (35 g) all-purpose flour
3¼ cups (450 g) water, plus more as needed
1 dried bay leaf
1 large garlic clove, crushed through a press
½ large bunch of cilantro, finely chopped
¼ large bunch of parsley, finely chopped
Buttered egg pasta or mashed potatoes, for serving

SERVES 4 TO 6

Season the beef with a generous 1 tablespoon salt.

In a large sauté pan or Dutch oven, heat 2 tablespoons of the oil over medium heat. Add three-quarters of the beef in an even layer and allow it to brown, undisturbed. The beef will immediately start to release a lot of liquid. After a couple of minutes, add the remaining beef, using a wooden spoon or spatula to move the beef around to make room. Continue to cook, stirring occasionally, until the beef is browned all over (it's okay if there's pink here and there) and mostly covered by its own juices, about 5 minutes. Cover, reduce the heat to maintain a gentle simmer, and cook for 1 hour.

Meanwhile, in a large skillet, heat the remaining 2 tablespoons oil over medium heat. Add the onion, carrots, and a pinch of salt and cook until the vegetables are meltingly soft and golden, 20 to 25 minutes. Adjust the heat as needed if the vegetables are browning too quickly.

Stir in the paprika and pepper flakes. Add the tomato paste and a splash of water to loosen it up and cook, stirring occasionally, to deepen its flavor, 3 to 4 minutes. Remove from the heat and set aside.

After about 1 hour of simmering, the liquid from the beef should be mostly evaporated, and when you poke a piece with a fork, it should feel tender but still have some resistance. If there's still a lot of liquid, tilt the pan and ladle some of the juices out and set aside for later. Increase the heat to medium and add the onion-carrot mixture (hold on to that skillet!) and a generous pinch of salt. Cook, stirring occasionally, for 5 minutes. At this point, all the liquid from the beef should be evaporated.

Sprinkle the flour all over the beef and stir to evenly coat. Cook, stirring frequently, for 3 to 4 minutes to remove the raw flavor of the flour. Add a splash of the measured water to the skillet you used to cook the onion-carrot mixture in, swish it around to clean the pan, and pour it into the goulash. Stir in the remaining water, any meat juices, and the bay leaf. If you don't have any meat juices, add an extra ¼ cup (60 g) water. Taste the sauce and season with salt and, if desired, more pepper flakes.

Bring to a simmer. Cover and adjust the heat to maintain a gentle simmer. Cook, stirring occasionally so that the bottom doesn't burn, until the meat is tender and the sauce is rich and glossy, 45 minutes to 1 hour.

Stir in the garlic and three-quarters of both the cilantro and parsley. Taste and season with salt if needed. Remove from the heat. Serve immediately, spooned over buttered egg pasta or mashed potatoes, and garnished with the remaining herbs. Store leftovers in the refrigerator for up to 4 days.

MAKARONY PO FLOTSKI

NAVY-STYLE PASTA

This simple pasta was originally served to men in the navy while they were out to sea. Their work was grueling, and so to keep them motivated, navy cooks cooked up macaroni (a delicacy then) and stretched it with *tushonka*—a canned stewed meat that held a special place in many a citizen's heart (just like Spam does for many Asian Americans today). Cheap, quick, simple, the dish became popular throughout Eastern bloc countries, especially after World War II, when fresh ingredients were scarce. For me it's a very nostalgic food, taking me right back to sleepovers with my cousin Nick. My aunt Olga would cook up a whole pot, and he and I would work through it over the course of the weekend (the macaroni doused in ketchup, of course) while we played countless hours of video games together.

With access to fresh, good-quality meat, we no longer need tushonka. We instead slowly simmer a cut of beef (any kind will do, although maybe save the rib eye for steak night) until very tender. It's then ground up and added to sautéed onion—a few splashes of the cooking broth and butter keeps the base extra moist and rounded—before the pasta is stirred in. Is *makarony po flotski* the lightest, healthiest dish? No. But when you want something simple yet hearty, you won't find a dish that better fits the bill.

....

Beef Treugolniki Filling (page 74)
Kosher salt
1 pound (450 g) pasta, such as elbow, rigatoni, ziti,
*   or penne*
3 tablespoons (45 g) unsalted butter

SERVES 4 TO 6

Prepare the beef filling in a large sauté pan or pot large enough to toss the pasta in (see Note).

Bring a large pot of water to a boil and generously salt. Add the pasta to the water and cook a little shy of al dente according to the package directions. Reserve ½ cup (120 g) of the pasta cooking water. Transfer the cooked pasta directly to the beef filling, along with the reserved pasta cooking water.

Return the sauté pan to a medium-low heat and continue cooking, stirring constantly, until the pasta is glossy and evenly mixed, 1 to 2 minutes. Remove from the heat and add the butter, stirring to melt and emulsify, adding more cooking water as needed if the pasta seems to be dry or not glossy.

Serve immediately. Store leftovers in the refrigerator for up to 3 days.

Note: *If your sauté pan isn't large enough to hold everything, drain the pasta, reserving a bit more cooking water than you might need, and return the pasta to the pasta pot. Then add the beef-onion base and ½ cup (120 g) cooking water.*

MAMA'S KOTLETI

MAMA'S CUTLETS

Kotleti are juicy, savory little meat patties that are breaded and pan-fried until golden and crispy. What started out as the specialty of an inn and restaurant in the small Russian town of Torzhok in the nineteenth century, eventually became a mainstay at every Soviet-era canteen, from Moscow to Tashkent. The original even impressed Tsar Nicholas I enough to feature it at his court several times; the latter iteration, let's just say, inspired much less enthusiasm.

With food rations no longer in the way, each ex-Soviet cook has their own special method of producing kotleti worth writing about. True to her Georgian culinary sensibility, my mom features plenty of fresh herbs, garlic, and a spoonful or two of *adjika* or crushed hot pepper in her recipe. While she used to rely on milk-soaked bread to keep her patties succulent, now it's a much healthier ingredient that does the job: zucchini!

My favorite way to eat a hot, still crispy *kotlet* is with buckwheat kasha, an herby salad of tomatoes and cucumbers (page 123), and *tkemali* (page 182). A true amalgam of our cross-cultural roots. These little "hamburgers" make great leftovers and, when turned into a sandwich, are the ultimate picnic or road-trip food. You can also easily halve this recipe (or freeze half for another time) if you're cooking for a smaller number.

• •

1 large yellow onion, quartered
1 cup (35 g) roughly chopped cilantro leaves and stems
¼ cup (9 g) roughly chopped parsley leaves and tender stems
1 large garlic clove, peeled but whole
1 medium zucchini (8 to 10 ounces / 225 to 280 g), trimmed
1 pound (450 g) ground pork
1 pound (450 g) ground dark turkey (93/7)
2 tablespoons adjika paste or relish, hot chopped peppers, or chili garlic sauce, plus more to taste
4 teaspoons kosher salt, plus more to taste
1 teaspoon freshly ground black pepper, plus more to taste
2 eggs
1½ cups (120 g) panko or fine dried breadcrumbs
Sunflower oil, light olive oil, or other oil with a high smoke point, for pan-frying

SERVES 4, WITH LEFTOVERS

In a food processor, combine the onion, herbs, and garlic and process until finely chopped. Transfer to a large bowl. Switch to the shredding disc, shred the zucchini, and add to the bowl. (Alternatively, finely chop the onions and herbs, crush the garlic in a press, and coarsely grate the zucchini.)

To the zucchini-onion mixture, add the pork, turkey, adjika, salt, and pepper. Begin to mix, squeezing the meat through your fingers, until the flavorings are fully and evenly incorporated into the meat. Hold the bowl in place with one hand while you knead the meat with the other: scoop the meat from the bottom with a closed hand, fold it over the top, and flatten it back down with the heel of your hand. Don't be afraid to get aggressive—you can even slam it back down! Continue until the fat is evenly integrated and the meat comes together in a homogeneous, slightly tacky, and sticky mass.

To test for seasoning, take a teaspoon of meat, set it on a plate, and microwave on high for 15 seconds. Taste and add more salt, pepper, and adjika if needed.

Cover and refrigerate for at least 30 minutes and up to 1 day to allow flavors to meld.

When ready to cook the kotleti, line a baking sheet with parchment paper. With slightly wet hands, divide the meat into 16 equal portions (about 100 g each) and shape into elongated oval patties about 3½ inches (9 cm) long. Transfer to the prepared baking sheet once formed. The patties are easier to handle when they're thoroughly chilled, so if desired, freeze for 30 to 40 minutes.

Set up a dredging station in two shallow bowls: Lightly beat the eggs in one bowl and place the panko in a second bowl. Take one patty and dip both sides into the egg, shaking to remove excess. Then fully coat in the panko. Carefully return to the baking sheet, reshaping and flattening it out as needed. Repeat with remaining patties.

Line a baking sheet with paper towels and set near the stove. Pour ¼ inch (6 mm) of oil into a large nonstick sauté pan or skillet and heat over medium heat until hot and shimmering (to test, throw a bread crumb in and if it immediately starts to sizzle, the oil is ready).

Working in batches, carefully lower the kotleti into the oil away from you and cook until the bottom is golden brown and crispy, 5 to 7 minutes. The kotleti should sizzle, not sputter or crackle, so adjust the heat as needed if they're browning too quickly or if it seems the temperature of the oil dropped too much. Carefully flip using two forks and continue to cook until the other side is golden brown and the meat is cooked through, another 5 to 7 minutes.

Transfer to the paper-towel-lined pan and allow to cool for 10 minutes before serving. Store leftovers in the refrigerator for up to 5 days.

SUMMER RAGOUT

While the word *ragu* might conjure up heaping plates of Italian pasta in meat sauce for many of us, for those throughout the former Soviet Union, the term invokes what the French refer to as ragout—a slow-cooked stew with or without meat. Many variations abound, but this one nods to one made in the Caucasus. After the meat is browned, it's simply a matter of layering vegetables and aromatics, and pressing them down to make sure everything fits. In the oven, the vegetables slowly collapse and release their own juices, which in turn soften and tenderize the meat. You start with only a touch of liquid, but by the end, even the very top layer of tomatoes is submerged in aromatic broth! While the ingredient list and prep time might seem a bit long, I can't stress how immensely satisfying, both in assembly and result, this one-pot ragout is.

The butter, while optional, adds richness and depth to the broth.
....

2½ to 3 pounds (1.14 to 1.4 kg) chuck roast, cut into 2-inch (5 cm) chunks and patted dry
Kosher salt and freshly ground black pepper
3 tablespoons sunflower oil or extra-virgin olive oil
2 medium yellow onions, thinly sliced
1 teaspoon dried basil (preferably purple)
¾ teaspoon paprika
3 medium Yukon Gold potatoes, peeled and cut into rounds ½ inch (1.3 cm) thick
½ pound (225 g) green beans, trimmed and cut into thirds
4 to 5 garlic cloves
2 small dried bay leaves
1 tablespoon tomato paste
1 dried red chili pepper (optional)
1 small bunch of herb stems, with or without the leaves (such as a combination of basil, cilantro, and parsley), tied together
3 bell peppers, cut into thick slices
1 jalapeño or serrano chili, thinly sliced
5 tablespoons (70 g) unsalted butter (optional), cut into slices ½ inch (1.3 cm) thick
3 medium zucchini, quartered lengthwise and cut crosswise into 3-inch (7.5 cm) pieces
3 large firm, but ripe tomatoes, cut into thick slices
½ cup (120 g) dry white wine

SERVES 6 TO 8

Preheat the oven to 350°F (180°C).

Season the beef all over with 1 tablespoon kosher salt and 1 teaspoon pepper.

In an 8-quart (7.5 L) Dutch oven or similar heavy-bottomed pot, heat the oil over medium heat until shimmering. Working in batches, add the beef in a single layer and cook until browned and a bit seared on the bottom, 4 to 5 minutes. Flip and brown the other side. Transfer to a plate and repeat with the remaining meat.

Let the pot cool down a bit and cover the bottom with half of the onions. Nestle the browned beef atop in an even layer. Season evenly with the basil and paprika and top with the remaining onions. Evenly arrange the potatoes on top. Season with salt and pepper. Top with the green beans. Scatter the garlic, bay leaves, tomato paste, and dried chili (if using). Top with the tied herb bunch. Pressing down as you go to make sure everything fits, continue to evenly layer with the bell peppers, jalapeño, butter (if using), another seasoning of salt and pepper, the zucchini (cut side down), and tomatoes. Pour the wine over the ragout and then generously season the tomatoes with salt and pepper.

Cut a round piece of parchment paper to fit the inside diameter of the pot and place on top before covering with the lid (don't skip this part, otherwise your tomatoes will stick to the lid!). It's okay if the lid doesn't fit tightly at first (it will as the stew cooks).

Transfer to the oven and bake until the vegetables have collapsed and are simmering in their own juices—the tomatoes will be partially submerged at this point—and the beef is tender, 2½ to 3 hours. Taste the broth and season with more salt if needed. Allow the stew to sit, uncovered, for 15 to 20 minutes to cool down before serving.

GOLUBTSY

STUFFED CABBAGE ROLLS

Depending on where you're from, you might also know these as *holubtsi* (Ukraine), *gołąbki* (Poland), *szárma* (Hungary), *sarmale* (Moldova and Romania)—the list goes on. Which is all to say: There are as many variations on golubtsy (meaning "little doves") as there are Central and Eastern European cooks that prepare them. Given that my family grew up in the Caucasus, these are a bit of a mash up. The filling—with its abundant use of herbs and light hand with the rice—is closer to what they would use in Armenia for *dolma*. Even the tomato sauce, reminiscent of Hungarian *lecsó*, is punchy. I know I'm biased, but the melding of these culinary worlds makes for truly the best stuffed cabbage I've ever had. You will have to dedicate an afternoon to making this dish, but the golubtsy—colorful and robust—will be worth it and will reward you for days.

We will sometimes make this with whole bell peppers, nestling the stuffed vessels in two layers in a large pot. The method is otherwise the same. For the holidays, we'll swap out the cabbage leaves for blanched collard greens (a substitute for hard-to-get grape leaves) and fit slices of tomatoes between the layers and torn bits of butter before simmering in water (no sauce)—our version of Armenian dolma.

Make the sauce and blanch the cabbage leaves a day or two in advance to break up assembly. Plain sour cream for serving works well, but for special occasions we'll take it one step further: Scoop about a cup of sour cream into a bowl, press a clove or two of garlic into it, and thin it out with water until it resembles thick plain yogurt.

· ·

CABBAGE
Kosher salt
1 large head green cabbage (see note), tough outer leaves removed

FILLING
2 tablespoons sunflower oil or extra-virgin olive oil
2 medium yellow onions (about 12 ounces / 340 g total), 1 finely chopped and 1 sliced into eighths
Kosher salt
3 garlic cloves, peeled but whole
¾ cup (25 g) cilantro, finely chopped
¾ cup (25 g) parsley, finely chopped
½ cup (15 g) dill, roughly chopped
A handful of fresh mint leaves, roughly chopped
1 pound (450 g) ground pork
1 pound (450 g) ground beef (85/15)
1¼ cups (300 g) cold water
Generous ¼ cup (60 g) long-grain rice, rinsed well
1 tablespoon crushed dried basil (preferably purple)
1 teaspoon freshly ground black pepper
1 teaspoon red pepper flakes

TOMATO SAUCE
2 tablespoons sunflower oil or extra-virgin olive oil
1 medium yellow onion, chopped
3 medium carrots, peeled and cut into ⅛-inch (6 mm) half-moons
Kosher salt
½ each red, green, and orange bell pepper, chopped
1 jalapeño, halved and thinly sliced
3 tablespoons tomato paste
3 medium firm-ripe tomatoes, peeled (see page 127), cored, and finely chopped
Granulated sugar (optional)

ASSEMBLY
2 cups (475 g) water, plus more as needed
½ cup (15 g) cilantro, finely chopped
½ cup (15 g) parsley, finely chopped
½ cup (15 g) dill, finely chopped
2 garlic cloves, crushed through a press
Sour cream, for serving
Crusty bread, for mopping

SERVES 10 TO 12

Prepare the cabbage: Bring a large pot of salted water to a boil.

While the water is coming to a boil, place the cabbage on a cutting board stem side up. Using a paring knife slightly angled toward the core, carefully cut a deep circle around the stem and around the core—you're aiming for a cone-shaped piece. Pull the piece out.

Once the water has come to a boil, carefully lower the cabbage into the pot. After a few minutes, you'll notice that the outer leaves will start to loosen from the head. Use a fork to pull them away. Continue to cook until the leaves are tender and the center around the rib is pliable. Transfer to a colander. Repeat until you've removed most of the leaves and are left with a core about the size of an orange. Remove from the pot and allow to cool.

Once the leaves have cooled, cut any exceptionally large outer leaves in half. Cut away the tough ribs— leaving a "v"-shaped gap at the base of each leaf. Set the prepared leaves aside.

Make the filling: In a small skillet, heat the oil over medium heat. Add the finely chopped onion and a generous pinch of salt and cook, stirring occasionally and adjusting heat as needed if it's browning too quickly, until the onion is soft and golden, 10 minutes. Remove from the heat and allow to fully cool.

In a food processor, combine the sliced onion, garlic, and herbs and process until everything is very finely chopped, but not mushy or pasty.

In a large bowl, combine the pork, beef, onion-herb mixture, cooled sautéed onion, water, rice, dried basil, 1 tablespoon of salt, black pepper, and pepper flakes. Mix, squeezing the meat through your fingers, until the flavorings and water are fully and evenly incorporated into the meat. Set aside.

Make the tomato sauce: In a large sauté pan, heat the oil over medium heat. Add the onion, carrots, and a big pinch of salt, and cook until softened, 8 to 10 minutes.

Add the bell peppers and jalapeño and cook until slightly softened, 5 to 6 minutes. Add the tomato paste and a splash of water to help loosen it up. Cook, stirring frequently, for 3 to 4 minutes to deepen its flavor.

Add the tomatoes and a pinch of salt and stir everything together. If the tomatoes are acidic, add a pinch of sugar. Partially cover, adjust the heat to maintain a gentle simmer, and cook, stirring occasionally, until the sauce has thickened and the tomatoes have lost their raw edge, about 25 minutes. Add a splash of water if the sauce starts to look too dry at any point. Taste and season with salt and sugar as needed. Set aside.

Assemble the golubtsy: Pour just enough water into a large, preferably 8-quart (7.5 L), heavy-bottomed pot or Dutch oven to cover the bottom. Set it next to your work surface.

Working with one leaf at a time, place a big spoonful of filling at the bottom third of the leaf. The amount of filling you use will depend on the size of your leaf, but I find it's usually around ¼ cup (60 g). You'll eventually get a feel for how much you can fit.

Fold the bottom edge of the cabbage over the filling to fully cover; roll it forward a bit to tuck the edge under. Fold the left side over the filling, and then the right. Then roll up the cabbage like a burrito. Any excess on the bottom can be trimmed away. Place inside the pot, tucked up against the wall of the pot. Repeat with the remaining cabbage leaves, nestling the golubtsy snugly against each other in an even layer. Arrange a second snug layer on top of the first. You should get around 28 to 30 golubtsy.

Thinly slice any tender bits of the core and left-over leaves and arrange them in an even layer over the golubtsy. Add the 2 cups (475 g) water to the pot—it should hit but not cover the top layer of the golubtsy. Place a plate over the center of the pot and bring to a boil over medium heat. Cover, adjust the heat to maintain a gentle simmer, and cook for 20 minutes. During this time, the golubtsy will release their own liquid and the filling aromatics will in turn flavor the liquid.

Taste the sauce and add more salt as needed. Pour the tomato sauce over the golubtsy and gently try to tuck some of it into the sides between the pot and the golubtsy. Cover and continue to gently simmer for another 15 minutes.

Taste the broth and add more salt if needed. In a small bowl, mix together the cilantro, parsley, dill, and garlic. Sprinkle the mixture all over the sauce. Remove from the heat. Allow the golubtsy to rest for 30 minutes before serving.

To serve, use a large spoon to push away some of the sauce to reveal the cabbage rolls beneath. Insert the edge of your spoon between two rolls and carefully lift the first roll out and transfer to your serving bowl. Generously spoon juices and sauce on top. Serve with a dollop of sour cream and good crusty bread for mopping. Golubtsy can be stored in the refrigerator for up to 3 to 4 days or frozen for up to 2 months.

Note: *Use the largest cabbage head you can find (4½ to 5 pounds / 2 to 2.25 kg), otherwise buy 2 medium cabbage heads (there's nothing worse than having to run to the store halfway through filling rolls because you're out of leaves).*

When tomatoes aren't in season, feel free to swap out the fresh tomatoes for one (14½-ounce / 411 g) can of crushed or diced tomatoes with their juices.

BUZHENINA

GARLIC-ROASTED PORK TENDERLOIN

Buzhenina is a simple roasted pork tenderloin stuffed with garlic that is usually served cold, thinly sliced, as part of a larger *zakuski* (small bites) spread for the New Year holidays. I personally enjoy the tenderloins straight from the oven when they're still hot and succulent, paired with boiled potatoes and Slavic-style sauerkraut. However it's served, a dousing of Tkemali (page 182) is its friend. Leftovers also make for a great *buterbrod* (tartine) topper. When shopping for the meat, make sure your tenderloin pieces are the same weight so that they cook up evenly together.

....

4 teaspoons kosher salt

2 teaspoons freshly ground black pepper

2 pork tenderloins (1¼ to 1½ pounds / 565 to 680 g each), silver skin removed and excess fat trimmed

6 garlic cloves, thinly sliced

SERVES 6 TO 8

In a small bowl, stir together the salt and pepper.

Working with one pork tenderloin piece at a time, use a sharp paring knife to make slits about ½ inch (1.3 cm) deep all over the pork, spacing them about 1½ inches (4 cm) apart. Season the pork with half of the salt and black pepper and rub it evenly over the surface and into the incisions. Stuff a garlic slice into each slit. Set aside and repeat with the second pork tenderloin.

Set the pork tenderloins side by side so that the thick end of one piece lines up with the thin end of the other—you want them fitting so that the overall circumference is even. Use kitchen twine to tie the two pieces at 1½-inch (4 cm) intervals. Transfer to a large bowl and cover with plastic wrap. Refrigerate for at least 6 hours and ideally overnight (and up to 2 days).

Let the pork come to room temperature 1 to 2 hours before you plan to cook it.

Preheat the oven to 350°F (180°C).

Pull out a sheet of aluminum foil 18 inches (46 cm) long and lay it on your work surface. Top it with a piece of parchment paper that is about the length of the pork tenderloin. Wrap the pork tenderloin in the parchment paper. Then bring the two long sides of the foil together, tenting it slightly, and crimp the edges together to tightly seal. Fold the sides over to further seal. Transfer the wrapped pork tenderloin to a baking sheet.

Bake until an instant-read thermometer inserted into the thickest part of the tenderloins reaches 140°F (60°C), 45 to 55 minutes depending on the size of your tenderloins. To check, you will have to slightly open the foil and puncture through the parchment paper.

Open the foil up and allow the pork to rest for 10 to 15 minutes before cutting into it if serving immediately (the temperature will continue to rise as the pork sits). If serving cold, allow it to come to room temperature and then refrigerate until thoroughly chilled.

When ready to serve, remove the pork from the foil and snip away the kitchen twine. Cut into thin slices and serve.

SHASHLYK

SHISH KEBABS

At its heart, *shashlyk* (from the Russian word *shashka* or "saber") is a rustic food—meant to be enjoyed al fresco on a hike in the countryside or at someone's dacha by the river. Of course, when I was growing up in the suburbs of Rhode Island, our backyard setting was a little less idyllic. But that didn't keep us from salivating as the scent of skewered chunks of meat slowly charring over an open flame wafted in the air. In the Caucasus, where shashlyk took its inspiration from, they favor lamb in Armenia and Azerbaijan (known as *khorovats* and *kebab*, respectively), but in Georgia, where it's called *mtsvadi*, you'll often find it with pork, which is how I know it best. Everyone has their own secret marinade, but if there's one thing everyone can agree on it's the onions: tossed in with the meat while it's marinating and then again as it comes off the grill. If I'm feeding a large crowd, I'll go ahead and double the recipe. You can also easily swap in boneless, skinless chicken thighs for the pork tenderloin. Serve shashlyk with Tkemali (page 182), Salat (page 123), and crusty bread or lavash to sop up the juices.

....

2 pounds (900 g) pork tenderloin, excess fat trimmed, silver skin removed, cut into 2½-inch (6.5 cm) chunks

3 tablespoons (45 g) mayonnaise, sunflower oil, or other oil with a high smoke point

2 tablespoons red wine vinegar

1 tablespoon dried adjika or Svanetian salt

1 to 2 teaspoons kosher salt, to taste

¾ teaspoon freshly ground black pepper

2 small yellow onions or 4 medium shallots, half thinly sliced for marinade and half thinly sliced before grilling

SERVES 4 TO 6 AS PART OF A LARGER SPREAD

In a large bowl, toss the meat with the mayonnaise, vinegar, adjika, salt, pepper, and half of the onions. Massage the seasonings into the meat until the onions are limp and the meat is coated well. Refrigerate overnight and up to 24 hours.

Take the meat out 1 hour before grilling. Thread the meat lengthwise on metal skewers so that they are nestled against each other but no pieces are squished. You should be able to fill four 12-inch (30 cm) skewers. Set aside.

Add the remaining sliced onion to a pot large enough to hold all of the shashlyk once off the skewers and set near your grill.

Set up your mangal or kettle grill (see Getting Shashlyk Right, page 155) for the skewers. Light one chimney full of charcoal. When the charcoal is completely gray and is no longer smoking, pour out and spread the coals evenly into the bottom of your grill, leaving one-third of the grill empty to create a low-heat zone. (If using a gas grill, heat all of the burners, save for one, on high, close the lid, and preheat for 15 to 20 minutes. Clean and oil the grates.)

Place the skewers on the grill directly over the charcoal (or on the grates if using gas). Cook, turning the skewers frequently, so that all the sides cook evenly. The meat should be golden brown, lightly charred in spots, but succulent on the inside; this will take 7 to 10 minutes to cook to medium. An instant-read thermometer inserted in the center of the biggest piece will read 135°F to 145°F (57°C to 63°C). If fat drips down and flares up or if some skewers are charring too quickly, move the skewers and charcoal to the low-heat zone. Of course, cooking shashlik (and any grilling endeavor in my opinion) is a bit of an art, so turn the skewers frequently, move them between the high and low heat zones as needed, and check the internal temperature early and often to make sure you don't overcook the meat.

As the meat is done, take the skewers off the grill. Working over the pot with the sliced onions, use tongs or a fork to slide the meat off the skewer and into the pot. Close the lid and give the pot a shake—the heat of the meat will soften the onions and the onions in turn will further flavor the meat. Allow the meat to rest for 5 minutes before serving.

Note: *Taste your adjika and if it's on the saltier side (or if you're using a dried spice blend with salt in it), start with the smaller amount of salt.*

GETTING SHASHLYK RIGHT

- **MARINATING:** Giving the meat a full 18- to 24-hour rest in its marinade will help tenderize and flavor it.

- **SKEWERS:** You'll want to use 12-inch (30 cm) V-shaped metal skewers that are flat (not round) so that they sit comfortably on the edges of the grill.

- **MANGAL:** Typically, shashlyk is cooked over a rectangular open-faced grill called a mangal. The grill is designed so that you can set the skewers across the narrow dimension of the grill to be propped up by the two sides of the grill and directly over the fire.

- **KETTLE GRILL:** If you don't have a mangal, you can easily jerry-rig a kettle grill. To do so, empty a 28-ounce (795 g) tomato can and remove the label. Fill it with sand or small rocks so that it doesn't move around while you're grilling. Remove the top grilling rack and place the can just beyond the center on the lower grilling rack to divide the grill into a bottom two-thirds section (your high-heat zone) and upper-third section (your low-heat zone). Arrange the heated charcoal around the can in the high-heat zone in an even layer on the bottom rack. The pointed end of the skewers will rest on the tomato can, fanning out to the grill's rim.

- **GAS GRILL:** In a pinch, use a gas grill (but you won't get that same kiss of smoke and fire as you would with charcoal).

CHAKAPULI

LAMB, TARRAGON, AND WHITE WINE BRAISE

Typically prepared with the arrival of spring, this Georgian lamb stew—redolent of herbs and pungent with fruity white wine and tart *tkemali* (sour plum sauce)—can be made all year long. It also happens to be extremely easy to make. Get the lamb going and prep and chop all your herbs while it's simmering away. I include a large lamb shank here because it contributes to a richer, more savory broth; I usually ask my butcher to cut it into three or four pieces for me. As for the tkemali, you want to use a green or yellow kind—find it at any Eastern European market or online if you didn't make your own. If you can't get your hands on it, lemon juice to taste will make a fine substitute. While it's delicious fresh, try making *chakapuli* a day in advance, if you can, to allow the flavors to meld overnight.

....

2 teaspoons kosher salt, plus more as needed
1¼ pounds (565 g) boneless lamb stew meat, fat trimmed, cut into bite-size pieces
1¼ pounds (565 g) lamb shank (about 1 large), cut into pieces 1½ inches (4 cm) thick
3 cups (720 g) water
⅔ cup (160 g) dry fruity white wine
2 bunches of green onions, white and light-green parts only, thinly sliced
2 cups (80 g) packed tarragon, finely chopped
1 large bunch of cilantro, finely chopped
½ medium bunch of parsley, finely chopped
1 serrano chili, seeded and finely chopped
4 medium garlic cloves, minced
3 to 4 large spoonfuls green or yellow tkemali, homemade (page 182) or store-bought
Good hearty bread, for serving

SERVES 4

Salt the stew meat and shank evenly on all sides. Arrange in an 8-quart (7.5 L) pot or Dutch oven in an even layer. Add the water so that it just barely covers the lamb—add a little more water if needed. Bring to a boil over medium-high heat. Resist the urge to skim any foam that rises. Add the white wine, cover, adjust the heat to maintain a gentle, bubbling simmer, and cook until the meat is very tender and easily falls apart, 1¾ to 2 hours. If at any point the liquid seems to be getting low, add water to keep the lamb submerged.

Stir in the green onions, tarragon, cilantro, parsley, chili, garlic, and about 3 spoonfuls of the tkemali to start. Gently simmer, covered, to soften the bite of the raw garlic and chili, 10 to 15 minutes.

Taste: The stew should be bright, herbaceous, and a bit tangy from the tkemali. Season with more salt and, if desired, the last spoonful of tkemali.

Serve with good, hearty bread. Store in the refrigerator for up to 5 days.

ROASTED SALMON WITH TSKAHTON

SALMON WITH OSSETIAN GARLICKY HERB SAUCE

Every Sunday, my mom's youth group when she was a teenager would gather after church at a host family's house to eat, sing, and play games. On one memorable occasion, they were invited over by an Ossetian couple, their five daughters, and son—exciting, given the fact that they were known to be excellent cooks. True to their reputation, the family put together a spread that had the teenagers falling over themselves out of delight. One dish stood out: delicate fillets of pan-fried white fish that were generously slathered in a garlicky, piquant sauce and left to chill overnight. The sauce not only kept the fish moist and tender but also infused it with its flavors.

After a bit of sleuthing, I discovered that the sauce is a variation of Ossetian *tskahton*. The traditional version calls for thick homemade sour cream or *matsoni* (yogurt) and walnuts in addition to fresh herbs and hot chili pepper. This recipe is as my mom jotted it down all those years ago and how she still makes it today. The addition of Georgian spices most likely a reflection of the family's time in Tbilisi; and the swap of mayonnaise for sour cream probably due to dairy shortages that plagued the Soviet era. We prepare tskahton most often with salmon, but it's a great sidekick to grilled, pan-fried, or roasted fish of any kind.

••

SAUCE
6 large sprigs dill, roughly chopped
2 small garlic cloves, roughly chopped
Kosher salt
¾ cup (180 g) mayonnaise or very thick high-fat
    sour cream
1 teaspoon ground blue fenugreek
1 teaspoon ground marigold
¼ teaspoon cayenne pepper, plus more to taste
6 to 8 tablespoons (90 to 120 ml) water

SALMON
1 thick fatty salmon fillet (1½ to 2 pounds / 680 to
    900 g)
2 to 3 teaspoons extra-virgin olive oil, depending
    on the size of the fillet
Kosher salt and freshly ground black pepper

SERVES 4 TO 6

Make the sauce: In a large mortar and pestle, combine the dill, garlic, and a generous pinch of salt and pound until a smooth paste forms (this could also be done in a food processor). Add the mayonnaise, blue fenugreek, marigold, and cayenne and stir together. Begin to stir in the water, a bit at a time, until a loose sauce forms. Taste and season with salt and more cayenne if desired. Transfer to a bowl or serving vessel. Allow to sit for at least 4 to 6 hours for the garlic to mellow before serving.

Prepare the salmon: When ready to cook the fish, line a baking sheet with foil. Position a rack in the upper third of the oven and turn the broiler on high.

Place the fish on the lined baking sheet, skin side down. Rub both sides with olive oil and season generously with salt and pepper. Broil until the salmon flakes easily with a fork, 5 to 10 minutes depending on the thickness of the fillet and strength of your broiler.

Serve with the sauce on the side for generous spooning. Any leftover fish can be smothered in the sauce and eaten the next day cold.

GARLICKY BEER SHRIMP

My mom would often pull out these garlicky beer-simmered shrimp for dinner parties, but I'd argue they make a wonderful weeknight dinner, too. They pack a punch, but the method is pleasantly restrained: Throw in a handful of minced garlic, a dash of paprika, a few splashes of a light lager, and finish with chopped parsley. That's it. You can peel the shrimp, but if you want to further cut down on prep and enjoy getting slightly messy and sucking all the juices out of them, keep the shells on. Serve spooned over rice or with good crusty bread for dipping into the sauce.

••

1¾ to 2 pounds (795 to 900 g) peeled and
    deveined shrimp
1 teaspoon kosher salt, plus more to taste
½ teaspoon freshly ground black pepper
2 tablespoons extra-virgin olive oil
8 large garlic cloves (40 g), thinly sliced or
    finely chopped
2 teaspoons sweet paprika
½ cup (120 g) light lager, such as Stella Artois
2 to 3 tablespoons unsalted butter
½ lemon, plus lemon wedges for serving
Handful of chopped parsley

SERVES 4 TO 6

In a large bowl, toss the shrimp with the salt and pepper. Set aside to marinate in the refrigerator (can be done up to 1 hour in advance).

In a large skillet, heat the oil over medium-low heat. Add the garlic and cook, stirring occasionally, until the garlic begin to take on a golden color and perfume the kitchen, 1 to 2 minutes. Stir in the paprika and cook for 30 to 45 more seconds.

Stir in the beer, shrimp, and butter. Cook, tossing frequently to nicely coat the shrimp, until they're deep, bright pink and firm, 4 to 6 minutes.

Remove from the heat and transfer to a platter. Squeeze the lemon half all over the shrimp and garnish with the parsley. Serve with more lemon wedges on the side.

SMOKED MACKEREL
WITH BUTTERED POTATOES

Smoked mackerel with boiled potatoes is my mom's favorite food. The soft, buttery potatoes take the edge off the brined fish, leaving you wanting more with each bite. I'm pretty sure she would be happy if she could sit down to this meal every day.

Here's the non-recipe recipe: Go to your nearest Eastern European grocery, walk up to the glass display of cured meats and seafood, and ask for a cold-smoked mackerel (*skumbriya*); see Note. Bring it home and keep it refrigerated while you turn your attention to the potatoes (Yukon Golds or something similar is best here). If you haven't noticed yet, Slavs are very intentional when it comes to our potatoes and how we cook them, adjusting the preparation to best suit the food it's paired with. You *could* give them the home-fry treatment as on page 131, but here, boiled is better. My mom likes to boil the potatoes whole and unpeeled; then at her plate, slip the skin away, cut them into rough coins, then pour melted butter over them. I personally like to peel and halve the potatoes before cooking; after they've drained, toss them in a few pats of butter and a handful of finely chopped dill. Both options will work.

Now back to the mackerel. When you're ready to eat, cut the head and tail off the fish (you can reserve them for plating), then slice the body into 1-inch (2.5 cm) segments—they'll look like little steaks. Plate the mackerel, along with your potatoes seasoned with a pinch or two of black pepper. Pull open a segment and watch out for bones as you dig in.

••

SERVES 1 OR 2

Note: *The smoked mackerel is brined whole and then smoked at a low temperature—keeping its flesh firm and silky rather than flaky.*

CHAPTER SIX

GRAINS AND LEGUMES

GRECHKA

ROASTED BUCKWHEAT

Buckwheat has only recently gained popularity in the US, but this pseudocereal (technically a seed) has been an important staple of the Slavic diet for centuries. Not only is it gluten-free and a complete protein, but *grechka*, as we call it, is also nutrient-dense. These healthful properties are just a bonus, though—we eat it because it's delicious, comforting, and versatile. Have it with warmed milk as a porridge for breakfast (as many Slavic children do), as a sidekick to *kotleti* (page 145) or any other meat or poultry dish, or as a hearty vegetarian main. Mushrooms, onions, and dill with buckwheat make for one of my favorite hearty pilafs.

There are two sorts of buckwheat, roasted (often referred to as kasha) and green (or raw). All of the recipes here call for roasted, as that is the variety we Slavs predominantly use. If you can, try to pick up your buckwheat at an Eastern European store (where the turnover for it is high) for the best results and flavor.

- -

2 cups (480 g) water
1 cup (200 g) roasted buckwheat groats (kasha)
2 tablespoons unsalted butter
1 teaspoon kosher salt

MAKES ABOUT 3½ CUPS (575 G)

In a medium saucepan over medium heat bring the water, buckwheat, butter, and salt to a boil. Cover, reduce the heat to low to maintain a steady, gentle simmer, and cook until all the water has been absorbed, 20 to 22 minutes. The buckwheat should be moist, fluffy, and tender.

Remove from the heat. Remove the lid, cover the pot with a kitchen towel, and cover again with the lid. Allow to sit for 15 minutes before fluffing with a fork and serving.

VARIATIONS

Breakfast Buckwheat: *Spoon the desired amount of cooked buckwheat into a bowl. Pour in enough hot milk to cover three-quarters of the buckwheat. Eat immediately, mixing the buckwheat in with the milk.*

Savory Buckwheat with Mushrooms, Onions, and Herbs: *Heat a 12-inch (30 cm) nonstick skillet or sauté pan over medium-high heat. Once the pan is hot, add 1 pound (450 g) sliced cremini mushrooms and cook, stirring occasionally, until the liquid the mushrooms release has mostly evaporated and the pan starts to dry out, 6 to 8 minutes. Reduce the heat to medium and stir in 2 tablespoons refined sunflower oil or unsalted butter, 1 diced medium yellow onion, and a generous pinch of kosher salt. Cook until the edges of the onion begin to brown and the mushrooms take on color, 12 to 15 minutes. Remove from the heat. Once the mushroom-onion mixture has slightly cooled, add to the cooled cooked buckwheat, along with ¼ cup (15 g) finely chopped dill and 2 tablespoons finely chopped parsley. Mix together. Taste and season with salt and freshly ground black pepper before serving.*

KASHA

While kasha here in the States mainly refers to buckwheat, kasha in Russian and other Slavic languages refers to any cooked whole grain, whether it's in whole groat or porridge form. So it's just as right to call buckwheat *grechnevaya kasha* as is it is to refer to semolina porridge as *mannaya kasha*.

LOBIO

HERBED KIDNEY BEAN STEW

The Georgian term for bean, *lobio*, also designates the array of dishes made with the country's legume of choice: red kidney beans. This "stew" is a staple of Georgian home cooking and encapsulates the earthy, spicy, and rustic flavors of the cuisine. It's traditionally served in little clay pots with a *mchadi*, or corn cake, for a lid. Heaps of fresh tarragon, basil, and other herbs are brought out, as well as pungent stalks of green onions, bright-pink radishes, and slabs of fresh, salty cheese. In the wintertime, pickled or fermented vegetables are common. A little bite here, a little taste there, all of it eaten together, preferably by hand. When I'm not feeling the pomp and circumstance, though, I settle for toast, feta, and a garnish of thinly sliced green onions.

Because it's so quick and easy to prepare—not to mention good for you—it's a frequent one-pot meal in our house. In a pinch, we have also prepared lobio with canned beans. In this case, use four cans of the best-quality kidney beans you can find, along with their liquid. Also, don't be deterred if you can't find blue fenugreek and summer savory. We have often made the dish without the two and still lick our bowls clean!

• •

KIDNEY BEANS
1 pound (450 g) dried red kidney beans, rinsed
Kosher salt
2 dried bay leaves or 1 fresh
1 small yellow onion, unpeeled, halved
3 garlic cloves, peeled but whole
1 strip of kombu (optional)

STEW
3 tablespoons sunflower or extra-virgin olive oil
1 large yellow onion, chopped
Kosher salt
1 teaspoon ground coriander
1 teaspoon ground blue fenugreek
1 teaspoon dried summer savory
½ teaspoon red pepper flakes
1½ tablespoons tomato paste
2 tablespoons apple cider or red wine vinegar
2½ cups (75 g) cilantro, finely chopped
¾ cup (25 g) parsley, finely chopped
4 to 5 large garlic cloves, minced or crushed in a press

FOR SERVING
Salty, fresh cheese, such as feta
Fresh herbs, such as tarragon and basil, roughly chopped
Green onions and radishes, sliced
Fermented cucumbers or other veg
Hearty bread

SERVES 4 TO 6

Prepare the kidney beans: Place the beans in a large pot and fill with enough water to cover by 2 inches (5 cm). Season with 2 tablespoons kosher salt. Let soak overnight.

When ready to cook, drain and rinse the soaked beans, transfer to a large heavy-bottomed pot, and add water to cover by 2 inches (5 cm). Add the bay leaves, onion halves, garlic cloves, kombu strip (if using), and 1 tablespoon kosher salt. Bring to a boil over high heat and boil, uncovered, for 10 minutes. Partially cover, reduce the heat to maintain a gentle simmer, and cook until the beans are very tender, 1 to 1½ hours.

Prepare the stew: Meanwhile, in a medium skillet, heat the oil over medium heat. Add the onion and a pinch of salt and cook until translucent and lightly golden, 5 to 7 minutes.

Stir in the coriander, blue fenugreek, summer savory, and pepper flakes. Cook for another minute. Add the tomato paste and a splash of water to help loosen it up and stir to combine. Cook, stirring frequently, to deepen its flavor, 2 to 3 minutes. Add the vinegar and deglaze the pan, using your spoon to scrape off any browned bits from the bottom of the pan. Cook for another minute. Remove from the heat and set aside.

Once the beans are done, discard the onion halves, garlic cloves, bay leaves, and kombu (if used). Keeping the heat on low, mash the beans with a potato masher (or the back of a wooden spoon) just enough to crush half the beans, leaving the rest intact. Stir in the onion mixture, increase the heat to maintain a gentle simmer, and cook for 5 to 7 minutes. If the beans seem very thick (you want them on the soupier side), add water to thin them out. Stir in the fresh herbs and minced garlic and cook for another minute or two. Remove from the heat. Taste and season with more salt or spices if needed.

To serve: Serve with cheese, fresh herbs, green onions, radishes, fermented vegetables, and good hearty bread.

Note: *The addition of kombu is a trick I learned from Joe Yonan's book* Cool Beans. *Not only does it help tenderize the beans, but it also contains enzymes that make them more digestible. A win-win!*

UZBEK PLOV

LAMB AND RICE PILAF

Weddings in the post-Soviet community I grew up in sort of blended together after a point. They'd follow the same ceremony and processions, seat guests at the same long banquet tables, and serve up the same menu of cold *zakuski* (small bites), hot plates, and desserts. *Plov*, Uzbekistan's national dish of lamb and rice, always made an appearance and was secretly the litmus test that we based our food judgments on (that, and how much caviar the bridal couple shelled out for). It wasn't until my friend Sasha, whose family emigrated from the Uzbek region of Fergana, had me over for a plov lesson with his father that I realized that the Slavified plov I had been served my whole life was only a poor imitation of what real plov, or *osh* in Uzbek, could really be.

Traditionally, plov is cooked in a large cast-iron pot called a *kazan* over an open fire. Large chunks of lamb are fried in copious amounts of rendered *kurdyuk* (lamb tail fat), along with sliced onions and mostly yellow carrots cut into matchsticks. Whole heads of garlic, fresh chili peppers, *zira* (cumin seeds), and other spices depending on the region, go in and the whole thing gets submerged in water, at which point the dish is called *zirvak*. This heady mix simmers away, growing in flavor and slowly tenderizing the meat, until it's ready for the rice. (Traditional plov is made almost exclusively with devzira, a medium-grain ruddy-colored rice that somehow absorbs all the flavors while still retaining individual grains.) Once the rice is added, it's all about finesse, getting the amount of water added and cook time just right so that the rice doesn't turn to mush. It takes years of trial and error perfecting this dish, as exemplified by plov masters called *oshpaz*, who dedicate their lives to the craft. If pulled off, though, you'll be rewarded with cumin-scented rice (this dish is all about the rice!) glistening in lamb fat and juices that is scooped onto a platter to reveal meltingly soft meat underneath. A simple, light salad

of tomatoes and onions (*achichuk*) is all that's needed to fill out the meal.

This Fergana-style recipe is largely based on the one Sasha taught me, with some adjustments (such as the addition of chickpeas, barberries, and other spices) gleaned from other plov I've had over the years. Devzira rice is not widely available but I've had a lot of success with Uzbek laser rice, although you will most likely have to special order it online. I've also known people to use Turkish baldo and Calrose rice, such as Kokuho, to good results. If you don't have a kazan, you will need a large heavy bottomed pot (preferably with sloped sides) or a Dutch oven and ideally a stainless-steel skimmer (*shumovka*) for handling the rice; otherwise a large slotted spoon will work. As I mentioned, this dish may take some trial and error, but I promise you'll have no trouble eating even the imperfect results.

••

⅔ cup (150 g) sunflower oil or light olive oil

1½ pounds (680 g) bone-in lamb shoulder blade, bones removed and set aside (it's okay if there's a bit of meat left on them), cut into 2-inch (5 cm) chunks, patted dry

½ medium yellow onion, sliced crosswise ⅛ inch (3 mm) thick

Kosher salt

1⅓ pounds (605 g) carrots (preferably a mix of yellow and orange), peeled, cut into thin matchsticks, and patted dry

1 tablespoon store-bought plov spice mix

1 tablespoon toasted cumin seeds, divided

2 small heads of garlic, a few layers of papery skin pulled off and the bottoms cut to slightly expose the cloves

2 to 3 small green and red chilis, such as serrano, or Fresno

2 tablespoons dried barberries (optional)

¾ cup (125 g) cooked chickpeas (optional), rinsed and drained

3 cups (600 g) rice, such as Uzbek laser, Kokuho Calrose, or Turkish baldo

SERVES 6 TO 8

In a large heavy-bottomed pot or Dutch oven heat the oil over medium-high heat until just shy of smoking. Fill a kettle to its full capacity with water and bring to a boil.

Add the bone pieces first and sear on both sides until browned, 2 to 3 minutes. Remove and set aside. Then arrange the rest of the meat in the pot in an even layer. Cook, turning frequently, until browned and seared all over, about 5 minutes.

Add the onion and a generous pinch of salt. Cook, stirring frequently, until softened and starting to brown around the edges, 1 to 2 minutes.

Add the carrots and a generous pinch of salt and cook, stirring frequently, until starting to soften, 3 to 4 minutes. Stir in the spice mix and 2 teaspoons of the cumin seeds. Cook, stirring frequently, until the carrots begin to take on some golden color around the edges and are easily cut in half by the edge of a spoon, another 3 to 4 minutes.

Tuck the garlic heads and chilis into the meat-vegetable mixture, along with the seared bone pieces. Add the barberries (if using). Add just enough of the boiling hot water from the kettle to cover everything. Once the water is in, the brew is called zirvak. Season with salt until the zirvak tastes a beat too salty. Bring to a boil. Then reduce the heat to a simmer and cook, uncovered, for 45 minutes to soften the meat and vegetables and flavor the broth the rice will be cooking in. In the last 5 minutes of simmering the zirvak, stir in the chickpeas (if using).

Place the rice in a medium bowl. Cover with cool water and use your hand to gently agitate and swirl the rice, then drain. Repeat, rinsing the rice 8 to 10 times, until the water runs clear. Drain well. Remove the garlic heads and chiles from the zirvak and set aside. Then add the rice in an even layer. Gently level it out with a skimmer or the back of a spoon. Pour in just enough hot water to cover the rice by ⅜ inch (1 cm). Even out the rice again.

Bring to a simmer and cook until the rice begins to swell, most of the liquid has been absorbed, and the mixture looks saucy, 12 to 15 minutes. Being careful not to disturb the meat and vegetables below, flip the rice periodically with the skimmer to bring the bottom layer to the top so that it cooks evenly. At the same time, if the center is bubbling and the rice at the edges seems to be lagging, bring the rice from the edges to the center and then even it out again with the back of your skimmer.

Drag some of the rice from the edges to the center to make a small mound. Make a large dent in the very center and sprinkle in the remaining cumin seeds. Tuck the garlic heads and chilies inside and cover it all back up with the rice. Place a plate just large enough to cover most of the mound. Reduce the heat to low, and cook, covered, until the rice is tender and the liquid is fully absorbed, 15 to 20 minutes.

Remove from the heat and let sit, covered, for another 15 minutes.

Fish out the garlic heads and chiles. Carefully mix the rice in with the meat and vegetables. Scoop and mound the plov onto a serving platter and top with the garlic heads and chilis. Serve immediately.

AZERI PLOV WITH SAFFRON, DRIED FRUIT, AND CHESTNUTS

When I was little, we had family friends—Nana, Nadir, and their son, Farid—who were from Baku and with whom we would often get together for dinner parties. As with most children, I was largely apathetic about the "dinner" portion of the evening, being more invested in maximizing playtime with Farid. On one occasion, however, Nana made this rice, and it rooted me at the table for once. Tinged yellow from a saffron-infused tea, the *plov* (pilaf) was studded with dried fruits, chestnuts, walnuts, sautéed onions, and coins of golden, crispy potatoes. I had never tried saffron until then, and its sweet, floral taste left such an impression on me that to this day, I still associate the bright-red pistils with Nana and her rice.

Nana graciously shared her recipe with me and let me tell you, it's just as good—and regal—as I remember it. Saffron-infused rice is very traditional in Azerbaijan, although the heavy hand with the dried fruit, especially tawny-toned apricots and raisins, is more reflective of Armenian cuisine. The plov would do well for a special occasion, served with roasted chicken or fish, braised lamb or beef, or even pork.

••

2 tablespoons extra-virgin or light olive oil, plus
    more as needed
2 large yellow onions, thinly sliced crosswise
Kosher salt
½ teaspoon ground turmeric
1 cup (160 g) golden raisins
1 cup (210 g) small dried apricots (halved if large)
⅓ cup (70 g) dried plums
Generous ¾ cup (150 g) peeled roasted chestnuts
    (see Note)
½ cup (60 g) walnuts
6 tablespoons (85 g) clarified butter or ghee
1 large russet potato, peeled and cut into coins
    ⅜ inch (1 cm) thick
3 cups (600 g) basmati or long-grain rice
A generous pinch of good-quality saffron threads
    (about ½ teaspoon)

SERVES 6 TO 8

In a medium skillet or sauté pan, heat the oil over medium heat. Add the onions and a big pinch of salt. Cook, stirring occasionally, until the onions are totally collapsed, tawny, and begin to frizzle at the edges, 15 to 20 minutes. Adjust the heat as needed if the onions are browning too quickly. Add the turmeric and cook for 30 seconds. Remove from the heat. Transfer to a medium saucepan and set aside.

Wipe out the skillet. Add a small drizzle of oil and return the pan to medium heat. Add the raisins and cook, stirring constantly, until they soften and begin to brown all over, 1 to 2 minutes. Transfer to the pan with the onions.

Repeat the process with the rest of the dried fruit and the nuts, wiping out the pan of any browned or burnt bits before moving on to the next ingredient and turning down the heat as needed. Cook the apricots and then the prunes for 2 to 3 minutes each. Add each to the pan with the raisins and onions. Do not stir in. Do the same with the chestnuts until browned all over and then the walnuts, until golden and toasted, 3 to 4 minutes each. When done, set the saucepan with the fruit-nut medley aside and do not mix together until ready to serve.

Heat a large, preferably 8-quart (7.5 L), nonstick pot or Dutch oven over medium heat. Add 3 tablespoons of the clarified butter. Arrange the potatoes in an even layer and season with a generous pinch or two of salt. Cook until golden and crispy, 5 to 7 minutes. Flip the potatoes. Remove the pot from the heat and set aside.

Fill a medium pot two-thirds of the way with water and generously season with salt. Bring to a boil. When the water is almost at a boil, place the rice in a medium bowl. Cover with cool water and use your hand to gently agitate and swirl the rice, then drain. Repeat four to five more times until the water is mostly clear.

Add the drained rice to the boiling water and stir a few times so that it doesn't clump. Parboil until the rice is al dente, 7 to 8 minutes. When you bite into a grain, it will be soft around the edges but opaque white and firm in the center. Drain the rice.

Using a large spoon, mound the parboiled rice in a pyramid over the potatoes. Poke a few holes in the pyramid with the handle of a wooden spoon or chopstick to allow steam to escape. Wrap the lid in a clean kitchen towel (use a rubber band to secure the ends of the towel to the lid handle) and set the lid over the pot to cover.

Set the rice-filled pot over medium heat. When the sides of the pot feel hot to the touch and you hear a simmering sound, reduce the heat to medium-low and cook for 15 minutes.

While the rice is minding its own business, as Nana would say, in a small heatproof bowl, pour 3 tablespoons just-boiled water over the saffron threads and steep for 10 to 15 minutes.

When the rice is ready, spoon the remaining 3 tablespoons clarified butter evenly over the rice, then drizzle the saffron tea (along with the pistils) over the rice in circles. Do not disturb the rice. Reduce the heat to low and cook for another 15 to 20 minutes, or until the rice is fully cooked and fluffy. If the rice still isn't fully cooked, drizzle a tablespoon or two of water over the rice, cover, and continue to cook, checking after 5 to 10 minutes. Keep covered until ready to serve.

When ready to serve, stir the fruit-nut medley together to evenly combine and warm through over low heat. Mound the fluffy rice onto a large platter. Loosen the potatoes and arrange in a circular pattern along the base of the rice. Make a divot at the top of the mound and scoop some of the fruit-nut medley to fill it. Serve immediately, along with the rest of the fruit-nut medley in a small serving bowl alongside it.

Note: *Vacuum-sealed packs of roasted and peeled chestnuts are often a seasonal fall and winter item found in the nuts and dried fruit section (although I've had luck finding them in July at some stores!). Otherwise, they are readily available online—I like the Blanchard & Blanchard brand.*

MAMALYGA

CHEESY CORNMEAL PORRIDGE

In my family, we refer to cornmeal porridge as *mamalyga*. I had always assumed the term was Georgian, given that we typically serve it piping hot as a vehicle for Chicken Bazhe (page 139) around the holidays. It wasn't until a few years ago, after reading Irina Georgescu's cookbook *Carpathia*, that I learned that it's actually derived from Romania and Moldova, where they spell it *mămăligă*, and it refers to the two countries' shared national dish of a kind of yellow polenta. Like the national hits of other republics, mămăligă slowly made its way into the Soviet culinary canon, and by the time my mom and her siblings were growing up in Tbilisi in the '60s and '70s, it was just part of daily lexicon. I had simply no idea.

But, while mămăligă may be Romanian/Moldovan in origin, this preparation is—at least loosely—Georgian. It's our approximation of *elarji*: a white corn porridge, called *ghomi*, that is mixed with *sulguni* (a semi-firm, slightly salty, mild cheese best known for its starring role in *khachapuri*). Here in the States, we mimic sulguni with mozzarella and feta and use whatever stone-ground cornmeal variety we can find at the store, usually polenta or grits (both of which have their own long-standing cultural traditions—the irony is not lost). All this to say that food, and how we come to it, doesn't always follow clear lines. Cook and enjoy—and do try it with that spiced walnut *bazhe* sauce.

....

6 cups (1.4 kg) water
1½ cups (255 g) coarse stone-ground cornmeal, such as grits or polenta
1 tablespoon kosher salt, plus more to taste
6 ounces (170 g) low-moisture whole-milk mozzarella cheese, coarsely grated
3 ounces (85 g) feta cheese, finely crumbled

SERVES 4 TO 6

In a large pot, bring the water to a boil. Vigorously whisk in the cornmeal and salt and keep whisking until the cornmeal swells and soaks up all of the water, 2 to 3 minutes. Reduce the heat and simmer, partially covered, stirring frequently, and adding more water as needed to keep it a thick, pourable consistency. Cook until cornmeal is smooth, creamy, and tender, 25 to 30 minutes.

Stir in the mozzarella and feta and mix until the mozzarella is melted. The cornmeal should be thick, gooey, and slightly tangy from the feta. Taste and add more salt if needed. Serve immediately.

CHAPTER SEVEN

FERMENTS, PICKLES, AND PRESERVES

STERILIZING JARS + STREAMLINED CANNING

My dear friend Daniel Perry, who makes the Virginia-famous preserves JAM according to Daniel, taught me the following streamlined method for sterilizing jars and canning preserves. I use this when I'm putting away low-risk jams, preserves, marmalades, and cooked acidic sauces such as *tkemali* (sour plum sauce, see page 182). For higher-risk foods, such as pickles, chutneys, salsas, and canned fruit and vegetables, I suggest following a recipe from a trusted resource, such as the *Ball Blue Book Guide to Preserving*.

Preheat the oven to 250°F (120°C). Line a baking sheet with a clean kitchen towel. Wash the jars with hot, soapy water and then arrange, open end down, on the lined baking sheet. Transfer to the oven and allow to dry for at least 20 to 25 minutes, or until you are ready to fill them with preserves. If just sterilizing the jars, you can remove them from the oven and allow to cool down before proceeding with your recipe.

Once the preserves are ready, turn off the heat or turn down to low (you never want the preserves to fall under 194°F / 90°C for the entire process). Take the jars out of the oven and fill with the preserves, leaving ⅛ to ¼ inch (3 to 6 mm) of headspace. Gently run a clean non-metal utensil (such as a wooden chopstick or plastic knife) along the inside of your jar to release any trapped air bubbles. Wipe the rims if necessary, and tightly seal with new snap lids that haven't been used before. Allow to cool completely. You know it's properly sealed if the lids pop. Whether you hear the pop or not, the best way to check is to remove the ring band and then pick up the jar by the snap lid. If it's vacuumed properly, it should stay put. Stored in a cool, dark place, preserves should last for 1 year.

MARINATED TOMATOES

A welcome foil to the heavy and rich mains of the season, a bowl of glistening crimson-red marinated (i.e., pickled) tomatoes at the holiday table is a must. Their blistered skins give way to a brine-plumped flesh that releases a gush of tangy-sweet aromatic juice on first bite. Messy, full of noisy slurps, and utterly delicious. The brine, too, is good enough to drink, although you can also use it to spike dressings, sauces, and even your martini! For most of the year, we buy big jars from the Eastern European store, but in the summer, the pickle is incredibly easy and satisfying to make with summer tomatoes.

You want to use peak-season tomatoes (ideally from your local farmers' market) that are cocktail-size. Think two bites versus three or four. This is the time I also start to come across dill flowers and their woody stems—just in time for pickling. If you can't find them, a couple of bruised dill stems will work well, too. Otherwise, experiment! Parsley or tarragon can be swapped for the dill or celery. Keep the garlic whole or sliced; omit the chili or swap it for something a bit sweeter, like Anaheim; or add thin round slices of a small onion or shallot.

••

1¼ pounds (565 g) firm-ripe cocktail-size tomatoes, rinsed
6 fresh celery leaves
2 dill flowers gone to seed and their thick, woody dill stems, the latter cut into twelve 2½-inch (6.5 cm) lengths
2 small bay leaves
3 to 4 garlic cloves, kept whole or sliced
1 small fresh red chili, such as cayenne or Fresno, kept whole but bruised with the hilt of a knife or sliced for more heat
2 cups (480 g) water
8 black peppercorns
4 allspice berries
2 tablespoons white wine vinegar
2 tablespoons granulated sugar
2 tablespoons kosher salt

MAKES 1 QUART (1 L)

Poke each tomato with a skewer or toothpick to allow the pickling liquid to penetrate it more easily. Set aside.

Arrange a couple of the celery leaves, all of the dill stems, 1 bay leaf, and 2 garlic cloves in the bottom of a sterilized 1-quart (1 L) glass jar. Fill the jar with the tomatoes, fitting them snugly against each other, and tuck in the chili, remaining garlic, and remaining celery leaves into any empty spaces along the way. Press down gently if needed to make that last tomato or two fit. Tuck in the dill flowers and remaining bay leaf.

In a small saucepan, bring the water to a boil. Pour the boiling water into the jar to completely submerge the tomatoes (it's okay if you don't use all of the water; empty the saucepan if there is any left). Seal the jar and allow to sit for 10 minutes. Pour the water back into the now empty saucepan (if arranged snugly, the tomatoes won't budge). While this step seems fussy, it not only measures exactly how much water you need, but also helps presterilize the ingredients since you're not canning them.

Add the peppercorns, allspice, vinegar, sugar, and salt to the water in the saucepan and bring to a boil. Immediately remove from the heat. Pour the liquid back over the tomatoes, making sure the tomatoes are completely submerged in the brine and that there's ⅛ to ¼ inch (3 to 6 mm) of headspace. Seal tightly and allow to cool to room temperature before transferring to the refrigerator. Ideally, allow the tomatoes to rest for at least 1 week before opening to allow them to absorb the brine. The tomatoes keep refrigerated for up to 2 months.

MARINATED RED PEPPERS

Having lived in a city with as much culinary diversity as Tbilisi, my mom sometimes has trouble pinpointing where a dish comes from. This method of preparing peppers is a good example: While it finds its roots in Armenia, everyone in Tbilisi made them in the early fall. Unlike roasted peppers, which are cooked to slippery, limp submission, the vegetables here are simmered just until they begin to slouch but still maintain a bit of snap. Both the stalks and leaves of celery are added to the tangy marinade, along with plenty of garlic and parsley. Serve them as an appetizer—on their own as part of a larger spread or pair with soft goat or hard sheep's milk cheese for an Armenian "bruschetta."

••

¼ cup (55 g) sunflower oil or other neutral oil
¼ cup (60 g) water
¼ cup (60 g) white wine vinegar
1 tablespoon granulated sugar
1 tablespoon kosher salt
1 small bay leaf (fresh or dried)
8 black peppercorns
1½ pounds (680 g) red bell peppers, quartered (or cut into sixths depending on size), membranes and seeds removed
1 medium celery stalk, halved lengthwise and cut crosswise into 2-inch (5 cm) pieces
3 to 4 garlic cloves, sliced
¼ cup (9 g) roughly chopped celery leaves with stems
¼ cup (9 g) roughly chopped parsley, leaves and tender stems

MAKES 1 QUART (1 L)

In ideally a 4-quart (4 L) pot (better to use a larger pot than smaller if you don't have this size), combine the oil, water, vinegar, sugar, salt, bay leaf, and black peppercorns and bring to a boil.

Immediately add the peppers, reduce the heat to maintain a rapid simmer, and cook, stirring often so that the peppers cook evenly, until the peppers have begun to collapse and lose their rigid shape, 10 to 12 minutes.

Stir in the celery, garlic, celery leaves, and parsley and continue to cook, stirring occasionally, until the aromatics have infused the brine, the celery stalks have softened, and the peppers are pliable but still offer some resistance when pierced with a fork, another 5 minutes.

Transfer the peppers and aromatics to a sterilized 1-quart (1 L) jar and pour the marinade over them. If the peppers aren't fully submerged, use a glass weight or stack a little ramekin inside so that when sealed, the ramekin presses down on the peppers to fully submerge them in the brine. Seal tightly and allow to cool to room temperature before transferring to the refrigerator. Allow to rest for at least 1 day before opening. Refrigerated, the peppers will last for 2 to 3 weeks.

FERMENTED CAULIFLOWER WITH BEETS

Come late summer and early fall, my mom would recount how her father became a bit manic in the kitchen: fermenting, pickling, marinating, and preserving—anything to extend the bounty of summer for as long as he could for the cold, sparse months ahead. These days we turn to preserving more out of capturing the essence of the season rather than out of necessity. But that doesn't mean our appetite for the sour and tangy (a hallmark of cuisines from both Eastern Europe and the Caucasus) has lessened. This recipe is an easy gateway into the world of fermenting and pickling. Just make sure you sterilize your jar ahead of time and use salt that doesn't have iodine or anticaking agents that will inhibit fermentation.

• •

3 tablespoons (30 g) kosher salt
3½ cups (840 g) water
½ medium head organic cauliflower (about
    14 ounces / 395 g), cored and cut into
    small florets
1 medium-small organic red beet (about 4 ounces
    / 115 g), peeled and cut into ⅜-inch (1 cm) wedges
3 garlic cloves, peeled but whole
3 dill sprigs, stalks bruised
2 small bay leaves
1 dried red chili, such as chile de árbol, toasted
2 teaspoons coriander seeds, toasted
½ teaspoon black peppercorns

MAKES 1½ QUARTS (1.5 L)

In a liquid measuring cup, stir the salt into the water until fully dissolved. Set the brine aside.

Pack the cauliflower, beets, garlic, dill sprigs, bay leaves, red chili, coriander seeds, and black peppercorns into a sterilized 1½-quart (1.5 L) glass jar, leaving about 1 inch (2.5 cm) of headspace.

Cover with the brine so that the vegetables are fully submerged. Weight down the vegetables with a glass weight or a small ramekin to prevent them from bobbing up to the top—you can even wedge a couple of celery or carrot sticks across the neck of the jar to accomplish this. Cover the jar with its lid, but don't tighten it. Leave it out in your kitchen away from a cool draft (you want it to be around 60°F to 75°F / 15°C to 24°C).

After about 2 days, the brine should have some bubbles on the surface and give off an acidic smell. Continue to let the vegetables ferment and start checking for flavor around day 4 or 5. I usually let mine go for 7 to 10 days. Once you're happy with the level of tanginess, seal and refrigerate. The vegetables will continue to ferment but at a much slower pace. Refrigerated, the vegetables should last for several months.

TKEMALI

SOUR PLUM SAUCE

I loved ketchup as a child. Absolutely *looooved* it. With potatoes, pasta, bread, and rice; on chicken nuggets, hot dogs, and Genoa salami roll-ups. Almost all food (save for scrambled eggs and mashed potatoes) was made tastier by the sweet amalgam of tomato concentrate and high-fructose corn syrup. Of course, there was always a bottle of *tkemali*, Georgian sour plum sauce, hanging around in the door of the fridge, but I was too busy making a beeline for the Heinz squirt bottle to notice.

As I grew older, I slowly (to everyone's relief) became more lax with my processed-meat and carb-only diet. I actually started to enjoy my family's home cooking and found that tkemali was a better match for its nuanced flavors. So instead of American ketchup, I started to douse everything in, what I like to think of as, its Georgian counterpart.

Tkemali is, yes, sweet, but also tangy and zesty. Garlic, coriander (both fresh and ground seeds), wild mint, and other herbs and spices flavor the full-bodied sauce. In Georgia, you'll find green, yellow, red, and dark-purple tkemali, depending on the variety of plums used. Here in the States, you can find bottles of tkemali sauce in most Eastern European stores, but I always find the homemade version superior. Use as an accompaniment to grilled or roasted meat and poultry, potatoes, and really everything in between. Or use it as an ingredient in a stew like Chakapuli (page 156).

. . . .

2¼ pounds (1 kg) firm, tart green or red plums (see box)
1 cup (240 g) water, divided
2 teaspoons kosher salt, plus more to taste
2 tablespoons granulated sugar, plus more to taste
½ large bunch of cilantro, roughly chopped
½ large bunch of dill, roughly chopped
1 to 2 basil sprigs, leaves picked and roughly chopped
1 serrano or cayenne chili, roughly chopped, plus more to taste
3 garlic cloves, roughly chopped
½ teaspoon ground coriander
½ teaspoon ground blue fenugreek
¼ teaspoon dried ombalo (pennyroyal mint) or dried mint (optional)

MAKES ABOUT 3½ CUPS (840 G)

Place the plums in a large pot and add ½ cup (120 g) water. Bring to a boil over medium-high heat. Reduce the heat to low, cover, and simmer, stirring occasionally, just until the fruit easily falls off the pit, 15 to 25 minutes. Transfer to a large bowl to cool completely.

Working over the large pot, run the fruit and its juices through a food mill. (Alternatively, put through a colander set over the large pot, pressing down on the fruit with your hands or a wooden spoon until only skins and pits remain.) Stir in the salt and sugar and taste. You want enough tartness to balance out the sweetness, but not so much that it causes you to pucker. Add a bit more sugar if needed.

In a food processor, combine the cilantro, dill, basil, half of the serrano (seeds and all), and the garlic. Pulse, scraping down the sides of the bowl as needed, until finely chopped. Set aside.

Bring the plum puree to a simmer over medium heat. Cook, adjusting the heat as needed to maintain a steady simmer, for 5 minutes. Stir in the herb-garlic mixture and the coriander, blue fenugreek, and ombalo (if using). Continue simmering for another 8 to 10 minutes. Stir in the remaining ½ cup (120 g) water to loosen it up.

Now the important part: Taste. If there's still a pucker to the sauce, stir in sugar a bit at a time until it's balanced. If you'd like a little more heat, add a bit more of the serrano chili. Check for salt, too. Simmer for a couple of minutes for the additional seasonings to meld into the sauce.

Allow the tkemali to cool completely. Store in an airtight container in the refrigerator for up to 6 weeks. It can also be canned (see page 176).

SOUR PLUMS

The hardest part about this recipe is procuring the right kind of plum. Sometimes green Persian plums will pop up at Middle Eastern markets around springtime, and I will make a batch of fresh green *tkemali* then. More often, though, I will wait until late summer to make it—using plums I've foraged or found at the farmers' market, after much tasting and quizzing the local fruit vendor.

The varieties I've had most success with are Santa Rosa, Greengage, and Cherry. While Italian plums are tart, do not use them. They're too meaty, with not enough juice for our purposes.

CRANBERRY "TKEMALI"

My Aunt Olga starts to make this knock-off *"tkemali"* as soon as cranberries start popping up at the grocery stores in the fall. It's a great condiment to have around during the holidays, going well with roasts, chops, sausages, and veggies like crispy potatoes.

....

One (12-ounce / 340 g) bag fresh or frozen cranberries
1½ cups (360 g) water, divided
½ cup (15 g) cilantro, finely chopped
2 small garlic cloves, crushed through a press or finely minced
¼ cup (50 g) granulated sugar
1 teaspoon kosher salt, plus more to taste
½ teaspoon red pepper flakes, plus more to taste
Generous ¼ teaspoon ground coriander
Pinch of dried ombalo (pennyroyal mint) or dried mint (optional)

MAKES 1 PINT (475 ML)

Put the cranberries in a medium saucepan and add 1 cup (240 g) of the water. Bring to a simmer over medium heat. Cook, stirring often, until the cranberries have popped and softened, 5 to 7 minutes. Allow to cool slightly. Transfer to a food mill or medium-mesh sieve and press the cooked fruit into a bowl (discard the skins and seeds). Return the puree to the saucepan.

Stir the cilantro, garlic, sugar, salt, pepper flakes, coriander, ombalo (if using), and the remaining water into the puree. Bring to a gentle simmer, adjusting the heat as needed, and cook for 10 minutes to soften the harshness of the garlic. Taste and season with more salt or pepper flakes if desired.

Allow the tkemali to cool completely. Store in an airtight container in the refrigerator for up to 1 month.

SLAVIC-STYLE SAUERKRAUT

In the early fall, my mom starts rummaging through the cabbage section for cabbage heads she deems suitable for *kvashenaya kapusta*, or sauerkraut. What she's looking for is white cabbage: similar in appearance to green cabbage, but when turned over, the base (and thus interior) is white. Compared to green cabbage, white has a denser yet softer texture that holds its shape well and doesn't release as much liquid during the fermentation process. It's also a bit sweeter in flavor. With her hands on the right stuff, my mom then makes a big batch of sauerkraut that will last us at least through the holidays. I've found in my own kapusta escapades that I can usually still get my hands on some proper cabbage in late winter/early spring. So if you miss that first window, all is not lost!

To serve this sauerkraut as part of a *zakuski* (small bites) spread, fill a shallow serving bowl with the sauerkraut. Top with a smattering of thinly sliced red onions and drizzle generously with unrefined sunflower oil. Other uses for this sauerkraut are Vinegret Salat (page 120); sour cabbage soup such as *shchi* or *solyanka*; or as a topping for sausages or even avocado toast! This recipe is easily scaled up or down depending on how much cabbage you have.

••

1 large or 2 small heads "white" cabbage, outer leaves removed (about 5 pounds / 2.25 kg)
2 large carrots (about 8 ounces / 225 g total), peeled
⅓ cup (35 g) cranberries (optional), fresh or frozen
3 tablespoons (30 g) kosher salt, plus more as needed
1½ tablespoons black peppercorns
1 teaspoon granulated sugar
3 bay leaves

MAKES ABOUT 4 QUARTS (4 L)

Get out an extra-large bowl for mixing. I mix the cabbage in two batches, which is how the recipe is written, but if you have an extremely large bowl to fit all the sliced cabbage, you can do it all in one go.

Before you start, make sure your hands are very clean! With your sharpest chef's knife, halve the cabbage head lengthwise through the core. Slice one-half of the cabbage into paper-thin, long strips. (Alternatively, use a mandoline to slice the cabbage on the thinnest setting.) Transfer the sliced cabbage to the bowl. Grate one carrot into the cabbage bowl. Sprinkle evenly with half of the following ingredients: cranberries (if using), salt, black peppercorns, and sugar. Toss the cabbage-carrot mixture, massaging it as you go to help break it down, until the cabbage turns limp and is very wet with its own brine, 3 to 4 minutes. If you're not seeing much brine, continue to massage more firmly until the cabbage has surrendered. Taste the cabbage: You want it to be a beat too salty. Adjust the salt as needed.

Working with a handful of cabbage at a time, arrange it in an even layer in a 4-quart (4 L) nonreactive pot and press it down with your fist to pack it in. Continue packing in the cabbage, fitting a bay leaf in every few layers, until no cabbage remains in the bowl. Pour in any brine that accumulated at the bottom of the bowl.

Repeat the process with the remaining cabbage, carrot, and seasoning ingredients. Pack into the pot, using the last of the bay leaves.

Line the top of the cabbage with a paper towel or clean muslin cloth and tuck the edges in between the cabbage and sides of the pot. Place a plate on top and weight it down with two 28-ounce cans of tomatoes to start (you can ditch the second one once enough brine has accumulated) or something of similar or heavier weight. Leave the pot out on your kitchen counter away from a cool draft or the heat of the oven. Within an hour or so, you will see that the cabbage is completely submerged in its brine. If there's not enough brine within a few hours or by the next morning, add a little water until the cabbage is submerged.

Days 1 and 2: Leave the cabbage for 2 full days, after which you should check the cabbage. The brine should have some bubbles on the surface and give off an acidic smell. Remove the weight and plate and peel back the paper towel. Using a skewer or chopstick, poke holes down to the bottom of the pot all over. This helps release gas and keeps the cabbage from turning too acidic. Cover again with the paper towel and weight it down.

Days 3 through 5: Continue releasing gas in this way one or two times a day through the fifth day. On the fifth full day, check the cabbage for flavor. It should be pleasantly tangy with a subtle sweetness to it (it will also be very smelly). We usually stop here, preferring sauerkraut with a milder flavor that still has some crunch to it, but if you prefer your sauerkraut to be stronger, leave it for a few more days or until you're happy with the flavor.

When the cabbage is done fermenting, discard the paper towel and keep in the pot or transfer to a nonreactive storage vessel. Cover and refrigerate (it will continue to ferment in the fridge but at a slower pace). Refrigerated, the cabbage should last for 6 to 12 months, although the texture will start to soften over time.

RASPBERRY JAM

On my first and only trip to Russia when I was twelve, I spent a week with my father's parents in their sleepy town of Konakova, about two hours northwest of Moscow. I remember dusty dirt roads; picking wild blueberries in a dense green forest, followed by a dip in the Volga River; a faded Soviet-era outdoor gym; and a dim corner store that sold orange-colored ice pops and milk in pouches. A sense of adventure imbued each new day, even as I chafed against the strict regimen and rules my grandparents adhered to (my grandfather served in the Soviet army as a colonel for decades).

Each day started with a nonnegotiable—and by the end of my stay, dreaded—bowl of *grechka* (buckwheat). But as regular as my morning kasha was, so was my afternoon treat: my grandfather's homemade raspberry jam. Syrupy and teeming with seeds, fruity yet floral, it was the very essence of sun-ripened fruit and unlike any store-bought jam I had ever known. I'd sit at their small wooden kitchen table and eat one buttery Ritz-type cracker after another, each generously dolloped with jam, until my stomach hurt. Here's my homage to that raspberry jam. A reminder that a measured life enjoys indulgences that much more.

••

2¼ pounds (1 kg) fresh raspberries
2¼ cups (450 g) granulated sugar
3 tablespoons (45 g) lemon juice

MAKES THREE TO FOUR 8-OUNCE (250 ML) JARS

In a large bowl, combine the fruit, sugar, and lemon juice. Cover and let macerate for at least 2 to 3 hours. This step pulls some of the juices from the fruit and creates a syrup. Leave at room temperature for up to 24 hours or in the refrigerator for up to 1 week.

When you're ready to make jam, put two small plates in the freezer. Prepare and sterilize the jars (see Sterilizing Jars + Streamlined Canning, page 176). Transfer the berries to a large, wide heavy-bottomed pot. Bring the mixture to a vigorous boil over medium-high heat and cook, stirring frequently and skimming any foam that arises, until the jam is dark, glossy, and has set. Because raspberries are so high in pectin, I've found it sets quicker than jam made with other fruit, so I start testing the jam around 5 to 7 minutes after it has started to boil.

To test, remove the jam from the heat. Drop a generous teaspoon of jam onto a chilled plate and return it to the freezer for 2 minutes. Take it out and give the jam a nudge with your finger. If it has formed a skin and wrinkles, you're good to go. (Bonus if you run your finger through the jam and it leaves a clean trail.) If it's not ready, cook for another 2 minutes and test again; repeat if necessary until it passes the test. Switch to the second plate if the first is starting to lose its chill.

If you want your jam a little less seedy, scoop half of it into a fine-mesh sieve set over the pot and, using your spatula, push the jam through the sieve.

Once set, divide among the prepared jars, leaving ⅛ to ¼ inch (3 to 6 mm) of headspace. Remove any air bubbles, wipe the rims if necessary, and seal. Invert the jars and let them sit for 2 minutes before flipping back over (this prevents all the fruit from settling down to the bottom). Let the preserves sit, undisturbed, for 24 hours before storing.

WHITE CHERRY AND HAZELNUT PRESERVES

It's always a good day when I come home to a bulging care package on my doorstep labeled "from Mama Larisa." It's often a grab bag, but, if I'm lucky, tucked between the layers of new blouses and cloth napkins, knickknacks and tinned fish, is a jar or two of homemade *varenye*, whole-fruit preserves. One year it was these glistening cherries, suspended in a viscous, tawny syrup along with hazelnuts and lemon slices. I was hooked. The fruit is stuffed with nuts and slowly simmered until it becomes candy-like—dark, translucent, with a bit of chew. Aside from enjoying with tea, the preserves are wonderful spooned over ice cream, yogurt, or even a decadent bowl of morning oatmeal. Thank you, Mama!

While we call it "white" cherry, it's in fact a yellow varietal. In the States, Rainier works well. The most important thing is that they be flavorful, so taste one before you commence this project. The nuts give the preserves a special touch but are by no means essential. The recipe also gives a range: Decide for yourself how many of the cherries you'd like to stuff, whether that's half or all of them. And don't stress if some hazelnuts fall out, as it is inevitable and will still be delicious.

· ·

2¼ pounds (1 kg) pitted Rainier cherries or other
    yellow varietal
⅓ to ¾ cup (55 to 100 g) hazelnuts, toasted and
    skinned
3 cups (600 g) granulated sugar
1 medium organic lemon, scrubbed and halved
½ vanilla bean, or 1 teaspoon vanilla bean paste

MAKES FIVE 8-OUNCE (250 ML) JARS

Stuff each cherry with a hazelnut, inserting the nut through the bottom of the fruit. In a large bowl, combine the fruit and sugar. Squeeze in the lemon juice from 1 lemon half. Cover and macerate for at least 2 to 3 hours. This step pulls some of the juices from the fruit and creates a syrup. Leave at room temperature for up to 24 hours or in the refrigerator for up to 1 week.

Transfer the mixture to a large, wide heavy-bottomed pot. Set over medium-high heat, stirring frequently but gently, until the sugar has completely dissolved and the mixture begins to simmer. Reduce the heat to maintain a gentle simmer and cook for 10 minutes, skimming any foam that arises. The cherries should look collapsed and mildly shriveled. Remove from the heat.

Use a small paring knife to halve the vanilla bean lengthwise. Use the back of a knife to scrape out the seeds into the preserves and add the spent pod. (Or add the vanilla bean paste.) Cut the remaining lemon half lengthwise and thinly slice crosswise into half-moons. Add the lemon slices to the pot. Cover and let the cherries sit out at room temperature until fully cooled or overnight.

When ready to make the jam, put two small plates in the freezer. Prepare and sterilize the jars (see Sterilizing Jars + Streamlined Canning, page 176). Set the pot of cherry mixture over medium-high heat and bring to a simmer. Adjust the heat to maintain a gentle simmer and cook, gently stirring occasionally and skimming any foam that arises, until the cherries are translucent and glossy and the syrup matches the color of the hazelnuts and has reached its setting point. Start checking around the 1-hour mark.

To test, remove the jam from the heat. Drop a generous teaspoon of jam onto a chilled plate and return to the freezer for 2 minutes. Take it out and give the jam a nudge with your finger. If it has formed a skin and wrinkles, you're good to go. If not (or if it's still runny), cook for another 2 minutes and test again; repeat if necessary until it passes the test. Switch to the second plate if the first is starting to lose its chill.

Once set, remove from the heat. Divide among the prepared jars, leaving ⅛ to ¼ inch (3 to 6 mm) of headspace. Remove any air bubbles, wipe the rims if necessary, and seal. Let the preserves sit, undisturbed, for 24 hours before storing.

WILL YOU HAVE TEA?

Chai is a steaming hot cup of strong black tea. The clink of the spoon against its walls, a lemon slice bobbing on its surface. Paired with a *buterbrod* (tartine) of sharp pockmarked cheese and razor-thin salami. There's no better way to start the day. In the evenings, it may be an herbal infusion of fresh mint leaves or a fruit tisane of black currants—the sweetener a few spoonfuls of *varenye* (whole-fruit preserves) or a conserve of berries on the side.

Chai is having a little post-meal treat, pulling out a few wafer cookies or a square or two of chocolate from the pantry. It's having guests over (invited or not) for a simple cake or snack when a whole dinner feels too much to commit to. The only unspoken rule being that you never drink *chai* on its own. It can be made with a tea satchel and sipped on the hurry or brewed into a strong concentrate (*zavarka*), diluted to guests' liking with fresh *kipyatok* (boiled water), and turned into a multihour affair.

For us in the diaspora, chai fuels, comforts, and anchors our daily life. It, like a faithful spouse, is there for us in sickness and in health. A nonnegotiable. As Fyodor Dostoevsky wrote in his *Notes from Underground*: "I say let the world go to hell, but I should always have my tea."

SPICED OVEN-ROASTED
PLUM PRESERVES

Unlike most preserves, which are cooked on the stovetop, these plums are slowly baked at a low temperature in the oven. It's less mess and requires less attention, so this method is great if you're just getting into preserve making. Over time, the plums shrink in on themselves and edge into prune territory, concentrating in flavor and developing a bit of a chew. The fruit syrup they are bathed in, on the other hand, takes on a dark-burgundy color and the warm spice of cinnamon and star anise. Make it in late summer, when plums are in full swing, for a preserve that will match the broody autumn days ahead.

You can also make this with 2 bay leaves instead of cinnamon and star anise, which will lend a warm vermouth-like spiciness to the preserves. I find a 10 × 14-inch (25 × 36 cm) pan works perfectly here, but anything in this range will work.

●●

2¼ pounds (1 kg) halved and pitted firm-ripe
    Italian plums or other dark-colored varietal
1 cinnamon stick
2 to 3 whole star anise
2 strips orange peel
3 tablespoons (45 g) lemon juice
2½ cups (500 g) granulated sugar

MAKES FOUR 8-OUNCE (250 ML) JARS

In a 10 × 14-inch (25 × 36 cm) or similar-size baking or roasting pan, arrange the plum halves skin side down in an even layer. Tuck the spices and peel in between the fruit. Pour the lemon juice over the plums and evenly scatter over the sugar. Cover and let macerate for at least 2 to 3 hours. This step pulls some of the juices from the fruit and creates a syrup. Leave at room temperature for up to 24 hours or in the refrigerator for up to 1 week.

Preheat the oven to 300°F (150°C).

Carefully stir the plums to make sure all the sugar is moistened and in the syrup. Transfer to the oven and bake for 1½ hours, stirring the syrup every 30 minutes to help incorporate any sugar that still hasn't dissolved. By the end, the plums will have shrunk and the syrup will look thin but will thicken as it cools.

Meanwhile, prepare and sterilize the jars (see Sterilizing Jars + Streamlined Canning, page 176).

Remove the whole spices and immediately divide the fruit among the sterilized jars and top with syrup, leaving ⅛ to ¼ inch (3 to 6 mm) of headspace. Remove any air bubbles, wipe the rims if necessary, and seal. Let the preserves sit, undisturbed, for 24 hours before storing.

SUGARED CURRANTS

My Aunt Olga's fridge is, for a lack of a better word, chaotic. Take a peek and you'll find multiple yogurt containers (good luck finding the one that actually holds yogurt), a door lined with expired condiments, crammed and perpetually stuck crisper drawers, and a pot (or two) of soup that requires Tetris-like skills to get out. If you dig around long enough, though, you'll find a jar of sugared currants—a no-cook "jam" that lasts through the winter season. The thought is that you mix the vitamin-C-packed fruit with so much sugar that you preserve it, along with all of its health benefits (or so my Aunt says). Make it when currants are in season, and in the months to come, stir a spoonful directly into your tea for both a sugar and immune boost.

While the sugar content does feel high, do not skimp, otherwise your fruit will go bad. You can also make this with raspberries or even cranberries. You can scale this recipe up or down; just keep in mind the ratio of 1:1 by weight or 1⅓:1 by volume.

••

*2⅔ cups (400 g) black or red currants, washed
    and dried*
2 cups (400 g) granulated sugar

MAKES ABOUT 1½ PINTS (850 ML)

If you have access to a meat grinder, run the currants through it, including skins, seeds, and all. If you don't have one, add the fruit to a food processor and pulse until you have a puree that still retains a hint of its pulp.

Transfer the fruit puree to a bowl and stir in the sugar until it's completely moistened and incorporated. Let it sit out for an hour or two. It'll be grainy and thin at first, but as the preserve sits, it will smooth out and thicken.

Transfer to a sterilized jar (see Sterilizing Jars + Streamlined Canning, page 176), tightly seal, and refrigerate. The preserves should last you through the winter.

SOUR CHERRY COMPOTE

A quick and easy fruit compote with a beautiful inky red syrup. Spoon over Blinchiki (page 48), Syrniki (page 41), and my favorite, Varenyky (page 58).

••

⅔ to ¾ cup (160 to 180 g) water (use the larger amount if using fresh cherries)
¼ cup (50 g) granulated sugar
¼ teaspoon kosher salt
2 cups (310 g) pitted sour cherries, fresh or frozen
2 teaspoons lemon juice
1½ teaspoons cornstarch

MAKES 1½ CUPS (380 G)

In a medium saucepan, combine the water, sugar, and salt and bring to a boil. Cook, stirring often, until reduced and a thin syrup has formed, 5 to 6 minutes. Add the cherries, bring to a simmer, and cook until the cherries are tender and begin to collapse, another 5 to 6 minutes.

In a small bowl, stir the lemon juice into the cornstarch and stir into the compote. Allow the compote to come to a full simmer again and cook for another 15 to 20 seconds before removing from the heat.

Allow to cool and serve warm or at room temperature. Store in the refrigerator for up to 1 week.

CHAPTER EIGHT

SWEETS

MEDOVIK

HONEY CAKE

Medovik is all the rage now, but that's nothing new for this iconic honey cake. During Soviet times, it was intensely popular and everyone's favorite homemade treat. It's truly a work of art—your guests will wonder how in the world you managed to get the graham-like layers so razor thin—but once you get the hang of it, you'll find that it doesn't take as much as skill as it does time. The peculiar cake batter starts out on the stove, but after a chill in the fridge, it will feel, roll out, and even bake up like cookie dough. The rounds come out thin and crispy, which is why the assembled medovik needs to sit overnight so that they turn into a soft sponge. As for the filling, my family has always preferred our custard-based buttercream mixed with dulce de leche to heighten the notes of honey, over the whipped sour cream the cake is often made with.

If you'd like to make a twelve-layer cake like you see in the photo, increase the cake and buttercream recipes by 1½ times. You can make the cake layers up to a week in advance and store in an airtight container or a bag at room temperature before assembling them.

. . . .

7 tablespoons (100 g) unsalted butter
¾ cup (150 g) granulated sugar
Scant ⅓ cup (100 g) light honey, such as wildflower,
    clover, or orange blossom
Rounded 1¼ teaspoons baking soda
1 teaspoon kosher salt
2 eggs
2¾ cups plus 2 tablespoons (375 g) all-purpose
    flour, plus more as needed
1 cup (120 g) walnuts, toasted
Plombir Buttercream (page 228) made with
    dulce de leche or sweetened condensed milk

SERVES 8 TO 10

In a medium saucepan, bring 1 inch (2.5 cm) of water to a simmer.

In a large heatproof bowl, combine the butter, sugar, and honey and set the bowl over the saucepan. Stir from time to time to help the butter melt. Once the butter has melted, whisk the ingredients to combine. Cook until the honey mixture is smooth and the sugar has dissolved a bit and doesn't feel as granular, 3 to 4 minutes (to check, rub the batter between two fingers). Meanwhile, in a small bowl, stir together the baking soda and salt.

Whisk the baking soda mixture into the honey mixture and cook for 1 to 2 minutes—the honey mixture will lighten in color, thicken, and grow in volume. Remove the bowl from the heat and wipe off the bottom before setting it on your work counter.

While whisking, add 1 egg at a time and mix to fully incorporate after each addition. Switch to a wooden spoon. Sift 2¼ cups (295 g) of the flour into the batter and mix to combine. Sift in the remaining flour in increments, stirring to combine—the batter should come together in one very soft, malleable mass. Cover with plastic wrap and refrigerate until the batter is no longer warm, about 30 minutes.

Meanwhile, preheat the oven to 400°F (200°C).

Cut four pieces of parchment paper the length of a baking sheet. Use a 9-inch (23 cm) springform cake pan or metal cake ring to trace a circle onto each piece of parchment paper.

Transfer the dough to a lightly floured surface and sprinkle the top with more flour. Knead, adding more flour if needed, to form a smooth, slightly tacky dough—like a semi-firm Play-Doh. Form into a log and divide into 8 equal portions (about 100 g each). Roll each piece into a smooth ball.

Place a piece of parchment on your work surface with the tracing side down and set a ball of dough in the center. Top with another sheet (tracing side up), lining it up so that the dough is in the middle of its traced circle. Roll out the dough between the two sheets into a round that is slightly larger than the traced circle. Use the top of your cake pan or ring to press down on the dough to outline a 9-inch (23 cm) round. Carefully peel the top sheet away. Dock the inside of the round all over with a fork.

Transfer the dough on the parchment to a cookie sheet or an overturned baking sheet and bake until the cake is golden brown and springs back when you press on it, 3 to 5 minutes. While it bakes, start working on the next round.

As soon as the cake is out of the oven, use a sharp knife to cut away the extra trimmings and set them aside. Remove the round from the parchment paper and immediately transfer it to a cooling rack. Repeat the process, reusing the parchment papers, until all of the pieces of dough are rolled out and baked.

Process all of the cake trimmings in a food processor until they're finely ground. Transfer to a small bowl. Then process the walnuts until finely ground. Add 3 spoonfuls of the walnuts to the cake crumbs and stir to combine. Transfer the remaining walnuts to another small bowl.

Once the cake layers are cool, place a dab of the buttercream on a cake plate or stand and place the first layer on top. Cut or tear one of the sheets of parchment paper into four long pieces and tuck them underneath the cake to keep the plate clean. Scoop about ⅓ cup (about 100 g) of the buttercream onto the center of the cake and evenly spread to the edges. Sprinkle all over with some of the ground walnuts. Repeat the process, stacking and frosting the cake (don't forget the walnuts!), until you have 8 layers. Once you get to the last layer, frost the top and sides of the cake with the remaining buttercream—it doesn't have to be perfect. Press the cake crumb / walnut mixture into the sides of the cake and sprinkle them over the top in an even layer. Remove the paper strips.

Ideally let sit for 5 to 6 hours at room temperature to better help meld flavors before chilling it overnight. The cake can be served chilled or, the way I prefer, at room temperature (simply take it out an hour before you plan to eat it). The cake can be made up to 2 days in advance—any leftovers will last up to 3 days.

IDEAL TORTE

When I first started my blog, Chesnok, back in 2015, I kicked it off with my mother's specialty honey cake: *ideal torte* (pronounced "ee-dee-al"). The story goes that her best friend, Tamara, decided to make this cake sometime in the 90s in post-Soviet Tbilisi, when gas, among other utilities, was scarce and was only made available, just barely, in the evenings. Her oven temperature was so low, it took her almost half the night to bake off the layers. Determined to still serve it, she frosted the cake and brought it to her party the next day—to rave reviews! The sponge layers were dense, chewy, almost candy-like. She never baked the cake any other way, and that's how my mom has, and now I have, made it ever since.

Unlike the multilayered Medovik (page 200), this torte has two modest layers that are sandwiched together and frosted with a dulce de leche buttercream; then topped with toasted walnuts and dark chocolate. I've lost count the number of times I've seen someone take a bite, pause, and let out a long "Mmm . . ." A sky-high medovik is good, but this one? Well, it's simply ideal.

··

CAKE
Unsalted butter, for the pans
4 eggs, at room temperature
1⅓ cup (265 g) granulated sugar
¼ cup (85 g) runny honey
1 teaspoon baking soda
½ teaspoon apple cider vinegar
2⅓ cups (325 g) all-purpose flour

BUTTERCREAM
1½ cups (340 g) unsalted butter, at room temperature
⅛ teaspoon vanillin, 1 packet (9 g) vanilla sugar (scant 2 teaspoons), or 1½ teaspoons vanilla extract
¼ teaspoon kosher salt
One (13.4-ounce / 380 g) can dulce de leche or Homemade Dulce de Leche (page 204)

ASSEMBLY
1½ cups (170 g) walnuts, toasted and roughly chopped
3 to 4 ounces (85 to 115 g) dark chocolate, cut into thin shards

SERVES 10 TO 12

Make the cake: Generously grease two 10 x 15-inch (25 x 38 cm) jelly-roll pans with butter. Line the pans with parchment paper, leaving overhang on both of the short sides, and grease the paper.

In a stand mixer fitted with the whisk, beat the eggs and sugar on medium-high until the mixture turns pale and forms thick ribbons, 8 to 10 minutes. Pour in the honey. In a small bowl, combine the baking soda and vinegar to create a bubbling paste. Add to the batter and beat to fully incorporate. Sift one-third of the flour over the batter and, using a rubber spatula, fold until just combined. Repeat with the remaining flour in two batches. The batter should have the consistency of super-thick sour cream (smetana).

Divide the batter between the prepared pans (about 430 g each) and use an offset spatula to spread the batter into an even layer. The batter will be a bit hard to spread, which is where the clips come in handy to hold the parchment in place. Let sit for 1 hour.

Meanwhile, position a rack in the center of the oven and preheat the oven to 300°F (150°C).

Baking one cake layer at a time, bake until the cake is a light golden brown and slowly springs back when lightly pressed, 12 to 15 minutes. Let cool in the pan for a couple of minutes before running a knife along the sides to loosen any edges from the pan. Use the overhang to lift the cake out of the pan and transfer it to a wire rack to cool completely. Repeat with the second cake layer.

Make the buttercream: Meanwhile, in a stand mixer fitted with the paddle attachment, beat the butter, vanillin, and salt on medium-high, scraping down the bottom and sides of the bowl periodically, until almost white in color and fluffy, 5 to 6 minutes. Add the dulce de leche a big spoonful at a time, pulsing the mixer until just combined and scraping down the bottom and sides of the bowl as needed before the next addition.

Assemble the ideal torte: Poke the cake layers all over with a fork. Place the first cake layer on a serving platter or a baking sheet. Top the layer with a little less than half of the buttercream and use an offset spatula to spread it into an even layer. Center the second cake layer over the frosted layer and nestle it on top. Frost the top and sides of the cake with the remaining buttercream—the edges don't need much, just a thin crumb coat. Sprinkle the walnuts evenly over the top, followed by the chocolate shards. Wrap tightly with plastic and let sit at room temperature in a cool, dark place for at least a day, ideally two—this will help meld the flavors and improve the texture of the cake.

Before serving, cut into diamonds or squares. Once the cake is cut into and served, any leftovers can be refrigerated for 3 to 4 days.

Note: *Once the cake is assembled, it does benefit from sitting at least a day to let all the flavors meld and the cake to soften. Traditionally, this cake is cut into diamond shapes.*

HOMEMADE DULCE DE LECHE

To make dulce de leche, strip a 14-ounce (397 g) can of sweetened condensed milk of its wrapper and place in a deep saucepan. Fill the pot with enough water to cover the can by 1 to 2 inches (2.5 to 5 cm). Bring the water to a boil, then reduce the heat so that you have a nice, gentle simmer. Cover and simmer for 2½ hours, adding more water as needed to keep it submerged at all times. Remove from the heat. Allow the can to cool completely before opening.

PRAGUE CAKE

Just as inventive as the whimsical cakes of the USSR were, so were the names bestowed upon them. Golden Key, Spartak, Bird's Milk, Bear in the North, and Fairy Tale, just to call out a few. Cakes with monikers of cities, like Kyiv and Prague, also abounded, even though, in the case of the latter, the dessert had nothing to do with the Czech capital. Invented by the famous Russian pastry chef Vladimir Guralnik of Moscow's famed Praga restaurant, *Prazhskii torte* (similar to Austrian Sacher torte) was *the* chocolate cake of its time. Citizens would stand in line for hours trying to snag one, and often failed. So, as they were often forced to do, they learned to make it at home. While there are a handful of components—a tender chocolate sponge, silky chocolate buttercream, Cognac soak, and apricot jam—none of them on their own are hard to make. The torte is decadent: A small slice will go a very long way.

CAKE
3 tablespoons (45 g) neutral oil, such as sunflower or safflower, plus more for the pan
1 cup plus 1 tablespoon (140 g) all-purpose flour
⅓ cup (35 g) Dutch-process cocoa powder
¾ cup plus 1 tablespoon (175 g) granulated sugar, divided
1 teaspoon baking powder
6 eggs, separated, at room temperature
¼ teaspoon kosher salt

COGNAC SOAK
½ cup (120 g) water
½ cup (100 g) granulated sugar
¼ cup (60 g) Cognac or brandy

COCOA-COGNAC BUTTERCREAM
3 egg yolks
3 tablespoons (45 g) water
One (14-ounce / 397 g) can sweetened condensed milk
2½ tablespoons (20 g) Dutch-process cocoa powder
¼ teaspoon kosher salt
Scant ⅛ teaspoon vanillin, or 1 teaspoon vanilla sugar or vanilla extract
1¾ cup (400 g) unsalted butter, at room temperature
2 tablespoons Cognac or brandy

ASSEMBLY
Generous ¾ cup (265 g) apricot jam, slightly warmed
7 ounces (200 g) bittersweet chocolate (70% cacao), finely chopped
7 tablespoons (100 g) unsalted butter
1 tablespoon light corn syrup or honey (optional)
Pinch of kosher salt

SERVES 8 TO 10

Make the cake: Preheat the oven to 350°F (180°C). Line a 9-inch (23 cm) springform or cake pan (at least 3 inches / 7.5 cm deep) with a round of parchment paper. Lightly grease only the paper with the oil.

In a bowl, combine the flour, cocoa powder, 1 tablespoon of the sugar, and the baking powder. Sift together three times.

In a stand mixer fitted with the whisk, whip the egg whites and salt on medium speed until the egg whites resemble a thick, dense white foam, 1½ to 2 minutes. With the mixer still running, gradually add the remaining ¾ cup (150 g) sugar a few tablespoons at a time. Continue to beat until the whites are thick, glossy, and opaque and hold stiff peaks, 3 to 5 minutes. Add the egg yolks one at a time, beating well after each addition. Slowly stream in the oil, mixing until fully incorporated.

Sprinkle one-third of the sifted flour mixture onto the batter and use a rubber spatula to gently but confidently fold it by hand until combined. Repeat with the rest of the flour mixture in two batches, being careful not to deflate the batter.

Gently guide the batter into the prepared pan and smooth out the top. Run a toothpick in a spiral motion, starting from the center and working your way out, to pop any large air bubbles.

Bake, without opening the oven door, until the cake springs back when pressed in the center and a tester comes out clean, 35 to 40 minutes.

Let it cool in the pan for 20 minutes. Run a paring knife between the edges of the cake and the pan to help release the cake and transfer to a wire rack to cool completely. Well wrapped, the cake will keep at room temperature for up to 2 days or up to 1 month in the freezer.

Make the Cognac soak: In a small saucepan, combine the water and sugar. Bring to a simmer over medium heat, stirring to help dissolve the sugar. Remove from the heat and add the Cognac. Set aside and allow to cool completely.

Make the buttercream: In a heavy-bottomed medium saucepan, whisk together the egg yolks and water. Add the sweetened condensed milk and mix to combine. Heat over medium-low and cook, whisking constantly, until the custard thickens to the consistency of sweetened condensed milk straight from the can and starts to bubble, 8 to 10 minutes (an instant-read thermometer will read between 195°F and 200°F / 90°C and 93°C). Sift in the cocoa powder and salt, add the vanillin, and whisk to combine. Set aside to cool to room temperature.

In a stand mixer fitted with the whisk, beat the butter on medium-high speed until very light and fluffy, scraping down the bottom and sides of the bowl periodically, 4 to 5 minutes. Reduce the speed to medium and add the cooled custard a big dollop at a time, beating to fully incorporate and scraping down the bowl as needed. Add the Cognac and mix to combine. Use right away or keep at room temperature in an airtight container for 1 day or in the refrigerator for up to 1 month.

Assemble the Prague cake: Cut the domed center off the top to even the cake out. Cut the cake horizontally into 3 even layers. Reserve the bottom layer for the top of the cake.

Place one of the other cake layers on a cake stand or plate. Brush the cake with ¼ cup (60 g) of the Cognac soak. Add ¼ cup (80 g) of the apricot jam and spread it evenly. Top with a generous

1¾ cups (about 300 g) of the buttercream and use an offset spatula to spread it into an even layer. Center a second cake layer over the first and press it down gently to secure it. Repeat with the soak, jam, and buttercream. Nestle the reserved bottom layer, flat-side up, on top. Brush with ¼ cup (60 g) Cognac soak. Warm the last of the jam again and strain through a fine-mesh sieve to remove any fruit pieces. Spread the strained apricot jam evenly over the top. Use the remaining buttercream to spread a very thin crumb coat over the sides to fill any gaps. (You will have some buttercream left over. Pair it with leftover cake scraps and soak for a chef's snack!). Refrigerate the cake until the jam no longer feels sticky to the touch and the buttercream is set, 3 to 4 hours.

When ready to glaze, bring 1 inch (2.5 cm) of water to a bare simmer in a medium pot over medium-low heat. In a heatproof bowl (that can sit over the pot of simmering water without touching the water), combine the chocolate, butter, corn syrup (if using), and salt and set over the pot. Stir occasionally to encourage melting and prevent the chocolate from burning. Once the mixture has melted and become smooth and glossy, remove from the heat. Allow to cool until it's about body temperature, 10 to 15 minutes, before glazing.

To glaze the cake, set it on a wire rack set over a baking sheet lined with parchment paper. Pour the glaze onto the center of the cake, and, working quickly, use an offset spatula to spread it across the top in an even and thin layer and to push the excess over the sides. Cover the sides completely.

If desired, rewarm excess glaze from the baking sheet and decorate the top with chocolate piping.

Refrigerate for 5 to 6 hours or overnight to allow the flavors to meld. Bring to room temperature at least 2 hours before serving. Refrigerated, the cake will last for 3 to 4 days.

NAPOLEON

They say that its exterior, coated in powdered-sugar-dusted flaky crumbs, symbolizes the snowy fields that helped defeat Napoleon's army in its invasion of Russia. Evolved from the French mille-feuille pastry of the same name, this Napoleon, with its many layers of golden pastry and rich, silken custard, is a darling in kitchens from Russia to Armenia and all the way to Uzbekistan. In my last book, *Everyday Cake*, I shared a variation my family makes using store-bought puff pastry and a whipped pastry cream (*crème légère*) filling. This recipe, on the other hand, is the real deal, asking you to mix your own dough (don't worry, it's not real puff) and make a *plombir* (read: extra luscious) buttercream. As for how to serve Napoleon, you have two options: Refrigerate the cake overnight to soften the layers or slice into it within hours of assembly. We prefer the latter, to preserve that heavenly textural contrast as much as possible, but I'll leave it up to you to decide.

••

1 egg
1 tablespoon apple cider vinegar
Ice-cold water, for the dough
2⅔ cups (345 g) all-purpose flour
1 teaspoon kosher salt
1 cup plus 2 tablespoons (250 g) unsalted butter,
    frozen
Plombir Buttercream (page 228) made with
    sweetened condensed milk, or Creme Mousseline
Powdered sugar, for dusting

SERVES 8 TO 10

In a liquid measuring cup, whisk together the egg and vinegar. Then add ice water until the mixture measures ½ cup (120 ml). Set aside in the fridge or freezer to chill.

In a large bowl, whisk together the flour and salt. Grate the butter on the large holes on a box grater, using a fork to mix it into the flour periodically to keep it from clumping. Working quickly, comb your fingers through the mixture to separate the butter shreds and evenly coat them in flour. As you work, rub the butter between your fingers to flatten then into flat shards.

Drizzle half of the liquid over the flour-butter mixture. Using a fork, toss the dry ingredients until no visible pockets of liquid remain. Add the remaining liquid, a few tablespoons at a time, and toss again to incorporate after each addition. When you squeeze the dough, it should hold together easily but still be a bit rough. With wide, open hands, scoop the shaggy mixture from the bottom and then bring it up and over, pressing it back down on the rest of the ingredients. Continue to gently knead the dough until all the dry, floury bits are incorporated and the dough is one cohesive mass. Scrape the dough onto a large piece of plastic wrap and use the wrap to help shape the dough into a log 6 inches (15 cm) long. Wrap and refrigerate for at least 2 hours, ideally overnight, and up to 2 days (frozen, the dough will keep for 2 months).

Preheat the oven to 425°F (220°C). Cut 6 pieces of parchment paper the size of a baking sheet.

Remove the dough from the refrigerator and divide into 6 equal portions (about 120 g each). Form each piece into an even, flat disc. Working with one at a time (while keeping the others covered and refrigerated), lightly flour a work surface and the dough. Roll out the dough into an 11-inch (28 cm) round, reflouring as needed. Place on a piece of parchment paper and dock all over with a fork. Transfer to a baking sheet and chill in the refrigerator while you work on the next disc. Repeat with the remaining pieces of dough, stacking the parchment papers with the rolled-out rounds on top of each of other as you go.

Once the first round has chilled for 20 minutes, transfer to another baking sheet and bake until the pastry is puffed up and evenly golden, 8 to 10 minutes. Transfer to a wire rack and allow to cool. Repeat with the remaining rounds.

Once cooled, working with one piece at a time, lightly place a 9-inch (23 cm) cake ring or cake pan onto the center of the pastry and use a paring knife to trim the pastry into an even 9-inch (23 cm) round. Transfer the trimmings to a medium bowl and repeat with the remaining pastry rounds. Break the trimmings into small and medium crumbs and set aside.

Lightly set the first layer on top of a cake plate or stand. Cut or tear one of the sheets of parchment paper into four long strips and tuck them underneath the cake to keep the plate clean. Scoop about ⅓ cup (about 100 g) of the buttercream onto the center of the first layer and evenly spread to the edges. Repeat the process, stacking and frosting the cake, pressing down on it periodically, to break any large bubbles, until you have 6 layers. Once you get to the last layer, frost the top and sides of the cake with the remaining buttercream—it doesn't have to be perfect, and you will have some buttercream left over. Press the cake crumbs into the sides of the cake and sprinkle them over the top in an even layer. Remove the paper strips.

Dust the top with powdered sugar and serve immediately or within 3 to 4 hours of assembly. As it continues to sit, the cake will get softer—if you prefer Napoleon this way, allow to sit over-night in the refrigerator before serving. Well wrapped, the cake will last in the refrigerator for 3 to 4 days.

Note: *If you've ever worked with pie dough, you've got this. Just keep the two cardinal rules in mind so that your pastry turns out as flaky and tender as possible. One: Always keep your ingredients and dough cold (if you see your butter softening too much or the dough starting to stick and feel unwieldy, just pop everything back in the fridge to give it, and yourself, some time to chill out). Two: Allow the dough plenty of time to rest, after both mixing and rolling, so that the gluten relaxes (this will also prevent shrinkage).*

BISKVITNYI TORTE

BERRIES AND CREAM SPONGE CAKE

This *biskvitnyi torte* (sponge), soaked in an Earl Grey–Cognac syrup and laden with macerated strawberries and a custard buttercream, holds a special place in my heart as it is my family's go-to birthday cake. The whole top is hidden under a bonanza of berries and then drizzled with chocolate. Then to really gild the lily, the sides are covered in cake crumbs (if you haven't noticed by now, a common theme in Slavic bakes—and evidence of the no-waste ethos). I have so many fond memories of spending afternoons in the kitchen with my mom and Aunt Olga before a big party, dividing and conquering all the components and assembly. We'd always bake it in the same 10-inch (25 cm) metal pan so that the gargantuan result was enough to feed our whole horde of sweet tooths (and then some). I learned this sponge method of whipping a meringue, then adding yolks, for the base from my aunt—it's a great and easy primer into the world of "egg-foam" cakes.

••

CAKE
Neutral oil, for the pan
1¼ cups (160 g) all-purpose flour
2½ tablespoons (20 g) cornstarch
¾ cup plus 1 tablespoon (175 g) granulated
  sugar, divided
6 eggs, separated, at room temperature
½ teaspoon kosher salt

EARL GREY–COGNAC SOAK
1 Earl Grey tea bag
3 tablespoons (45 g) granulated sugar
½ cup (120 g) boiling water
2 tablespoons Cognac or brandy

MACERATED STRAWBERRIES
1 pound (450 g) strawberries, hulled, halved or
  quartered if large
3 tablespoons (45 g) granulated sugar
Pinch of kosher salt

ASSEMBLY
Plombir Buttercream (page 228) made with
  sweetened condensed milk, or Creme Mousseline
Hulled fresh strawberries, blueberries, and
  raspberries
1 ounce (28 g) dark chocolate (optional), melted

SERVES 8 TO 10

Make the cake: Preheat the oven to 350°F (180°C). Line a 9-inch (23 cm) springform or cake pan (at least 3 inches / 7.5 cm deep) with a round of parchment paper. Lightly grease only the paper.

In a bowl, combine the flour, cornstarch, and 1 tablespoon of the sugar. Sift together three times.

In a stand mixer fitted with the whisk, whip the egg whites and salt on medium speed until the egg whites resemble a thick, dense white foam, 1½ to 2 minutes. With the mixer still running, gradually add the remaining ¾ cup (175 g) sugar a few tablespoons at a time. Continue to beat until the whites are thick, glossy, and opaque and hold stiff peaks, 3 to 5 minutes. Add the egg yolks one at a time, beating well after each addition.

Sprinkle one-third of the flour mixture onto the batter and use a rubber spatula to gently, but confidently fold it by hand until just combined. Repeat with the rest of the flour mixture in two batches, being careful not to deflate the batter.

Gently guide the batter into the prepared pan and smooth out the top. Run a toothpick in a spiral motion, starting from the center and working your way out, to pop any large air bubbles.

Bake, without opening the oven door at any point, until the cake springs back when pressed in the center and a tester comes out clean, 35 to 40 minutes.

Let it cool in the pan for 20 minutes. Run a paring knife between the edges of the cake and

the pan to help release the cake and transfer to a wire rack to cool completely. Well wrapped, the cake will keep at room temperature for up to 2 days or up to 1 month in the freezer.

Make the Earl Grey-Cognac soak: Add the tea bag to a large mug and pour in the boiling water. Cover with a small plate and allow to brew for 4 to 5 minutes. Remove the tea bag. Gradually add the sugar, stirring to dissolve before adding more. Once all the sugar has dissolved, stir in the Cognac. Set aside to cool completely.

Macerate the strawberries: In a medium bowl, toss the strawberries with the sugar and salt. Let sit for about 30 minutes, stirring occasionally. The strawberries will soften significantly and release their juices to create a pool of bright-red syrup. Use a fork to crush the strawberries to create a chunky, jammy mash. Set aside.

Assemble the cake: Cut the domed top off the cake (⅛ to ¼ inch / 3 to 6 mm) to even it out and set the trimmed piece aside for later. Cut the cake horizontally into 3 even layers. Reserve the bottom layer for the top of the cake.

Place one of the other cake layers on a cake stand or plate. Brush the cake with 2 tablespoons of the soak. Spoon half of the macerated strawberries over the top in an even layer. Top with about 1¼ cups (about 250 g) of the buttercream and use an offset spatula to spread it into an even layer. Center a second cake layer over the first and press it gently to secure it. Repeat with the soak, strawberries, and buttercream. Nestle the reserved bottom layer, flat-side up, on top. Brush with 3 tablespoons (45 ml) of the soak. Use some buttercream to spread a very thin crumb coat over the top and sides to fill any gaps. Refrigerate the cake for 30 minutes to set the buttercream.

Meanwhile, take the reserved cake trimming and break it into crumbs in a medium bowl.

Use the remaining buttercream to evenly frost the top and sides of the cake. Press the crumbs into the sides of the cake. Fully cover the top of the cake with berries. If desired, drizzle with melted chocolate. Refrigerate for 5 to 6 hours or overnight to allow the flavors to meld and the cake layers to soak. Bring to room temperature at least 2 hours before serving. Refrigerated, the cake will last for up to 4 days.

APPLE SHARLOTKA

If you own my last book, *Everyday Cake*, then you are probably already familiar with sharlotka. Simple and not-too-sweet, this apple tea cake seems to be up every home cook's sleeve—sometimes, it may be the *only* thing they bake. The recipe—even more pared down than my last one—is easy enough to remember and it all comes together in less time than it takes for your oven to preheat. Whether you've got unexpected guests knocking on your door or you're fending off a major sugar craving (and failing), sharlotka will fit the bill. Once in the oven, the lemon-scented fruit cooks and softens just enough to still retain a satisfying bite while the batter turns into a soft sponge with a meringue-like crust that shatters when cut into. It's our go-to "Should we make something for dessert?" cake, and I hope it becomes yours, too!

You want to use sweet-tart baking apples, like Pink Lady, Granny Smith, or Jonagold.

....

Unsalted butter or neutral oil, for the pan
Grated zest and juice of 1 small lemon
4 medium apples (about 1¾ pounds / 795 g total),
*   cored and cut into ½-inch (1.3 cm) chunks*
4 eggs, at room temperature
1 cup (200 g) granulated sugar
¼ teaspoon baking soda
1½ teaspoons vanilla extract
½ teaspoon kosher salt
1 cup (130 g) all-purpose flour
6 to 8 thin shards of cold unsalted butter
Powdered sugar, for dusting
Whipped cream or ice cream, for serving

SERVES 6 TO 8

Preheat the oven to 350°F (180°C). Grease a 9-inch (23 cm) square pan or similar 2½-quart (2.4 L) baking dish. Line with parchment paper, leaving overhang on two sides.

Set aside 1 teaspoon lemon juice for the batter. In a medium bowl, toss together the apples, lemon zest, and remaining lemon juice. Set aside.

In a stand mixer fitted with the whisk, whip the eggs on high speed until uniformly yellow and very foamy, about 1 minute. Gradually add the granulated sugar in four additions, beating well before adding more. Continue to beat until thick ribbons form (when you lift the whisk, the batter will drizzle off into a thick stream that will slowly dissolve into the batter in the bowl), 8 to 10 minutes.

In a small bowl, mix together the baking soda and the reserved 1 teaspoon lemon juice into a fizzy paste. Reduce the mixer speed to low and add the paste to the batter, along with the vanilla and salt. Mix to combine.

Sift half of the flour into the batter and, using a rubber spatula, gently fold it in by hand until just combined. Sift and fold in the remaining flour.

Arrange half the apples in an even layer in the pan. Gently guide half the batter over the apples, spreading and pressing down into an even layer. Repeat with the remaining apples and batter. Tuck the shards of butter evenly into the batter.

Bake until the cake is a deep golden brown and firm and a paring knife inserted into the center comes out clean, 35 to 45 minutes.

Allow the cake to cool for 30 minutes before using the overhang to lift it out of the pan and transferring it to a wire rack. Dust with powdered sugar and serve warm or cooled with whipped cream or ice cream. Well wrapped, this cake keeps at room temperature for 3 to 4 days.

BELOCHKI

LITTLE "SQUIRREL" CAKES

As fun to make as they are to serve and eat, these petite cakes are frosted and covered in crumbs to resemble *belochki*, little bushy squirrels. The yellow butter cake itself is light, tender, and moist, while the frosting is one you'll want to eat by the spoonful. The recipe makes a lot, so think of them as your Slavic cupcakes—good for parties and potlucks. Against common cake wisdom, we find belochki just as delicious chilled as they are at room temperature.

••

Unsalted butter or neutral oil, for the pan
3 cups (390 g) all-purpose flour
4 teaspoons baking powder
1½ teaspoons kosher salt
Grated zest of 1 lemon
1½ cups (300 g) granulated sugar
1 cup (225 g) unsalted butter, at room temperature
5 eggs, at room temperature
1½ teaspoons vanilla extract
Generous ¾ cup (200 g) sour cream, at room temperature
Plombir Buttercream made with sweetened condensed milk (page 228), or Crème Mousseline (page 229)

MAKES ABOUT FIFTEEN 3-INCH (7.5 CM) CAKES

Preheat the oven to 350°F (180°C). Lightly grease a 13 × 18-inch (33 × 46 cm) baking sheet and line the bottom with parchment paper.

In a medium bowl, whisk together the flour, baking powder, and salt.

In a stand mixer fitted with the paddle, rub the lemon zest into the sugar until it is fragrant and has taken on a yellowish hue. Add the butter and beat on medium speed until light and fluffy, 4 to 5 minutes, scraping down the bottom and sides of the bowl often. Add the eggs one at a time, beating well after each addition and scraping down the bowl as needed. The mixture will look a bit curdled at this point—that's okay. Beat in the vanilla.

Reduce the speed to low and add the flour mixture in three additions, alternating with two additions of the sour cream. Mix until just combined and scrape down the bowl as needed. Scrape the batter into the prepared baking sheet and spread into an even layer.

Bake until the cake is golden and the center springs back when pressed, 22 to 28 minutes, rotating the pan front to back halfway through.

Transfer to a wire rack and let cool completely in the pan. Run a table knife between the edges of the cake and the pan and invert to remove the cake from the pan onto a work surface.

Using a 3-inch (7.5 cm) biscuit cutter (or the rim of a large glass), cut out rounds in the cake—you should get 15. Take whatever is left and break it into crumbs in a medium bowl.

Cut a round in half horizontally into 2 thin layers. Spread an even layer of buttercream over the bottom half. Top it with the second layer, cut side down. Transfer to a baking sheet and repeat with the remaining rounds. If you have time, refrigerate for 30 minutes—resting helps set the crumb, making it easier to frost.

Frost each round all over with the buttercream. Working over the bowl of crumbs, press the crumbs into the top and sides of the cake until you have a "little squirrel." Repeat the process until all the rounds are frosted and crumbed. Allow to sit for a few hours at room temperature or in the refrigerator for flavors to meld before serving. The frosted cakes can be covered and refrigerated for up to 4 days.

KEKS ACCORDING TO GOST

GOST, an acronym for *gosudarstvennyi standart*, or state standard, regulated everything from the design of vacuum tubes to recipes for jam in the Soviet Union. You knew, for better or for worse, exactly what you were getting. As a result, a lot of my mom's old baking recipes are written "according to GOST." Take this *keks*, for example, a classic pound-cake-style loaf studded with raisins. For my mom, it tastes just like the one from her childhood—sold at the local bakery by the gram—because it *is* the same one. The rum soak for the raisins and citrus zest are definitely not part of the original recipe, but they add a subtle je ne sais quoi. (And okay, we go a little heavier on the dried fruit, too, but just look the other way.) Keep in mind that keks may be a bit different from what you're used to. It's somewhat dense, but otherwise very buttery and crumbly, with a lovely burnished crust. It's a taste of the past, and it pairs exceptionally well with tea.

· ·

2 cups (280 g) raisins
⅓ cup (80 g) light rum, dark rum, or water
Unsalted butter and all-purpose flour, for the pan
2¼ cups plus 1 tablespoon (300 g) all-purpose flour
1 teaspoon baking powder
1 teaspoon kosher salt
1 cup plus 2 tablespoons (225 g) granulated sugar
1 teaspoon vanilla sugar
Grated zest of 1 lemon or ½ orange
1 cup (225 g) unsalted butter, at room temperature
180 g lightly beaten eggs (about 3½ large eggs), at room temperature
Powdered sugar, for dusting

SERVES 6 TO 8

In a medium bowl, toss the raisins with the rum and set aside, stirring occasionally, to soak for 2 to 3 hours and up to overnight. The raisins should absorb most of the rum during this period.

Preheat the oven to 325°F (160°C). Generously grease and flour a 9 × 5-inch (23 × 13 cm) loaf pan, preferably light-colored.

In a medium bowl, whisk together the flour, baking powder, and salt. In another medium bowl, combine the sugar and vanilla sugar. Add the citrus zest and rub it into the sugar with your fingers until the sugar is infused with the citrus aroma and flavor.

In a stand mixer fitted with the paddle, beat the butter on medium speed until light and fluffy, about 3 minutes (this can also be done in a large bowl using a hand mixer). Turn the speed down to medium-low and gradually add the granulated sugar a bit at a time. Increase the speed to medium again and continue beating until the mixture is very light and fluffy, 3 to 4 minutes. Reduce the speed to medium-low and gradually add the beaten egg, beating well after each addition and scraping down the bottom and sides of the bowl as needed.

Drain the raisins, making sure all excess liquid drains—pat dry if needed. Add to the batter and mix on low to incorporate. Add half of the flour mixture and beat until just combined. Scrape down the bowl and gently fold in the remaining flour mixture by hand. Scrape the batter into the prepared pan and smooth out the top.

Bake the cake until a tester inserted in the center comes out clean, 1 hour 20 minutes to 1½ hours.

Let the cake cool in the pan for 20 minutes. Run a knife between the cake and sides of the pan and turn the cake out onto a wire rack to cool completely.

Once the cake has cooled, set it on a platter and generously dust it with powdered sugar until the cake is fully blanketed. Cut into thin slices to serve. Well wrapped, the cake keeps for up to 5 days at room temperature.

TRUBOCHKI

CREAM HORNS

These *trubochki*, or "little horns," would always be the first to go from our holiday cookie platter. They're super impressive looking, but straightforward to make: Roll out some puff pastry (store-bought is fine), cut into thin long strips, and then wrap around special metal cones before baking off. Though the hollow pastries are usually filled with sweetened condensed milk whipped with butter, our preference is crème mousseline—which is not only lighter and silkier, but more refined.

You will need twenty 5½-inch (14 cm) baking cone molds. You can also use smaller 3½-inch (9 cm) cones or even cannoli metal tubes. If using this smaller cone size, cut the pastry sheet in half crosswise after you've cut them into strips. This recipe makes a lot of trubochki, so feel free to halve the recipe if baking for a smaller group.

• •

Melted unsalted butter or neutral oil, for the molds
All-purpose flour, for dusting
One (17.3-ounce / 490 g) box frozen puff pastry, thawed but chilled
Egg wash: 1 egg, lightly beaten with 1 tablespoon milk, cream, or water
Crème Mousseline (page 229) or Plombir Buttercream made with sweetened condensed milk (page 228)
Powdered sugar, for dusting

MAKES 20 PASTRY HORNS

Line two large baking sheets with parchment paper. Lightly brush the baking molds with the melted butter or oil to grease.

On a lightly floured surface, unfold 1 puff pastry sheet (keep the other refrigerated). Roll out the dough into a 10½ × 15-inch (27 × 38 cm) rectangle. Trim the long sides to make them even. With a short side facing you, cut the dough vertically into strips 1 inch (2.5 cm) wide—you should get 10.

Take one strip and gently tug along its length to stretch it to measure 20 inches (50 cm). Grab a baking mold and, starting at the pointed end, wrap the pastry strip around the mold in a spiral, with each layer overlapping slightly by about ¼ inch (6 mm). I find it helpful to direct the dough with one hand, while I twirl the mold with the other. Once you get to the end, press down on the seam to seal, making sure it's not covering the edge of the mold. Place on the baking sheet seam side down and refrigerate. Repeat with the remaining strips and refrigerate for 30 minutes to chill the dough. Repeat the process with the other puff pastry sheet.

Meanwhile, position racks in the top and bottom thirds of the oven and preheat the oven to 375°F (190°C).

Once all the pastry horns are chilled, brush them all over with egg wash. Transfer to the oven and bake the horns until the pastry is golden brown and firm, 15 to 20 minutes, switching racks and rotating the pans front to back halfway through.

Transfer to a wire rack to cool. I find that it's easiest to unmold the pastry while everything is still hot. So as soon as your fingertips can handle the heat, hold on to the mold with one hand while you gently and carefully push the pastry off with the other. Allow to cool completely.

Transfer the crème mousseline to a piping bag fitted with a regular or fluted tip. It's best to use and pipe the mousseline immediately—just leave the filled trubochki at room temperature uncovered. Fill each pastry horn with the mousseline and dust the outsides with powdered sugar.

Transfer to a serving plate. Serve immediately or ideally within 3 to 4 hours of filling. (If making in advance, do not store in an airtight container, otherwise they will get soggy.) Any leftovers can be wrapped in foil and refrigerated for up to 3 days.

ROGALIKI

SLAVIC-STYLE RUGELACH

In Georgia, these little roll-up cookies, a specialty of southern Russia and Ukraine, were referred to as *cigaretki,* "little cigarettes." Traditionally the dough is yeasted, but my Aunt's recipe is closer to American Jewish rugelach. The filling gives big baklava vibes with its honeyed raisins and nuts and the sour-cream-laden dough is buttery and crisp and rolls out like a dream. But unlike their Jewish counterpart, these *rogaliki* concentrate their filling right in the center, rather than thinly spreading it—giving you a big ol' dose of the good stuff when bitten into.

··

DOUGH
1 cup (225 g) unsalted butter, at room temperature
2 tablespoons granulated sugar
1 teaspoon kosher salt
1 egg yolk
One (8-ounce / 225 g) container sour cream
2 cups plus 2½ tablespoons (280 g) all-purpose
    flour, plus more for dusting

FILLING
⅔ cup (75 g) chopped toasted walnuts
¾ cup (115) golden raisins
¼ cup (50 g) granulated sugar
Generous pinch of kosher salt
2 tablespoons (45 g) runny honey
1 tablespoon (15 g) egg white

Powdered sugar, for dusting

MAKES 32 SMALL COOKIES

Make the dough: In a large bowl, using a wooden spoon, mix the butter, sugar, and salt until well combined. Mix in the egg yolk and then the sour cream. The mixture will look a bit curdled—that's okay. Add the flour all at once and mix just until it comes together into a shaggy dough.

Turn the dough out onto a work surface and gently knead a few times until all the dry, floury bits are incorporated and the dough is one cohesive mass.

Divide the dough in half, form into round discs, and wrap in plastic wrap. Refrigerate for at least

2 hours and up to 2 days before proceeding. (If making ahead, the dough can be frozen for up to 2 months.)

Make the filling: In a food processor, pulse the walnuts, raisins, granulated sugar, and salt until finely chopped. Add the honey and egg white and pulse until combined and the filling holds together. (Alternatively, finely chop the walnuts and raisins by hand and stir everything together.)

Assemble the rogaliki: When ready to bake, line two baking sheets with parchment paper.

Working with one disc of dough at a time on a lightly floured surface, roll the dough out into a 14-inch (36 cm) round. Dust the surface, rolling pin, and dough as needed to keep it from sticking.

With a sharp knife or pizza cutter, cut the dough into 16 equal wedges. Place a rounded 1 teaspoon of filling at the base of each wedge. Fold the bottom edge over the filling and then continue to roll the dough up like a croissant until the pointy end is tucked under the cookie. Lightly push down to secure the base. Transfer to the prepared baking sheet, point side down. Transfer to the refrigerator and chill for 20 to 30 minutes. Meanwhile repeat process repeat with the second disc of dough. (The assembled cookies can be frozen for up to 2 months.)

Bake the rogaliki: While the cookies are chilling, position racks in the top and bottom third of the oven and preheat the oven to 375°F (190°C).

Bake the cookies until puffed and starting to turn golden on top, 18 to 22 minutes, switching racks and rotating the sheets front to back half-way through.

Transfer the cookies to a wire rack to cool. Generously dust with powdered sugar before serving warm or at room temperature. Any leftover cookies can be stored in an airtight container at room temperature for up to 1 week.

ORESHKI

WALNUT-SHAPED COOKIES WITH DULCE DE LECHE

I can't think of a more Soviet dessert than these "little nuts." Comprising buttery shortbread and a dulce de leche filling, *oreshki* were invented by the Soviet state and enjoyed not only throughout the former republics but in the Warsaw Pact countries as well. For instance, in Romania, they are known as *nuci* and in Hungary, *dió sütemény*. The most intriguing thing about these sandwich cookies is that they were originally made on the stovetop in a specially designed hinged pan (called an *oreshnitsa*, literally "something that makes nuts") with molds in the shape of nutshells. Some families might still have their oreshnitsa from the old country, but I give you permission to buy yours online, just like I did. For many, oreshki are a taste of childhood, so don't be surprised if, when presented to those of us from the diaspora, we fall upon them like wolves.

••

DOUGH
⅔ cup (135 g) granulated sugar
1 egg, at room temperature
2 teaspoons baking powder
1 teaspoon vanilla extract
¾ teaspoon fine sea salt
½ cup (115 g) unsalted butter, melted and slightly cooled
½ cup (120 g) mayonnaise, at room temperature
3¼ cups (425 g) all-purpose flour
Neutral oil, for the pan

DULCE DE LECHE FILLING
½ cup (115 g) unsalted butter, at room temperature
Scant ⅛ teaspoon vanillin, or 1 teaspoon vanilla sugar or vanilla extract
Generous pinch of kosher salt
One (13.4-ounce / 380 g) can dulce de leche or Homemade Dulce de Leche (page 204)

Powdered sugar, for dusting

MAKES 40 TO 45 COOKIES

Make the dough: In a large bowl, whisk together the granulated sugar, egg, baking powder, vanilla, and salt until the mixture has slightly lightened, about 1 minute. Whisk in the melted butter and the mayonnaise and mix until fully incorporated.

Switch to a wooden spoon. Add half the flour and mix to incorporate. Add the remaining flour and mix to fully incorporate. The dough should be soft, malleable, with a bit of a sheen, but not tacky. Wrap in plastic wrap and refrigerate for 45 minutes.

Remove the dough from the refrigerator. Pinch off a rounded 1½-teaspoon piece of dough and roll it into a ball. For a 9-mold oreshnitsa, it should weigh 10 grams. Set it on a tray or baking sheet. Continue until no dough remains—you should get 80 to 85 pieces.

Very lightly grease the inside cavities of the oreshnitsa. Set atop a burner and preheat over medium heat for a few minutes until very hot. Place a ball of dough into each cavity (it should sizzle upon contact) and close the pan. While holding the handles closed, cook until the outside of the cookies are lightly browned, 1 to 1½ minutes. To check how far along they are, quickly flip the pan and open it. If not done yet, flip back over and continue to cook.

Once lightly browned, flip the pan and cook for about another minute, or until the cookies are golden on top and lightly browned on the inside. Tip the shells into a large bowl. Repeat the process until all the dough is baked. Allow to cool completely. Stored in an airtight container, the unfilled shells will keep for 1 week at room temperature.

Make the dulce de leche filling: In a stand mixer fitted with the paddle, beat the butter, vanillin, and salt on medium speed, scraping down the bottom and sides of bowl as needed, for 1 to 2 minutes to smooth it out. Add the dulce de leche and beat until light and fluffy, 3 to 4 minutes.

Assemble the oreshki: Use a paring knife or scissors to trim any excess from the shells. Working with one shell at a time, use an offset spatula or little spoon to fill each shell with the dulce de leche so that it is flush with the sides. Once the shells are filled, form the oreshki by pressing two halves together. Transfer to a serving plate and dust with powdered sugar. The cookies are crispy the day that they are made but soften overtime, which is how many prefer them. Stored at room temperature (do not refrigerate, or you will ruin the texture!), the oreshki will last for 4 to 5 days.

VARIATION

Baked Oreshki: *You can also make the oreshki in the oven by forming them in individual molds. Preheat the oven to 350°F (180°C). Place a ball of dough into the center of a mold and, using your thumb, press in the dough to evenly line the inside—it should be ⅛ inch (3 mm) thick. Trim any excess. Transfer the mold to a baking sheet with the dough side up. Repeat until all the molds are lined, arranging the molds in an even layer on the baking sheet. Working in batches, depending on the size of your baking sheet, bake the cookies until lightly golden on both sides, 18 to 22 minutes. To check for doneness, remove one of the molds using a pair of tongs and invert. If the cookie doesn't fall out, lightly tap to help release it. Keep baking if not golden yet. Once baked, removed from the oven and allow to cool for 10 minutes. While the cookies are still warm, invert the molds to release the cookies. Flip the cookies so that the cavities are facing up and allow to cool completely before filling.*

FURTHER NOTES ON ORESHKI

- The hinged metal pan that makes oreshki will work only with gas stoves. If you don't have a gas stove, you can bake the cookies in individual metal molds in the oven (see Variation). Just know that the cookies come out a little less crispy this way.

- I recommend getting a 9-mold oreshnitsa, which produces just the right size cookie.

- I also recommend laying out a piece of foil around your burner (just cut a hole out from a square) to catch the grease that will reliably leak out while the cookies cook.

- Just like the first pancake, the first round of shells never quite turns out. Cook time depends on your stove and oreshnitsa, so expect it to take a couple of rounds to find your groove. Once you do, it'll be smooth and quick sailing from there.

MINT PRYANIKI

MINT COOKIES

This recipe is for my mom, who loved these mint-flavored cookies as a child. They're light and tender and get rubbed in a syrup that gives *pryaniki* their signature opaque-white mottled glaze. Served with tea (or a big glass of milk!), they make for a great snack or post-meal treat.

....

DOUGH
4⅔ cups (605 g) all-purpose flour, plus more for dusting
1¼ cups (250 g) granulated sugar
1½ teaspoons kosher salt
1 cup (240 g) whole milk
3½ tablespoons (50 g) neutral oil
1 egg
1 egg yolk
1¼ teaspoons peppermint extract
1 teaspoon vanilla extract
1 tablespoon baking powder

GLAZE
½ cup (100 g) granulated sugar
3 tablespoons (45 g) water
½ teaspoon peppermint extract
4 drops of lemon juice

MAKES ABOUT 36 COOKIES

Preheat the oven to 350°F (180°C). Line two baking sheets with parchment paper.

Make the dough: In a large bowl, whisk together 1 cup (130 g) of the flour, sugar, and salt.

In a small saucepan, scald the milk over medium heat—until bubbles appear around the edges of the pan. Pour the scalded milk into the flour-sugar mixture and whisk until combined and lump free. Quickly whisk in the oil, followed by the whole egg, egg yolk, and peppermint and vanilla extracts. Set aside to cool for 10 to 15 minutes.

Meanwhile, in a medium bowl, whisk together the remaining 3⅔ cups (475 g) flour and the baking powder.

Fold in half of the flour/baking powder mixture into the large bowl and once it's mostly incorporated, add the remaining half. When the dough starts to become tough to mix, switch to your hands and knead the dough a few times to bring it together. It will be a tad sticky. Cover the bowl with a plate and refrigerate for 15 to 20 minutes, or until it's no longer warm, to make it easier to work with.

On a lightly floured surface, turn out the dough, press it into a disc, and dust it with flour. Roll out the dough into a round ⅜-inch (1 cm) thick. Using a 2-inch (5 cm) biscuit cutter (or the rim of a glass), cut out rounds and transfer to the prepared baking sheets, leaving 1 inch (2.5 cm) of space between them. Gather the scraps and reroll to cut out more rounds.

Bake until the cookies are firm to the touch and golden on the bottom, 13 to 17 minutes.

Allow to cool completely before glazing.

Make the glaze: In a small saucepan, heat the sugar and water over medium-low heat, stirring to help the sugar dissolve. Once it comes to a simmer, cook until the syrup reaches about 230°F (110°C), about 5 minutes. The syrup will slowly drip from the spoon, and when you continuously tap a drop of syrup between your index finger and thumb, it'll produce a thin white thread after some time. Remove from the heat and add the peppermint extract and lemon juice. Allow to cool for a few minutes.

Finish the pryaniki: Place half of the cookies in a large bowl and drizzle half of the syrup over them. Using your hand, rub the glaze all over into the cookies—it doesn't need to be a thick layer, just enough to coat. Once they're sufficiently coated, place them on a wire rack and allow the glaze to set for a couple of hours before eating. Store in an airtight container at room temperature for up to 5 days.

GATA

ARMENIAN BUTTER PASTRY

This buttery, flaky Armenian pastry—called *gata* or *nazook* depending on where you're from within Armenia—falls somewhere between a rugelach and strudel. It was very popular in Georgia when my family lived in T'bilisi (and continues to be), although there they know it better as *kada*. It's still a cherished recipe for us and elicits nothing less than giddy delight when it comes out for tea. As it should! What it lacks in bells and whistles, *gata* makes up for in its striking cross section of spiraled layers.

To achieve the mesmerizing effect, the short-crust-like dough is rolled out, covered with a vanilla-scented streusel called *khoritz*, and then folded up like a carpet. A crosshatch pattern on top gives it its trademark look, as do the serrated edges of each individual pastry (you'll have to source a "crinkle" cutter). In my opinion, gata is best fresh from the oven, when the golden, crispy exterior gives way to a still-warm melt-in-your-mouth inside. That's why I'll often make and freeze the pastries ahead of time so I can bake them off as the occasion (craving) arises.

••

Note: *If you've worked with pie dough before, you'll have a leg up in preparing this pastry. Make sure your dough is always cold, and if it starts to soften or stick too much, don't be afraid to stick it back in the fridge. If your kitchen is especially hot, stick your bowl with the dry ingredients in the freezer for 20 minutes to help keep the butter chilled. Formed and portioned pastries can be frozen for up to 2 months. Bake straight from the freezer and allow for a few extra minutes in the oven.*

DOUGH

2 egg yolks, fridge cold
Generous ¾ cup (200 g) sour cream, well chilled
3 cups plus 1 tablespoon (400 g) all-purpose flour
1 teaspoon kosher salt
1⅓ cups (300 g) unsalted butter, frozen

FILLING

2 cups (260 g) all-purpose flour, plus more for dusting
10½ tablespoons (150 g) unsalted butter, frozen
1 cup (200 g) granulated sugar
1 packet (9 g) (scant 2 teaspoons) vanilla sugar, or ⅛ teaspoon vanillin
¼ teaspoon kosher salt

ASSEMBLY

2 egg whites, for brushing the inside
1 egg yolk, for the egg wash

MAKES 16 TO 18 PASTRIES

Make the dough: In a small bowl, whisk the egg yolks into the sour cream and set in the fridge or freezer while you work.

In a large bowl, whisk together the flour and salt. Grate the butter on the large holes of a box grater into the flour, using a fork to mix it in periodically so that the butter doesn't clump. Working quickly, comb your fingers through the mixture to separate the butter shreds and evenly coat them in flour. As you do this, rub the butter into the flour until the mixture resembles coarse crumbs.

Make a well in the flour-butter mixture and pour in the sour cream / egg yolk mixture. Using a fork, stir the liquid into the butter-flour mixture until no visible pockets of liquid remain (you'll be tempted to add more liquid, but don't). With wide, open hands, scoop the shaggy mixture from the bottom and then bring it up and over, pressing it back down on the rest of the ingredients and gently knead. Rotate the bowl a quarter-turn and repeat—the dough will slowly start to come together. Continue to gently mix

GATA, CONTINUED

and knead the dough this way until all the dry, floury bits are incorporated and the dough is one cohesive mass. Divide the dough in half, form each into a rectangle, and wrap in plastic wrap. Refrigerate for at least 2 hours, ideally overnight, and up to 2 days.

Make the filling: Place the flour in a medium bowl. Grate the butter into the bowl on the small holes of a box grater, using a fork to mix it into the flour every few tablespoons so that the butter doesn't clump. Stir in the granulated sugar, vanilla sugar, and salt and then use your hands to rub the flour-butter mixture together until it resembles coarse sand and holds together when you squeeze a handful. Refrigerate while you roll out the dough.

Assemble the gata: Line two large baking sheets with parchment paper.

Take one block of dough and let it sit out at room temperature to slightly soften, about 5 minutes.

I also like to smack the dough with the rolling pin, turning it occasionally, to make it more pliable and to even it out.

Roll out the dough on a very well-floured surface, dusting the dough with more flour as needed to prevent it from sticking, into a 15 × 17-inch (38 × 43 cm) rectangle. If at any point the dough begins to soften too much, return it to the fridge to chill it down before proceeding.

Brush the dough with beaten egg white and sprinkle half the filling in an even layer, leaving a ¾-inch (2 cm) border around the edges. Gently press the filling into the dough. Then, starting at the long edge nearest to you, fold the dough 1 inch (2.5 cm) over the filling. From there,

carefully roll up the dough like a carpet into a log shape. If the dough sticks to the counter as you roll, use a bench scraper to help release it. For a slightly cleaner look, you can also fold the shorter border edges in before rolling.

Using light pressure, slightly flatten and even out the log with the rolling pin. Refrigerate the log for 30 minutes (or freeze for 20 minutes) to firm up and set the dough. In the meantime, roll out and fill the second block of dough and place it in the fridge to chill once you're done.

When ready to bake, preheat the oven to 350°F (180°C).

Working with and baking one log at a time, brush the top and edges of the log with the beaten egg yolk and use a fork to make a cross-hatch pattern on top. Using a "crinkle" or wavy-ridge pastry cutter (a serrated or sharp

knife or bench scraper will also work), cut the log at a diagonal into pieces 1½ to 2 inches (4 to 5 cm) thick. (Cutting them into 2-inch / 5 cm triangles is also traditional.) Use a spatula to carefully transfer the gata onto the baking sheet, leaving 2 inches (5 cm) of space between the pastries. If you have time, chill the pastries for another 20 to 30 minutes.

Bake until the tops are dark golden brown and the sides are firm and crisp, 30 to 35 minutes, rotating the pan front to back halfway through. Remove from the oven and allow to cool while you bake the other set of pastries.

Serve while still warm or at room temperature. The gata are best the day they are baked, but will keep at room temperature, covered and wrapped with a tea towel, for up 2 days.

PLOMBIR BUTTERCREAM

If you can't tell from all the cream-filled cakes and pastries in this chapter, my family staunchly believes that the more cream a dessert has the better. Unlike many Slavic buttercreams that have you solely beating butter with sweetened condensed milk, this one also has you add pastry cream. For you pastry chefs, you'll recognize it as a crème mousseline—enhanced with sweetened condensed milk to make it extra luscious with a rich, milky flavor that is reminiscent of *plombir*, the beloved ice cream of the USSR.

This buttercream has a reputation for being a bit finicky, but I've found two things that keep it—and myself—from breaking down. First, all the components have to be around the same warm room temperature before mixing. Second, you can absolutely make the pastry cream ahead of time, but once the sweetened condensed milk is added in, it's best used immediately. It does not respond well to being made in advance, especially once refrigerated.

••

PASTRY CREAM
1⅔ cups (400 g) whole milk
3 egg yolks
½ cup (100 g) granulated sugar
¼ cup (32 g) cornstarch
¾ teaspoon kosher salt
⅛ teaspoon vanillin, 1 packet (9 g) vanilla sugar (scant 2 teaspoons), or 1½ teaspoons vanilla extract
Pat of unsalted butter

TO FINISH
1¼ cups (280 g) unsalted butter, at room temperature, cubed
¾ cup (200 g) sweetened condensed milk or dulce de leche (page 204), at room temperature
Kosher salt

MAKES ENOUGH TO FROST 1 MEDOVIK, 1 BISKVITNYI TORTE, OR 15 BELOCHKI

Make the pastry cream: In a small saucepan, heat the milk over medium heat until scalding (edges begin to bubble).

Meanwhile, in a heavy-bottomed 2-quart (2 L) saucepan, whisk the egg yolks, and granulated sugar until a very pale-yellow paste forms. Add the cornstarch and salt and whisk to fully incorporate.

Add a few tablespoons of the hot milk at a time, mixing quickly after each addition, until a loose paste forms. Pour the rest of the milk in a slow stream, stirring constantly. Cook over medium heat, stirring constantly, until the custard thickens and big bubbles begin to "burp" in the center of the pot. Continue to cook until the custard is thick and glossy, 2 to 3 minutes. Remove from the heat. Stir in the vanillin. Use a fork to coat the surface with a pat of butter to prevent a skin from forming. Cool completely. The pastry cream can be made ahead and refrigerated for up to 5 days.

Finish the plombir buttercream: Before continuing, make sure everything is at a warm room temperature (68°F to 70°F / 20°C to 21°C) or the buttercream will not whip up properly.

In a stand mixer fitted with the whisk, beat the butter on medium-high speed, scraping down the sides of the bowl as needed, until very light and fluffy, 3 to 4 minutes. Reduce the speed to medium and add the pastry cream one big spoonful at a time, beating well after each addition and scraping down the bottom and sides as needed. The buttercream should be very light and fluffy at this point (if not, see Note). Gradually stream in the sweetened condensed milk a few tablespoons at a time (or a big spoonful if using dulce de leche), beating well after each addition and scraping down the bowl as needed. Taste and add salt if needed. Continue to beat for another minute until the buttercream is rich, luscious, and silken. Use immediately.

Note: *If the buttercream seems dense or greasy, don't panic! Scoop some of the buttercream (about ¼ cup / 75 g) and slightly melt in the microwave or saucepan. Scrape it back into the buttercream and then whisk on medium speed until it's smooth and fluffy again.*

VARIATION

Crème Mousseline Buttercream: *In the pastry cream recipe, increase the sugar to ¾ cup (150 g) and omit the sweetened condensed milk in the buttercream. I find that it's a more stable buttercream (you can make in advance and easily revitalize it), but ideally it should be used (or piped) immediately. Can be swapped in for the plombir buttercream in the Napoleon (page 208), Biskvitnyi Torte (page 210), and Belochki (page 215) recipes.*

GOGOL MOGOL

When pulling recipes for this book, I noticed that many of the instructions had you start out with whipping up a *gogol mogol*. In English terms, that would be beating the eggs and sugar together until thick ribbons form. I was surprised because, when I was growing up, gogol mogol sometimes *was* the dessert. The concoction—sweet, billowy, reminiscent of meringue but richer—was billed as healthy for children and, in fact, was especially saved for when they fell ill. I'm not sure what doctor signed off on serving raw eggs to immune-compromised youth, but as a gogol-mogol-eating child once myself, I certainly did not complain. Many versions of it abound, but this is the one I know and love. Sometimes I'll add a splash of liquor . . . for medicinal purposes.

. . . .

1 egg
2½ tablespoons granulated sugar
Splash of Cognac, rum, or orange liqueur

SERVES 1 (OR MORE; SCALE AS NEEDED)

Crack the egg into a coffee mug and add the sugar. Using a hand mixer fitted with one whisk attachment (or in a small bowl with both beaters), beat on high speed for 5 to 6 minutes until the concoction is thick, cream in color, and has tripled in volume. It should no longer taste eggy at this point. If desired, add a splash of liquor and mix until just combined. Eat immediately with a spoon.

SUMMER KOMPOT

Think of this homemade juice—made throughout Central and Eastern Europe (even as far as Kazakhstan!)—as another way to preserve and make use of summer's bounty. Many recipes have you can your *kompot* for imbibing in the colder months, but this one is for enjoying in the here and now. And it couldn't be easier: Simmer whole fruit in water and then sweeten it to taste. The end result is flavorful with a rich mouthfeel, plus there's bonus: stewed fruit to munch on once you reach the bottom of your glass! A refreshing drink and dessert all in one.

This recipe is more of a guideline—use what fruit you have on hand. Frozen works, too! Make it in the fall with apples or pears; dried fruit and whole spices (like vanilla bean or cinnamon) would be welcome as well. Whatever combo you come up with, it'll be leaps and bounds better than any store-bought juice.

In a large pot, combine the fruit and water. Bring to a boil. Reduce the heat to medium-low and allow to simmer until the fruit softens, about 10 minutes.

Stir in the sugar and gently mix until it fully dissolves. Taste and add more sugar as needed to achieve the desired sweetness. Allow to cool to room temperature.

Refrigerate for a few hours or until thoroughly chilled. Stored in the pot or in an airtight container in the refrigerator, the kompot will last up to 1 week. To drink, ladle a few pieces of the fruit (if desired) and juice into a glass and serve.

....

1 pound (450 g) stone fruit, pitted and quartered
½ pound (225 g) sweet or sour cherries, pitted
6 to 8 ounces (170 to 225 g) fresh berries, such as
    raspberries, blackberries, red or black currants
10 cups (2.4 kg) cold water
¼ cup (50 g) granulated sugar, plus more to taste

MAKES 3 TO 3½ QUARTS (3 TO 3.5 L)

ACKNOWLEDGMENTS

Oh gosh, where do I begin! This book, in some ways, has been ten years in the making, and there have been so many people along the way who have encouraged and supported my path to writing it.

To my Charlottesville community, where, in some ways, it all began. Phyllis and Will for hosting me for my first Georgian cooking class. Kate and Eric. Nina and David. Vu, Peter, Catalina, Janey, Keith, Terra, Kasia and Corry, Molly and Rob, Kristen, Sara, Eric H., and on and on. You all pulled me through one of the most difficult periods of my life and helped set me on my path to realizing my dreams. You will always *always* hold a special place in my heart.

Kelsey, whose support has taken so many different forms over the years. I really lucked out with the best friend lottery. Libby and Annie, I love you two. My Seattle crew—Karolina and Andy, Sarah and John—for always being up for a good dinner party (that sometimes doubled as recipe testing). Naoise, for being my Russian *sestrichka* from another life. Thank you for all the laughs and for always being game to be a sounding board.

Book Larder for everything, but especially for the community and opportunity to teach and hone so many recipes that made their way into this book. So grateful for my Book Larder crew: Lara, Mira, Jen, Amanda, Dee Dee, Virginia, and Zoe.

And what would I do without my recipe testers: Talia, Anastasia, Annie C., Sophia, Anna, Katy, Annie A., Karsyn, Kairu, and Hollyce, and everyone else (you know who you are!). I am so appreciative of the time, money, and energy you all put into making the recipes what they are and for pushing me to be a better writer!

Linnea, for your friendship, bread mastery, and for letting me pester you with questions. Olia Koutseridi, for your help and support from afar. Sasha, for being my *plov* Jedi master. Nana, for your time and recipe—Yana and Babushka Galya, too. Ben and Megan, for generously opening up your beautiful home and allowing me the space to write. Nazuk, for your friendship most of all, but also for letting me crash at your place during what ended up being a whirlwind week in the city. And the Mahdi family—most importantly and especially Deko—who took Anton in and showered him with so much love and care so that I could work on this book.

Kate Leahy, none of this would have happened if it wasn't for your introductions!

Susan Roxborough, for encouraging me to take my time and do things the proper way. It was worth it. Kathy Gunst, for your mentorship and confidence in my voice. I don't know how I would've started writing otherwise. My fabulous agent Amy Collins: For your doggedness, unrelenting optimism, and for seeing and believing in this book right from the start. And of course my editor and publisher Jenny Wapner. When you first reached out to me, I was a struggling, sleep-deprived new mom who couldn't fathom taking on the project of a cookbook. Thank you for your persistence, patience, and visionary intuition. I couldn't imagine writing this with anyone else but you and Hardie Grant NA. And speaking of Hardie Grant: Carolyn Insley (you're the best!), Natalie Lundgren, Maddy Kalmowitz, and Liz Correll. Thank you for all your hard work! And of course, Lizzie Allen—thank you for bringing your design eye to this project and creating a gorgeous book.

To the brilliant team who brought the recipes to life: Dane, you are a magician with lighting; Liza, if only I could make food look half as good as you do; Raina, for knowing exactly how to set the dreamiest of scenes, not to mention allowing us to take over your home; Jane, for your keen eye and for making sure we were all well fed; Emily and Brayden, for all your help; and Bob, for buying me dinner when I needed it most; and, lastly, Montgomery Place Farms and Caroline Gilroy, for generously allowing us to photograph at your farm and farm stand.

To everyone in my family. For all the meals we've shared together over our lifetimes. Tyeta Olga, Natasha, Nadya, and Vera—thank you all for teaching me everything you know, both in and outside the kitchen. If no one reads this book, I at least take comfort in knowing that I've preserved your recipes, our culinary heritage, for the next generation. To the Eschenroeders, for accepting me into your wonderful, heartfelt family and for all your unwavering support. I'm so grateful for all of you! My husband, Lee, without whom I would not have the time and space to do any of this. Thank you, my love. And of course, finally, Mama. For everything you've poured into this book—it's as much yours as it is mine.

INDEX

Hardie Grant North America
2912 Telegraph Ave
Berkeley, CA 94705
hardiegrant.com

Library of Congress Cataloging-in-Publication Data is available upon request.
ISBN: 9781958417577
ISBN: 9781958417584 (eBook)

Printed in China
Design by Lizzie Allen
Prop styling by Raina Kattelson
Food styling by Liza Jernow
First Edition

MIX
Paper | Supporting
responsible forestry
FSC® C020056
FSC
www.fsc.org

POLINA CHESNAKOVA was born in Ukraine to Russian and Armenian parents from the country of Georgia. She was raised in a tight-knit Rhode Island community of refugees from all over the former Soviet Union, and has cooked and baked in a handful of professional kitchens. She's had her blog (now newsletter) *Chesnok* since 2015, and her work has been published in *Saveur*, *Epicurious*, *The Washington Post*, and Food52. She has written two cookbooks: *Hot Cheese* and *Everyday Cake*. She worked for Book Larder in Seattle and presided over the cooking class program as the Culinary Director from 2021–2023. She lives in Rhode Island with her husband, Lee, and son, Anton.